C PROGRAMMING
IN A
UNIX™ ENVIRONMENT

INTERNATIONAL COMPUTER SCIENCE SERIES

Consulting Editors   **A D McGettrick**   University of Strathclyde

                          J van Leeuwen   University of Utrecht

SELECTED TITLES FROM THE SERIES

C PROGRAMMING
IN A
UNIX™ ENVIRONMENT

Judy Kay & Bob Kummerfeld

University of Sydney

ADDISON-WESLEY
PUBLISHING
COMPANY

Sydney · Wokingham, England · Reading, Massachusetts
Menlo Park, California · New York · Don Mills, Ontario
Amsterdam · Bonn · Singapore · Tokyo
Madrid · San Juan

To Betty, Clarrie, Kamilla, Lina and Sam.

©1989 J. Kay and R.J. Kummerfeld

The programs in this book have been included for their instructional value. They have been tested with care but are not guaranteed for any particular purpose. The publisher does not offer any warranties or representations, nor does it accept any liabilities with respect to the programs.

Many of the designations used by manufacturers and sellers to distinguish their products are claimed as trademarks. Addison-Wesley has made every attempt to supply trademark information about manufacturers and their products mentioned in this book. A list of the trademark designations and their owners appears on p. xii.

Cover designed by Crayon Design of Henley-on-Thames and printed by The Riverside Printing Co. (Reading) Ltd.
Typeset by Morton Computer Services Ltd, Scarborough.
Printed and bound in Great Britain by T.J. Press (Padstow), Cornwall.

First printed 1988.
Reprinted with corrections in 1989.

British Library Cataloguing in Publication Data
Kay, J.
   C programming in a UNIX environment.—
   (International computer science series).
   1. Computer systems. Operating systems:
   UNIX. Programming languages: C language
   I. Title   II. Kummerfeld, R.J.   III. Series
   005.42

   ISBN 0–201–12912–4

Library of Congress Cataloging in Publication Data
Kay, J.
   C programming in a UNIX environment/J. Kay, R.J. Kummerfeld.
      p.   cm. — (International computer science series)
   Bibliography: p.
   Includes index.
   ISBN 0–201–12912–4
   1. C (Computer program language)   2. UNIX (Computer operating
system)   I. Kummerfeld, R. J.   II. Title.   III. Series
QA76.73.C15K39 1988
005.26—dc19   88–19399
                          CIP

Preface

Since the mid-seventies, use of UNIX and C has been growing steadily. Initially it was limited to universities and research institutes, but availability and popularity has increased dramatically. Major microcomputer software houses are now writing their new software in C and rewriting important existing software in C. Part of the appeal of C is its portability. Compilers for it are available for a range of machines from the very large to the very modest and it is easy to write programs that can be ported over the full range of these machines.

C in a UNIX environment enables a programmer to be very productive. The language is powerful: one can express algorithms elegantly and it allows natural implementations of programs at all levels, from pure applications to the lowest level systems tasks. The other side of this power is that good C programming requires skill, experience and discipline.

Who should read this book?

This book is for people who are already proficient at programming in one language and want to be able to use C well. Experienced programmers and students who have completed a solid first course in programming should be able to learn C from this book. Since many people learn Pascal as their first language, we have taken particular care to help the Pascal programmer convert to C: we highlight language differences that are likely to cause difficulties and we provide exercises on new concepts.

Programming style

We have put considerable emphasis on programming style. We consider this critical to writing *safe* code that is readable and maintainable. We have seen many C programs by people who obviously learnt Pascal first and continue to use Pascal idiom when they write C. We have also seen too many C programs that were written as if there were a fee charged for the use of functions that are standard in the UNIX environment. Right from Chapter 1, we encourage the reader to acquire C idioms and a sense of where standard tools might be applied.

Our style has developed over ten years of programming on a variety of systems and applications programming tasks. We have seen a vast range of C programming styles and have developed a standard approach to program layout and form that we find helpful.

Of course, programming style tends to be a rather personal thing and you may well find that it takes a while to get used to ours. We take pains to explain the reasons behind our particular programming conventions and layout. With time you will develop your own style that will most likely be different but we urge that you use ours as a starting point. It has enabled us to cope better with the development of several complex systems.

Versions of UNIX and C

Although a C standard is emerging, its long term impact is hard to predict. Most aspects of C are fairly stable and we had no difficulty in describing those. For less stable aspects (as well as ones we would like to see change), we alert the reader to some of the possibilities, or, in the case of more minor details, we adhere to the language description in the published *UNIX Programmer's Manual*, Volume 2.

We have described C and UNIX aspects as they are in UNIX Version 7. This is a subset that is common to most current UNIX systems, including System V and Berkeley 4BSD.

The form of this book

The approach that we have used, where possible, is to introduce concepts with an example first. Only then do we expound the general principle. We have found that most students find it easier to start with concrete instances of an idea before trying to generalize to abstract notions.

The order of presentation is guided by two other criteria: earlier chapters act as foundations for later chapters and simpler, more familiar concepts are presented before the more difficult and unfamiliar. Our coverage of C is complete. However, there are several sections in which we advise you to skim on a first reading.

Throughout the text you will find exercises. It is important to *do the exercises* as you get to them. They reinforce important or difficult ideas. Exercises are also used to introduce material that is best appreciated after you have tried the task set. We have included the answers at the end of the book because we consider the exercises to be an important part of your active learning.

Aside from the overview in Chapter 1, each chapter explains an aspect of the language with minimal use of language facilities that are treated in other chapters. This should make it easier for you to learn about the language by reading sections as you need them.

The first chapter gives a wide overview of many of C's features. This should provide a context for the rest of the book. We assume that you want to get into C quite quickly and so the first chapter uses sample programs to present many aspects of the language.

Chapters 2 to 5 provide a detailed coverage of C. Chapter 2 starts with the control structures. We have chosen to present these first because they are one of the simpler aspects to master. Most likely you will find most of this chapter easy going. The most difficult part is the way that C treats the value zero as false (and non-zero as true) in loop and selection control statements.

In Chapter 3 we deal with the data types that C provides and we cover the large number of operators that are available for combining them. We start with a thorough treatment of the integer types. Then follow the types that are close to the integers: the character type, and the enumerated (scalar) type. Next come the floating point types. The last of the simple types is the pointer, which can point to data of any type. Finally, we deal with the rather messy topic of conversions between types, a subject that looks a lot worse than it turns out to be in practice.

Chapter 4 covers various aspects of writing and using functions. It deals with scope, storage classes, rules for initialization and standard approaches to writing functions with a variable number of arguments. By this stage of the book, you will be ready for the section on running substantial C programs that are stored in several files. We show how you can create and maintain your own libraries.

We complete the coverage of C in Chapter 5 with the treatment of its aggregate data types. We deal with structures and arrays first, then strings. Using these we show how to process program arguments. Next come unions. Finally, we give some of the ways to combine various structures in lists, trees and other recursive data structures and we show how C enables you to achieve a degree of data abstraction.

Chapter 6 treats the preprocessor and Chapter 7 deals with the libraries that are standard in the UNIX environment. Because both of these are very important in all C programs, we introduce some aspects of them earlier in the book and we frequently refer to sections of Chapter 7. Then Chapter 7 gives a broad treatment of the massive collection of resources that come as libraries of functions that do I/O, allocation of storage, character operations, manipulation of strings, standard sorting and searching tasks, plotting and mathematical functions as well as functions to interact directly with the UNIX system, ones that provide information about users and processes and others that deal with a terminal capabilities database. We also cover some standard data definitions. This chapter includes examples in the use of functions and notes on how to avoid pitfalls; many C programmers have to acquire much of this information through bitter experience. This is a chapter that you should dip into as the need arises. No-one could come to it and absorb all the information on a first reading.

Then to tie it all together, we present a substantial programming example in Chapter 8. As we develop a program that relies upon UNIX facilities, we demonstrate the use of program development tools and our approach to C programming.

Appendices 1–3 give a language summary using syntax diagrams and a collection of tables that summarize important aspects. Appendix 4 outlines what you can expect from C standardization efforts.

Acknowledgements

We are grateful to Tony Gerber for his meticulous reading and invaluable comments. We thank Piers Lauder for his contributions, particularly the exercises and problems he suggested. We are also indebted to the publisher's anonymous readers who provided numerous suggestions.

J. Kay
R.J. Kummerfeld

Contents

Trademark notice
UNIX™ is a trademark of AT&T.
VAX™ and PDP11™ are trademarks of Digital Equipment Corporation.
Berkeley 4.2BSD™ is a trademark of the University of California, Berkeley.
HP 7220™ is a trademark of Hewlett Packard.
IBM PC Venix™ is a trademark of International Business Machines
Corporation.
Motorola™ and MC68000™ are trademarks of Motorola Corporation.
POSIX™ is a trademark of the Institute of Electrical and Electronics
Engineers Inc.

Chapter 1
Introductory Concepts and Overview

This chapter introduces a good deal of C at a level that should enable you to read and write simple programs. It moves very quickly to give a broad overview of

- the C language
- some preprocessor facilities and
- some functions from the standard libraries.

We also show how to run programs.

1

1.1   Introduction

It is important to learn the form of a language. In this book, we help you to learn C *idiom* as well. This chapter illustrates the language as it is used by experienced C programmers. By this we mean not just the language, C, but also its preprocessor's facilities and the valuable collection of functions available in the standard libraries. Virtually all C programs use the preprocessor and functions from the standard libraries. We use example programs to introduce all of these aspects, and as each important issue arises we indicate where you can find the complete treatment in the book.

1.2   A simple input/output program

We characterize simple interactive input and output with a tiny program that converts a temperature from fahrenheit to centigrade. Here is a sample session with this program.

```
Please enter a fahrenheit temperature 67
67 fahrenheit is 19 centigrade
```

Now study the program that produces it.

```
/*
**      converts a temperature from
**      fahrenheit to centigrade
*/

main()
{
    int     ftemp;  /* the fahrenheit temperature */

    printf(" \nPlease enter a fahrenheit temperature " );
    scanf(" %d" , &ftemp);
    printf(" \n%d fahrenheit is %d centigrade \n" ,
        ftemp, (ftemp − 32) * 5 / 9);
}
```

1.2.1   Program structure

Essentially, this program has the following structure:

```
main()
{
```

> *declarations*
>
> *statements*
>
> }

Our *notation* uses an ordinary typeface for characters that must appear *exactly* as shown (terminal symbols) and italics to *describe* what should appear (non-terminal symbols). So, the main() and the curly braces must appear exactly as shown. Inside the curly braces, you must have first the **declarations** and then the **statements** that constitute main.

A C program is a collection of **functions**. One must be called main and this runs first. Note that the line

    main()

does *not* have a semicolon at the end of it. (Pascal programmers beware!)

The curly braces and the declarations and statements that they enclose are called a **block**. You can see that we have indented all the code within the block from the enclosing curly braces. This is a matter of style: the compiler is blind to it. We have found that programs are easier to develop and maintain when you can readily see which curly braces match.

1.2.2   Declarations

C requires that you declare all variables and that declarations appear at the beginning of the block. In the program above, the declaration has the form

    int   *identifier*;

Note that int is a **keyword** or **reserved word** and you may not use one as an identifier. (A full list of keywords and details of allowable identifiers are in Chapter 3.)

1.2.3   Output using printf

The first action of this program is to call the standard function printf to print the prompt

    Please enter a fahrenheit temperature

Although printf is *not* part of the language C, it is supplied with the standard library that comes with C in a UNIX environment (and is usually provided with other C compilers). In this case, printf has a string argument that specifies what is to be printed. Note that a new line is indicated by \n.

If you look at the other call to printf later in the program, you can see a more sophisticated use of the function. In general, printf must have at least one **argument**, which is a **string** that describes the **format** of the output. Observe that strings are enclosed in double quotes. When the value of an integer variable is to be printed, its position in the output is indicated by a %d in the format string. In the second printf, the output starts with a new line then a decimal integer followed by the string, "fahrenheit is". Next comes the format specification for another decimal integer, followed by "centigrade" and a new line. Although printf has quite powerful formatting facilities, only the simpler and more common ones are introduced in this chapter. (The complete treatment is in Chapter 7 where we discuss the standard libraries.)

After the format string, printf takes a sequence of arguments. These are the expressions whose values are to be printed. So this program prints ftemp and then the value of the expression that converts a fahrenheit temperature to centigrade.

1.2.4 Input using scanf

To do input, we have used another standard function scanf. As you can see, the form of the scanf is quite similar to that of the printf, with a string that describes the form of the input followed by a list of variables to be used. However, there is one important difference in the variable list here. In the printf function, we could simply list the name of each variable we wanted printed. For scanf, we must use a call in the form

```
scanf(" %d" , &ftemp);
```

where the ampersand, &, is essential (because all C arguments are **call by value**). Functions like scanf, that return a value (in this case the number that was entered by the user of the program) need the **address** of the location in which the function can leave a new value. C programs make heavy use of the address-of operator, &, for this purpose.

So, in our example, it is the address of the variable ftemp that is passed to scanf which reads a decimal number from the input and stores it in ftemp. Of course, the argument itself (the address of the variable ftemp) is *not* altered by scanf.

1.2.5 Comments

Comments can appear almost anywhere in a program and they are delimited by /* and */. They may span several lines. You can probably deduce the few places in which you cannot put a comment. For example, if you tried to put a comment in the string argument to printf, it would become part of the string that was printed. Nor can you have a comment in the middle of a keyword or identifier. The general form of a comment is

> /*   *anything you like*   */

You should note that once the compiler detects the beginning of a comment it scans over anything other than */ and so, if you accidentally forget to close a comment, the C compiler ignores all the program text to the end of the next comment.

Our programs follow a consistent style where comment blocks start with /* and end in */ aligned with ** in between to make a continuous line. This makes comments stand out and it is easier to see that they are properly terminated.

EXAMPLE ——————————————————————————

In the program we just studied, the temperatures had to be provided as integers. Given that the floating point number type is float, we can work out how to change the program to deal with non-integral temperatures and print the results accurate to three decimal places. Note that we need the descriptions of printf and scanf on pages 175 and 177 in Chapter 7 to work out how to adjust the formats.

```
/*
** converts a temperature from
** fahrenheit to centigrade
*/
main()
{
    float    ftemp; /* the fahrenheit temperature */

    printf(" \nPlease enter a fahrenheit temperature " );
    scanf(" %f" , &ftemp);
    printf(" \n%.3f fahrenheit is %.3f centigrade \n",
        ftemp, (ftemp − 32) * 5 / 9);
}
```

We have mixed integer and floating point type numbers in the temperature conversion expression. This works because C automatically converts the ints to floats.

1.3 Running a C program

We now work through a short terminal session that runs a very simple C program. We assume that you know enough about UNIX to log on and use the editor to create a file. (Otherwise, you are advised to see one of the UNIX books listed in the Bibliography.)

First you create a file containing the program text. This **source** file's name must have the suffix .c. Suppose that the temperature conversion program, of the preceding section, were in a file called fahr_to_cent.c. Now study the annotated sequence of UNIX commands that compiles and runs the program (we show the UNIX prompt as a dollar sign):

```
$ ls
fahr_to_cent.c
```

Compile the program, with the compiled form (called the **executable binary**) going to fahr_to_cent:

```
$ cc fahr_to_cent.c -o fahr_to_cent
```

and see the program source and binary:

```
$ ls
fahr_to_cent
fahr_to_cent.c
```

Run the program:

```
$ fahr_to_cent
Please enter a fahrenheit temperature 67
67 fahrenheit is 19 centigrade
$
```

Note that we have used the cc command with the −o flag. Had we omitted it, the object version of the program would have been put in a file called a.out. It is good to make a habit of using the −o flag so that you can give meaningful names to object files.

In general, then, you can run a small program thus:

- Create a program text in a file whose name has the suffix .c.
- Compile the program using the command cc.
- Run the program by typing the name of the object file produced by the compiler. (The default name is a.out.)

A typical sequence of UNIX commands for compiling and running a program in a file called whatever.c is as follows:

```
cc whatever.c −o whatever
whatever
```

EXERCISE

1.1 Type and run the last program. By introducing some errors and seeing their effect, you can become familiar with your compiler's diagnostics and other effects of simple errors. Here are some errors you might try:

- Place the program in a file that does not have the .c suffix.
- Try main();.
- Omit some of the semicolons.
- Omit the closing brace.
- Omit the & on the scanf argument.

Comments on Exercise 1.1 We have tried these errors (and many other unintended ones) on a range of systems and compilers. There is considerable variety in the diagnostics we have seen. For example, some systems respond to the first problem, a file without the .c suffix, with this rather mysterious message:

ld:*filename*: bad magic number

(To understand this, you need to read about the process involved in compiling a program on page 22: the bizarre message actually comes from the loader because the C compiler treats files with the wrong suffix as library files and passes them directly to the loader, which finds that the file is not in the right format.)

The quality of error messages that syntax errors generate is pretty dependent on your particular compiler. Most likely, you will find that error messages are not particularly explicit. (The contrast with most Pascal compilers is striking.) Commonly, you get the message, syntax error, with a line number that is usually close to, but after, the error. Some of the errors that we suggested you try can produce a vast output of parasitic messages, which is why we recommended that you try them under controlled conditions on your machine.

Of course, the last error we suggested, omission of the ampersand when using scanf, should pass the compiler without comment. When you run the program, it will read the data into some arbitrary part of memory.

1.4 Control flow and data structures

The program that we study in this section illustrates C idiom and several important concepts. It reads English text and finds the most frequent letter. Frequencies are calculated without regard to whether the letters are upper or lower case. So given some text like

> In considering any new subject, there is frequently a tendency, first, to overrate what we find to be already interesting or remarkable; and, secondly, by a sort of natural reaction, to undervalue the true state of the case, when we do discover that our notions have surpassed those that were really tenable. [A. Lovelace page 44, Notes on the Manabrea's Sketch, Babbage's Calculating Engines, Spon 1889]

it produces the output

> most frequent letter was e

The outline of a program for this task is

> while the next character is not an end of file
> {
>   if it is an upper case letter
>   increment that letter count
>   else if it is a lower case letter
>   increment that letter count
> }
> for each letter count
>   if that letter count exceeds the largest so far
>   update the largest so far
>
> print the most frequent letter

Although the program below uses a number of features of C that are probably unfamiliar to you, try to read it. We discuss it in the rest of this section.

```
/*
** Reads the text on input and prints the
** most frequent letter,
** (On ties, first letter is printed)
*/

#include   <stdio.h>    /* needed for EOF */
#include   <ctype.h>    /* needed for isupper and islower */


int  freq[26] = {0};     /* letter frequencies */
int  commonest = 0;      /* position of commonest so far */
int  ch;                 /* current character */
int  j;

main()
{
    /*
    ** Calculate the frequency of each letter
    */
    while ((ch = getchar()) != EOF)
    {
        if (isupper(ch))
            freq[ch - 'A']++;
        else if (islower(ch))
            freq[ch -'a']++;
    }

    /*
    ** Find the largest of the letter counts
    */
    for (j = 1; j < 26; j++)
        if (freq[j] > freq[commonest])
            commonest = j;

    printf(" most frequent letter was %c \n",
            commonest + 'a');

}
```

1.4.1 Preprocessor commands

The first new feature appears in the lines that start with #include. These cause text from the files called stdio.h and ctype.h to be included at this point in our program. Strictly speaking, these lines are not part of the C language; they are for the **preprocessor** which is invoked automatically when you compile a C program. Note that the preprocessor lines do *not* have a semicolon: by contrast, C statements are terminated with one.

In general, the #include command takes the text in the named file and *includes* it at that point in the program. We need the standard I/O library file, stdio.h, because the program refers to EOF, which is the standard symbol used to represent the end of file value and EOF is defined in stdio.h. Similarly, the library file ctype.h has the definitions for isupper and islower.

1.4.2 Declarations and initializations

The program block starts with several declarations including one for a twenty-six element array that keeps the number of occurrences of each letter. All the data in this program are an integer type, int. Observe that the declarations also initialize freq and commonest to zero. There is actually quite a bit to learn about initializations. For example, in the array initialization, we have actually set only the first element to zero. By default, the remainder is initialized to zero. We have a good deal more to say about initializations in Chapters 4 and 5.

You can see that the variable ch is used to hold a character. C has a character type, char, that should be used for character data. However, in this instance we need to declare ch as int because the standard I/O library function getchar returns an int value. It needs to do this as it must be able to return any character and a special *additional* value for end of file. You will note that when we want to print a character, the printf format string has %c so that the printf function will correctly interpret that int data as a character. In addition to the type int, C has floating point number types, pointers and several variants on ints.

Until Chapter 5, the only data structure we use is the **array**, as in the program above. Chapter 5 covers more unusual uses of arrays, strings and structures which permit data structures with different types of data. (They are like the Pascal record.)

An important characteristic of C programs is that counting generally starts at zero. So the elements of the array freq have indices 0 to 25.

Our style puts each declaration on a separate line. We could have replaced the four lines of declarations by the following single line:

```
int        freq[26] = {0}, ch, commonest = 0, j;
```

Our style makes individual declarations easier to see and to annotate with comments. It also proves more convenient to modify programs when additional declarations are needed or existing ones become redundant.

1.4.3 Control structures

Now let us move our attention to the control flow. The outer while loop gets a character from input, assigns it to the variable ch and keeps doing this as long as the character read is not the end of file character. Let us look more closely at this loop as it has a number of important features. The **assignment expression**

```
ch = getchar()
```

uses the standard function getchar to read the next character on input. This value is assigned to ch and the *whole expression* has the value of that character. Since this expression has a value, we can conveniently use it in the loop control by checking it against EOF. From the outset, you need to appreciate that expressions are fundamental building blocks in C. The most important consequence of this is that expressions, like the assignment expression above, have values which can be used. It is widespread C idiom to use the value of assignment expressions like this. So, the while loop is controlled by the expression

```
(ch = getchar()) != EOF
```

which checks that the character read is not an end of file. The inequality test operator is != (and the equality test operator is ==).

We can convert an assignment expression into an **assignment** *statement* by putting a semicolon after it, as we have done in a later line of the program:

```
commonest = j;
```

In this case we want the *effect* of the assignment expression. We make no use of the *value* of this assignment expression.

Note that the semicolon is a statement **terminator**. So you must put one at the end of every statement. (In Pascal, semicolons are *separ-*

ators: beware of omitting them in C!) Also, as we have said, pre-processor commands do *not* have a semicolon at the end of the line.

Now consider the details of the block controlled by the while loop. The first test

        if (isupper(ch))

uses definitions from the standard library file ctype.h which has many useful character tests. In general, these provide code that is more efficient and clearer than the equivalent you would be likely to produce. So you should use them.

We could have written the upper case test using

        if ((ch >= 'A') && (ch <= 'Z'))

which compares ch against A and Z. Note that **right quotes** enclose character constants. The logical **AND** operator is **&&** (the **OR** operator is ||). You may think that there are rather a lot of parentheses: one set is required by the syntax of the if statement and the other explicitly defines the order of evaluation within the expression. As it happens, >= and <= have higher precedence than && and the parentheses are not necessary: however, we recommend them for clarity. We have more to say on this when we deal with operator precedence in Chapter 3.

When the program encounters an **upper case letter**, it performs the **increment statement**

        freq[ch − 'A']++;

which is equivalent to, but shorter and clearer than, the following:

        freq[ch − 'A'] = freq[ch − 'A'] + 1;

As you will see in Chapter 3, C is quite rich in operators. The increment operator ++ is very heavily used in a variety of ways.

We have used code like

        ch − 'A'

which does arithmetic on characters. This is convenient and enables a conversion between the character read and the appropriate index into the array freq. The fact that the array indices start at zero makes this code tidy.

This code also assumes that the alphabetic characters are contiguous, as is the case with the ASCII character set. Since all UNIX systems are based on the ASCII character set, it is the norm for C programmers to write code like this. (Pascal programmers will have been drilled to avoid such ASCII dependency; such care is justified if you do need to run programs on non-ASCII systems but it seems that the majority of C programmers do not regard this as worth the inconvenience.)

This program finds the highest value in freq with a for loop. Its **control line** has three components:

- an initialization expression
- an expression whose value controls the loop termination and
- an expression that is executed after the completion of each loop repetition.

This makes C's for loop both powerful and simple. There is no magic incrementing of a counter variable; the program execution is all written explicitly. The syntax of the for ensures that all the loop initialization and control appear at the beginning of the loop.

EXERCISES

1.2 Rewrite the for loop at the end of the program as an equivalent while loop.

1.3 You will recall that our initialization of freq actually set only the first element to zero. When the list of initialization values for an array has fewer elements than the array, the remaining elements are set to zero. This is useless where you need to initialize a large array to values other than zero. An explicit and complete initialization is clearer. Write a loop that sets each element of freq to zero.

1.4 This and the next exercise give you some practice with the concept of an assignment expression. What does the following code segment do?

```
if (getchar() == zot)
    doA();
else
    doB();
```

1.5   The following is a rather ugly piece of code. What does it do?

```
for (j = -1; (j = j + 1) < 26; )
    freq[j] = 0;
```

1.6   What does the following code segment do?

```
for (j = -1; (++j) < 26; )
    freq[j] = 0;
```

1.7   The ctype library provides an isalpha. Look at page 216 in Chapter 7 to see how to use it. Then alter the program to use it with isupper (and avoid using islower).

1.8   We have used getchar to read characters in the program above. The corresponding function for printing a character ch is putchar(ch). Write a program that copies input to output, using getchar and putchar.

1.5   A program composed of several functions

The program we treat in this section demonstrates how to write functions other than main. It also illustrates a good deal about **strings** and **characters** and introduces **scope** and some additional control structures.

Our program detects nested comments in C programs. Because comments are delimited by /* and */, the careless omission of a closing */ can turn what you had intended to be code into a comment. (Pascal has the same problem.) Most C compilers give no warning about nested comments. So, if you are a paranoid programmer you might make regular use of a nested comment detector.

Our approach is to report any occurrence of /* within a comment. To do this, our program reads a C program, one character at a time from input. It must be able to determine when the character just read is within a comment and to do this it needs to determine when it is in a string (since a /* or */ within a string does *not* delimit a comment). In addition, the program keeps track of the current line number so that it can report the location of errors.

In keeping with the philosophy of UNIX, we write this program so that it does one *simple* task and does not duplicate actions performed by other programs. So, we assume that the comment checker is to be used in conjunction with the compiler and it checks programs that the compiler passed without any error messages. This saves us checking for a multitude of error conditions, like an unexpected end of file or new line.

1.5.1   The main function

First, let us study the main function. It starts with a #include as we saw in Section 1.4.1. Next is another preprocessor command, #define, which defines the **symbolic constants**, TRUE and FALSE. (These are similar to Pascal's constant definitions, except that #define permits you to define symbols that represent constant *expressions* as well as simple constant values.) In general, various symbolic constants like this can be used to make the purpose of your code clearer. The convention is that defined symbols are given upper case names. In general, C treats a zero as false and a non-zero as true, but we prefer to define symbols that make the meaning of our code clearer.

Now consider the overall structure of main. The while statement is very similar to that in the frequency program of the last section. It reads one character per loop iteration and terminates on finding EOF. The nextchar function is like the standard library function, getchar, except that it updates the line counter as well as reading a character. Within this loop is an if statement that recognizes the beginning of a comment and invokes the comment function to skip through the program to the end of the comment. On the basis of the character read by nextchar, the switch statement handles the three cases: a string, a comment or a slash.

Consider the switch statement. When the character just read is a double quote, the string function is invoked to scan to the end of the string. The next case is a single quote which marks the beginning of a character and is handled by the character function. The last case is that of a slash. This might indicate the beginning of a comment. But it might equally well be the division operator in an arithmetic expression and so the program sets gotslash to TRUE so that if the next character read is *, the start of a comment can be recognized. If the character read does not match any of these, the switch statement has no effect. (This is much more convenient than Pascal's case statement which requires that you explicitly cover each possible case.)

Next, look at the if statement. Now, a comment start is recognized when the second last character read was a slash (indicated by gotslash having the value TRUE) and the character just read is an asterisk. When this happens, we invoke comment and then the continue statement moves control to the next repetition of the nearest enclosing loop; in this case the while statement.

```
/*
**   check for nested comments
```

```
*/
#include    <stdio.h>
#define     FALSE    0
#define     TRUE     1


int  lineno = 1;


main()
{
    int  gotslash = FALSE;
    int  ch;

    while ((ch = nextchar()) != EOF)
    {
        if ((gotslash == TRUE) && (ch == '*'))
        {
            comment();
            continue;
        }
        gotslash = FALSE;

        /* At this point, not in a comment,
        ** string or character
        */
        switch (ch)
        {
        case '"':    string(); break;
        case '\'':   character(); break;
        case '/':    gotslash = TRUE; break;
        }
    }
}
```

Another jump statement is the break which we have used in the switch. Normally, execution in a switch statement *falls through* from one case to the next. (Pascal programmers take note!) So, you usually need a break at the end of the code for each case in a switch. In addition to break and continue, C has a goto which you need to use if you want to escape beyond the nearest enclosing loop. This use of the break might seem counter-intuitive. After all, we saw that the continue inside our if statement caused a jump to the next repetition of the nearest enclosing *loop*. Indeed, a continue always goes to the nearest enclosing loop, but the break has two uses: in a switch it just escapes the switch, but in all other situations it too escapes the nearest enclosing loop.

1.5.2 The comment and string handling functions

Now let us consider the other functions in this program, starting with a similar pair: comment, which skips through comments searching for a */ that defines the end of a comment, or a /* that marks the beginning of a nested comment; and string, which scans through a string until the closing double quote. These functions are based on the fact that once in a string, you continue to be in a string until you encounter a double quote character and you cannot have a comment within a string. Similarly, once in a comment only a */ gets you out. The overall form of comment is an infinite loop that is created by a for loop with no terminating condition. Within that loop is a switch that gets a character and uses its value to determine the action to perform. Note that we do not need a variable to keep the value of the character read. The first case deals with the problem the program addresses, nested comments, and the other case detects the end of a comment and then uses the return statement to escape the function, back to the calling function (in this case main).

```
void
comment()
{
    int   c;

    for(;;)
    {
        switch (nextchar())
        {
        case '/' : while ((c = nextchar()) == '/')
                        ; /* skip slashes */
                   if (c == '*')
                       printf("nested comment at line %d\n",
                              lineno);
                   break;
        case '*' : while ((c = nextchar()) == '*')
                        ; /* skip stars */
                   if (c == '/')
                           return;
        }
    }
}
```

Note the syntax of this function. It is similar to that of main. In writing your own functions, you start with a **header** that gives the function type and name and then comes the **block**. As we mentioned earlier, a C program is a collection of functions of which main is just the one that is executed first. We have declared the comment function to be of type void. This indicates that it does not return any value. We must admit that this is not yet widespread practice amongst C programmers, but it should be because it ensures consistency in the function's use and its definition. (Note that we have put the word void on a separate line; this ensures that the function name is at the beginning of the line and we do this because it proves useful when you want to use an editor to find a function definition.) The many other issues relating to functions are covered in Chapter 4.

The only data used in this function is lineno which maintains the number of the current line. It was declared *outside* the main function. As you can see we were able to use it in the main function and it is also accessible to the other functions in the program. So, its scope is **global**. Variables that are declared within the braces of the function block are **local** to that function and can be accessed only in the block of their declaration. Procedures *cannot* be nested (as in Pascal). So the data within a file can be global, local to a function or local to a block within a function.

Now consider the string function which is very similar to the last. The only case that needs discussion is the handling of the backslash, which precedes special characters. Since C uses the backslash as an escape character, you can put a double quote within a string as in the following example:

```
printf(" an example with  \"  − a double quote" );
```

To interpret this properly, our program has to skip over the character after a backslash when it scans through a string:

```
void
string()
{
    for (;;)
    {
        switch (nextchar())
        {
        case '"':    return;
        case '\\':   nextchar(); break;
        }
    }
}
```

1.5.3 The character handling function

The character function below should skip over a C character constant. Simple characters just have the form

   '*character*'

but we have already seen some more complicated cases, like the new line character \n. These special characters have a backslash followed by another character. (We shall see in Chapter 3 that there are yet other forms of character constants that this version of character does not handle.)

```
void
character()
{
     if (nextchar() == ' \ \ ')
          nextchar();
     nextchar();
}
```

1.5.4 The function that gets input

Finally, we need the function nextchar which reads a character and increments the line counter:

```
int
nextchar()
{
     int  c;

     if ((c = getchar()) == ' \n')
          lineno++;
     return c;
}
```

We use this function wherever a character has to be read because we want to ensure that the line counter is incremented in just one place in the code. We define nextchar as int, the same type as getchar. (Recall that we need to be able to return a value for EOF as well as any of the characters.) This function also illustrates how you can return a value for a function, using the return statement with an argument. In general, the form is return *[expression]*;

where the value of the function is that of the expression. (The square brackets indicate that the expression is optional.)

You will notice that our program is composed of several very small functions. This is typical in C. As you will see in Chapter 4, it is usual for substantial programs to be organized in several files, with each file holding a set of related functions. This contrasts with Pascal's idiom which makes for one large program.

EXERCISES

1.9 A return in a function returns control to the calling program. What would you expect a return in main to do?

1.10 You have seen how to use #define to establish a constant value. Now the only reason that we used the preprocessor's #include facility was to define EOF. Given that getchar returns the value −1 when it encounters an end of file, modify the program to avoid the #include and consider the merits of this approach.

1.11 We have written the comment function with a for statement that has no termination condition in the control line. We have also used a switch statement even though there are only two cases. Try rewriting comment using a while and if.

1.12 If you were actually developing a program like this you might well want some intermediate or debugging output. How would you get the characters echoed as they are read?

1.6 Running single file programs

We have already seen how to run a tiny program. Typically, programs have many functions split across several files. Each file can then be compiled separately as the functions within it are developed. For the moment, we just deal with issues that are relevant for programs that are in a single file. Chapter 4 treats multifile programs and Chapter 8 demonstrates how to use program development tools.

1.6.1 Checking for potential problems—lint

First let us consider the UNIX utility, lint. Its action is analogous to what you might do when you try to take all the little bits of lint off a garment which is otherwise clean. You may think of a program as syntactically 'clean' if the compiler accepts it without complaints and produces an a.out file. Of course, a syntactically correct program may still have errors and lint finds code that looks suspicious. We ran lint on the nested comment detector program with this command:

> lint comment.c

and it produced two messages:

> printf returns value which is always ignored
> nextchar returns value which is sometimes ignored

The first line tells us that printf returns a value and we have not used it. (The value that printf returns indicates whether it completed successfully or not.) The second message points out that nextchar returns a value and we sometimes use it, and in other places we ignore it. In a language like Pascal, such things are detected by the compiler and this is true of many of the problems that lint detects. There are two reasons for the difference. Firstly the Pascal language definition forbids several potentially dangerous practices that C permits. Secondly, there are some errors that cannot be identified by the compiler: for example, you can compile parts of C programs separately and so the compiler cannot find incompatibilities between code in a file it is compiling and the code in other files. We have introduced lint here because we think that you should develop the habit of using lint always. However, we will not treat it thoroughly until Chapter 4, after we have covered the various aspects of functions and scope that are critical to an appreciation of the range of lint's facilities.

Return now to the message that our use of printf generated. There are three possible reactions. First, you could simply ignore the lint error message. But if you are developing a substantial program and you want it to be of high quality, you would want your program to be quite lint-free. To do otherwise invites the risk of accidentally ignoring significant error warnings. The second approach would be to check the value that printf returns. In many applications, this may not be necessary as printf failure is unlikely and obvious. Our last option is to ignore the returned value but to make this explicit by casting it to void with a line of this form:

```
(void)printf( ... );
```

We can use the same approach in the cases where we do not use the result returned by nextchar. We have more to say about such type casts in Chapters 3 and 4.

1.6.2   What happens when you run a C program

If you are to interpret all the diagnostics that you might get, you need to understand what the cc command does. Figure 1.1 illustrates the process that takes a C source program in a file called prog.c, passes it through the preprocessor, the compiler, the assembler and, finally, the loader. As you can see, there are two intermediate files, prog.s and prog.o. If all goes well, these are temporary and they disappear by the end of the compilation leaving only a.out (and prog.c).

The first phase in compiling a program is the preprocessor's pass over the file. You will rarely get error messages from the preprocessor. When you do make mistakes in preprocessor commands, their effect is usually to produce code with errors that are detected by the *compiler*.

The preprocessor hands the program over to the compiler, which itself may involve several passes. We have shown the preprocessor and the compiler in one box because one thinks of these as being very closely coupled. The bulk of error messages come from the compiler as it attempts to parse a program and produce an assembly language version. If you really want or need to see this version, use

```
cc −S prog.c
```

and the assembly program will be available in prog.s.

In the next stage, the *assembler* (which is called as) translates the assembly code form of the program into a **relocatable binary** in prog.o. There should be no errors at this stage (since the compiler produced the code). If you want the intermediate .o files kept, use the −c flag on the cc command. You will see the uses for this when we discuss multifile programs in Chapter 4.

The loader completes the process, producing the **executable binary** in a file called a.out. (Or, if you compile using cc with the −o flag, you can give the binary a meaningful name.) It is not unusual to get errors at this stage. One of the most common occurs when a function or other external symbol is missing from your program and the loader reports that it cannot find it. You will see examples of this when you try the next exercises. The first few of these exercises are to help you learn how to interpret your compiler's diagnostic messages.

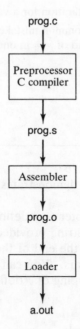

Figure 1.1   The action of the cc command.

EXERCISES

1.13   Enter any program and try to compile and run it with one of the functions missing. (Note that if you decide to type the nested comment checker, you will need to compile it with the global declarations first and main last; in Chapter 4, we show how to successfully compile a program with the functions in any order.)

1.14   Now try putting a semicolon at the end of the #defines.

1.15   Take any program you have typed and alter it to try to get preprocessor error messages.

1.16   Now get some practice with lint.

- See what happens if you change some of the function calls to have more or fewer arguments, or arguments of the wrong type. Note that the compiler can help within a single file but you need lint in other cases. So try mismatched arguments for functions that are called and defined within the same file as well as some of the standard functions (which are obviously not in the same file as their call).

- Try adding a spurious declaration for a variable.
- Now try one of the very common mistakes made by beginning C programmers, typing = instead of == in one of the if controlling expressions.
- Also try a loop like this:

  ```
  for(;;);
  ```

Comments on Exercises 1.13-1.16

1.13 Omission of a function demonstrates an error that is detected by the loader.

1.14 As you will see in Chapter 6, #define does a replacement of the defined symbol by the string provided in the definition. So when you put a semicolon at the end of the line, this is included in the places the symbol appears. You can generate some very mystifying errors by careless typing of #defines.

1.15 A command like

```
#deform EOF     −1
```

produces a genuine preprocessor error message.

1.16 Different systems set different default lint flags. So, on some systems lint complains every time you use printf without using the returned value (or casting it to void). On others there is no message. We recommend that you run lint with all flags set.

1.7 Perspectives

Before we go any further, it is valuable to set C in its historical context and discuss some common complaints about it.

C was developed in the early 1970s, just a little later than Pascal. Like Pascal, C reflects ideas that come from Algol60, but from there the two languages differ in the way they developed and the central motivations for their design.

C was created by Dennis Ritchie at Bell Laboratories, growing in parallel with UNIX on a PDP11 minicomputer. It was developed as a systems programming language and came from a sequence of others, with the typeless languages BCPL and B as its immediate predecessors. It reflects its history in many ways.

- It has the coherence of a language designed by one person.

- Because Ritchie used C extensively before it came into widespread use, he was able to refine and develop it into a language that works well in many applications.
- It is small enough to run on many types of machines.
- It allows the systems programmer to get close to the machine.
- It does not reflect the thinking of the programming schools that are concerned with program verification.

Now let's look at some common complaints about C.

Complaint 1: C does not have modern constructs

As the examples discussed in this chapter indicate, C does have control structures that support structured programming. It offers several selection and iteration control structures (described fully in Chapter 2). It has several built-in data types and the user can define enumerated types, arrays, aggregate data structures and combinations of these. Although C does not directly support data abstraction, it does have facilities that enable a programmer to achieve a similar effect. In this respect, it offers more than Pascal does.

Complaint 2: C is a high level assembler

Because C is a powerful language and has been used to write most of the UNIX operating system, it is widely assumed that it must be rather like an assembler. Many operating systems, especially older ones, are written in assembler. This is partly due to tradition: on old machines, the high level languages that were available were usually inadequate for systems programming. Although C gives the programmer most of the power that an assembly language program permits, it is not at all like an assembly language. It has elegant control and data structures.

Complaint 3: C does not have I/O

Input and output are *not* part of the language C. However, there is a collection of input and output functions in the standard I/O library. These are available on all UNIX systems and with most other implementations of C. So C certainly does have I/O: it is simply not defined as part of the language.

The I/O functions are (or can be) written almost exclusively in C and you can write your own I/O if you wish. This contrasts with Pascal in which I/O must be part of the language.

Complaint 4: C is not a strongly typed language

This is true: it is not a strongly typed language. (As we have already seen, we can use int to hold a character and then print it as a character using %c in the printf to define the type for printing.) Many compilers, especially older ones, are lax about enforcing all of C syntax and type requirements. They commonly fail to even warn of such violations.

Complaint 5: C is a dangerous language

This remark is somewhat related to particular implementations. It *is* true that some implementations of C permit some very dangerous practices to pass without even a warning from the compiler. It may be gratuitous to say that C is not dangerous but most implementations of it are. However, many of the existing compilers reflect C's history and stricter compilers are becoming available.

Even ignoring the issue of particular implementations, C is probably not appropriate as a language for teaching programming to beginners. The limitations imposed by a language like Pascal help a beginner. Good C programming does require that the programmer exert considerable self-discipline. The most widespread C compilers seem to have been written with the philosophy that competent programmers should know what they are doing and the compiler should not get in the way. So, you need to make a practice of using lint and you should follow the style and practices advised throughout this book.

SUMMARY

We have looked at or mentioned various aspects of the language C:

- block structure and functions
- parameter passing mechanism (call by value)
- use of &, address-of operator, to return values from a function
- comments
- scope of identifiers
- data types
- declarations and initializations for ints
- the array data structure (indexes starting at 0)
- semicolon as statement terminator
- assignment expressions
- equality test operators, == and !=

- increment operator, ++
- logical operators, &&, || and !
- control structures, for, while, if, if else, switch, break, continue and return
- use of \ as an escape character (as in \" in strings)
- special characters, \n and \t
- the type void for functions

and of the C preprocessor:

- #include for file inclusion
- #define for defining constant symbols

and of the C standard libraries:

- the I/O functions, printf, scanf, getchar and putchar
- standard symbol, EOF
- standard character tests, isupper, islower and isalpha

We saw how to run a program by compiling a file with the suffix .c using the C compiler, cc, to produce an executable binary (with default name a.out).

Chapter 2
Control Flow

2.1	Introduction		2.4	Selection
2.2	Statements and block		2.5	Loops
	structure		2.6	Jumps
2.3	Controlling expressions			Summary

The statements that control the flow of execution are:

- selection constructs: **if**, **if-else** and **switch**
- loops: **while**, **do-while** and **for**
- jump statements: **break**, **continue**, **return** and **goto**.

As you have already met most of these in Chapter 1, the treatment here is terse. This chapter has detailed coverage of the more difficult aspects that were glossed over in Chapter 1.

2.1 Introduction

C has fairly conventional control flow structures. By default, the program statements are executed strictly in the sequence in which they appear, starting with the first statement in main, then going to the second, the third ... inexorably through until the last. This chapter describes the statements that can alter the default straight line flow of control.

But before we can deal with these control structures, we discuss the *statements* and *blocks* that are controlled and we see how controlling expressions work. The Pascal programmer will find these rather foreign because C has no built-in boolean type to control selection structures and loops; it uses integer expressions. As we saw in Chapter 1, we can often get by quite well if we just read the loop control expressions as if they were booleans. However, this is not always true, and in this chapter you will come to grips with control expressions.

2.2 Statements and block structure

C is a block structured language in which a statement may be either

- a **single statement**, which is always terminated by a semicolon or
- a **block**, which is a sequence of declarations and statements enclosed in curly braces { }.

Now let us see these in terms of the following code segment that is taken from the main function of the comment checker program in Chapter 1. The while statement controls a block containing three statements: an if statement, an assignment and a switch statement. The if statement controls the execution of two statements: a call to the comment function and a continue statement. As we noted in Chapter 1, the statements within each block are indented from the line that controls their execution.

```
while ((ch = nextchar()) != EOF)
{
    if ((gotslash == TRUE) && (ch == '*'))
    {
        comment();
        continue;
    }
    gotslash = FALSE;
    /* At this point, not in a comment, string or character */
```

```
        switch (ch)
        {
        case ' " ' :    string(); break;
        case ' \ ' ' :  character(); break;
        case ' / ' :    gotslash = TRUE; break;
        }
    }
```

EXAMPLE _____

Why doesn't the following code find the maximum of an arbitrary sequence of positive numbers terminated by the value of SENTINEL?

```
#define SENTINEL        0

    int     j;
    int     max = 0;

    scanf(" %d" , &j);
    while (j != SENTINEL)
        if (j > max)
            max = j;
        scanf(" %d" , &j);
```

The answer is that braces are missing around the if and **scanf** statements. So the indentation does not reflect the actual block structure: the second **scanf** is *not* part of the loop. (Of course, this problem applies in Pascal, too.)

_____

2.3 Controlling expressions

Selection structures and loops use a controlling expression whose value defines whether the controlled statements are to be executed. So, for example, an if has the following form:

> if *controlling expression*
> *statement*

We can usually read this as follows:

> *if the controlling expression is true*
> *the statement is executed*

As foreshadowed in the introduction to this chapter, the actual situation is not quite as simple as this because C has no logical or boolean type. So the view that an expression is *true* or *false* is not accurate. In fact, the controlled statements are executed when the expression gives a *non-zero* value.

So, a statement like

```
if (j > max)
    max = j;
```

can be read as follows:

> *if j is greater than max*
> *assign the value of j to max*

But, in strict terms, it would read

> *if the expression (j > max) has a non−zero value*
> *assign j to max*

and we should note that relational expressions like (j > max) have the value zero when they are false. In general, expressions behave thus:

- expressions evaluating to *zero* act like *false*;
- expressions evaluating to *non-zero* values act as *true*.

You will recall that in the second programming example of Chapter 1 we defined our own symbols TRUE and FALSE. This enabled us to write code that was slightly longer but clearer than we could have produced using the fact that zero controlling expressions act as false.

We have already introduced several logical and relational operators. Before we launch into the control structures, we summarize them all.

!x	not x

x < y	x less than y
x > y	x greater than y
x <= y	x less than or equal to y
x >= y	x greater than or equal to y

x == y	x equal to y (*not* the same as the assignment operator =)
x != y	x not equal to y
x && y	x logical-AND y
x || y	x logical-OR y

The dotted lines mark precedence levels, with all operators between a pair of horizontal lines having the same precedence and the groups of operators with highest precedence appearing earlier in the table. Of course, you can write expressions with brackets and then you do not have to worry about precedence rules. Indeed, since bracketing is the safest approach, this what we recommend you do.

EXERCISES

2.1   Given that x is an int, when is the function called action invoked in these two if statements?

```
if (x)
    action();

if (x != 0)
    action();
```

2.2   Given that flagset is an int, explain what the following code fragment appears to do:

```
if (flagset)
    action();
```

2.3   Look back to the comment checking program in Chapter 1 and rewrite main as necessary so that the identifiers TRUE and FALSE are not needed.

2.4   Selection

C has three selection structures. The first two that we treat, if and if-else, look very alike. The third, switch, permits multiway branches on the basis of constant cases. All of these should be straightforward for the Pascal programmer, who will appreciate the greater power of C's switch cases which can be any constant *expression*.

2.4.1   if

You have already seen several uses of the if statement in this and the last chapter. Now we discuss its general form. But first consider the following simple if statement in a code segment which calculates an average by dividing sum by n. This if statement ensures that the division is only done when n is non-zero:

```
if (n != 0)
    av = sum / n;
```

When the expression n != 0 is false (actually zero) the statement is skipped. As you will be aware from the last section, we could have written the code as this equivalent but less natural form:

```
if (n)
    av = sum / n;
```

We certainly do *not* recommend such code and, of course, you will use the clearer form given first. However, you may well meet poorly written programs that do use the shorter, more obtuse form.

The general form of the if statement is

```
if (expression)
    statement
```

where the statement is executed if the expression is non-zero (true).

2.4.2   if-else

This structure selects between two statements as in the following example, which calculates an average when it can and prints an error message otherwise:

```
if (n != 0)
    av = sum / n;
else
    printf(" No data. \n" );
```

The general form of the if-else statement is

```
if (expression)
    statement
```

    else
       statement

The first statement is done when the expression is non-zero (true) and, otherwise, the second executes.

2.4.3 Dangling else

The if and if-else statements look very alike and this poses a potential ambiguity which C resolves very simply, by defining else to belong to the closest if above it in the text. (This is the same 'dangling else' problem and solution as in Pascal.) You need to take care that you write the code that you intend. So an if-else within an if looks like this:

```
if (expression-1)
    if (expression-2)
        statement-A
    else
        statement-B
```

but to nest an if within an if-else you need braces, like this:

```
if (expression-1)
{
    if (expression-2)
        statement-A
}
else
    statement-B
```

EXERCISE

2.4 The indentation in the following code is misleading. Why? What would you do to make this code actually work as its indentation and sense suggests it should do?

```
if (safe)
    if (val < TOL)
        printf(" Meets tolerance" );
else
    printf(" dangerous" );
```

2.4.4 switch

This multi-way selection structure is used in the code below to print a character, digit, with an appropriate ordinal suffix.

```
switch (digit)
{
case '1' : printf(" %c−st" , digit); break;
case '2' : printf(" %c−nd" , digit); break;
case '3' : printf(" %c−rd" , digit); break;
case '4' :
case '5' :
case '6' :
case '7' :
case '8' :
case '9' :
case '0' :
     printf(" %c−th" , digit); break;
}
```

When the character in digit is one, the first printf is executed and then the break transfers control from the switch. Note that without the break, execution would **fall through** to the next case. The cases that re-quire "th" as a suffix use this fall through. Because you can order cases as you wish, using fall through to the next case is the general mechan-ism for combining cases that you want to treat alike. Should digit have a value other than those digits covered by the cases specified, the whole switch statement is skipped. Unfortunately, ranges such as those in the above example cannot be abbreviated.

The general form of the switch is as follows:

```
switch (switch-expression)
{
     [declarations]
case constant-expression : statement list
     ...

[default:statement list]
}
```

Note that the switch expression can be any expression that gives a simple non-floating point type. Observe that you may have declarations at the beginning of the block controlled by the switch (although, in practice, they are rare). Each case must be a **constant expression** which means that its value must be defined at compile time; it cannot contain any variables or function calls. It can be any, arbitrarily complex constant expression that is either integer or one of the types that can be regarded as mapping on to the integers. (This includes the character and enumerated types, discussed in Chapter 3.) So, following our convention that constant symbols are given upper case names, these expressions are permissible case expressions:

```
case 847 :
case 4 * SPECIAL + OFFSET :
case EOF :
case 'a' :
```

They may be ordered as you choose but each case must be unique.

In general, you need a **break** after each **case** to prevent control from falling through to the next **case**. You should take care about using fall through as an intentional programming device other than to get the effect of ranges as in the example above (where the range of digits that take the same suffix are handled together). Should you use fall through, take care to document it carefully so that future modifications will take account of it.

The **default** case is optional. In its absence, the **switch** is skipped when the **switch** expression gives a value other than those specified in **case** expressions. When it is present, it acts as a catch-all and is particularly useful for trapping error conditions which arise because of a case that should never occur.

As we have already noted, the **cases** may only involve constant expressions; where this is inadequate, you need to use a sequence of if-else statements, as we show in the next section.

EXERCISES

2.5 Which of the following are acceptable **case** constant expressions? Assume the convention that upper case is used for #defined constant symbols and other identifiers are variables.

```
case 76 :
case num * 2 :
case SVAL * 2 :
case 84.6 :
```

2.6 How does the following code segment differ from the example at the beginning of Section 2.4.4 and how can you make its behaviour identical?

```
switch (digit)
{
case '1' :            printf(" %c−st" , digit); break;
case '2' :            printf(" %c−nd" , digit); break;
case '3' :            printf(" %c−rd" , digit); break;
default:              printf(" %c−th" , digit);
}
```

2.4.5   else-if

Although this is not really a separate structure, it is a common use of nested if-elses where a multiway branch requires variable case selector expressions, as in the example below which prints a comment on a grade:

```
if (grade > 90 )
      printf(" excellent" );
else if (grade > 70)
      printf(" good" );
else if (grade > 50)
      printf(" acceptable" );
else if (grade > 45)
      printf(" almost acceptable" );
else
      printf(" dreadful" );
```

Each if test covers a part of the range of values that constitute a particular assessment. Normal indentation conventions would make each else-if one level further indented so that the last printf would be four levels deeper than its present position. However, this else-if form of the if-else is usually indented as above to reflect the fact that it is really a multiway branch.

The general form of the else-if multiway branch is

```
if (expression-1)
      statement
else if (expression-2)
      statement
...
else
      statement
```

2.5 Loops

The looping statements are while, do-while and for. The while and do-while correspond to Pascal's *while* and *repeat* loops but, as we have already seen in Chapter 1, the for loop is very much more powerful than Pascal's.

As we also saw in Chapter 1, it is usual C idiom to make loop control expressions work hard: in addition to controlling the loop, they commonly have a side effect such as reading data or incrementing a counter.

2.5.1 while

A simple use of the while loop is shown in the following code segment that reads and prints a sequence of numbers, stopping at a special sentinel value, STOPPER:

```
while ((scanf(" %d" , &value) == 1) && (value != STOPPER))
    printf(" %d" , value);
```

This is similar to loops we saw in Chapter 1. Each loop iteration reads a number and compares it to STOPPER. If the number read is the same as STOPPER, the loop completes. Otherwise, the number is printed and the next iteration follows.

Another code segment that illustrates a common C idiom is shown below. It skips over white space:

```
while (isspace(nextch = getchar()))
    ;
```

The control line does all of the work, reading a character, assigning it to nextch and using the standard function isspace to check whether it is a white space character (this can be any one of space, tab, newline or formfeed). Each loop iteration reads one character. This continues just as long as the character read is a white space character. On loop exit, nextch will be the first character that is not white space. The semicolon, alone and indented, indicates that the null statement is executed (and no actions are performed aside from those in the loop control expression).

The general form of the while statement is

```
while (expression)
    statement
```

The statement is repeatedly executed as long as the expression is true (non-zero). If the expression is zero initially, the statement is never executed.

EXERCISE

2.7 Rewrite the while loop that reads and writes a sequence of numbers up to the STOPPER sentinel value, but take the scanf out of the control line.

2.5.2 do-while

The following example uses a do-while loop to read and print integers to a sentinel:

```
do
{
    scanf(" %d" , &number);
    printf(" %d" , number);
}
while (number != STOPPER);
```

It differs from the code in the last section in that it prints the sentinel value.

The do-while structure is less commonly used than the while. Its general form is

```
do
    statement
while (expression);
```

where the statement is executed at least *once* before the termination expression is evaluated and the statement is repeated until the controlling expression is false (zero).

2.5.3 for

The following code fragment uses a for loop as a simple counting loop that reads exactly num numbers:

```
scanf(" %d" , &num);
sum = 0;
for (i = 1; i <= num; i++ )
{
    scanf(" %d" , &value);
    printf(" %d" , value);
}
```

This uses i as a loop counter variable. The for-control line sets i to one initially, and tests whether i has exceeded the value of num on each entry to the loop. On each completion of the loop, i is incremented by the expression, "i++". Should num have the value zero, the for loop will not be executed at all.

Of course, the for loop is much more powerful than this simple counting loop might suggest; the for has all the power of a while loop. So we can recast the code segment that reads a sequence of numbers to a sentinel value like this:

```
for ( ; (scanf(" %d" , &value) == 1) && (value != STOPPER); )
    printf(" %d" , value);
```

which is equivalent to the code that used a while loop to read to a sentinel.

The general form of the for loop is

> for (*initialization; continuation-test; loop-increment*)
>   *statement*

As indicated above, the for loop is controlled by the three expressions that are separated by semicolons. The first expression sets up initial conditions for the loop. The second is tested at the beginning of each loop iteration and if it is true (non-zero), the statement is performed. The final expression is evaluated at the completion of each loop iteration and is frequently used as an increment as in the counting loop at the beginning of this section.

As we saw in Chapter 1, any or all of the controlling expressions can be null. In the case of a null initialization expression, no initialization is performed. When the termination test expression is omitted, the loop is repeated until an escape statement takes control flow out of the loop, as we saw in the example of Chapter 1 (and which we will treat in the next section). The third expression's omission means that the null expression is performed on each loop completion.

EXERCISE

2.8 In the code segment above, what is the value of the loop counter after a normal exit from the loop?

2.6 Jumps

We have already seen the continue, break and return statements used in Chapter 1. So we can deal with them briefly here. The only new jump is the unstructured goto.

2.6.1 continue

We saw the use of the continue in the main function of the comment checker program:

```
while ((ch = nextchar()) != EOF)
{
    if ((gotslash == TRUE) && (ch == '*'))
    {
        comment();
        continue;
    }
    gotslash = FALSE;

    /* At this point, not in a comment, string or character */
    switch (ch)
    {
    case '"':    string(); break;
    case '\'':   character(); break;
    case '/':    gotslash = TRUE; break;
    }
}
```

This continue occurs within an if statement and takes control to the next iteration of the while loop that reads another character from input.

The general form is

beginning of nearest enclosing loop
{

```
        ...
    continue
        ...
}
```
end of nearest enclosing loop

and the execution of the continue takes control to the end of the *current iteration* of the nearest enclosing loop.

2.6.2 break

As the example above also shows, the break is used to escape the cases of a switch statement. It can also be used to escape a loop. As we noted in Chapter 1, it is somewhat overloaded; within a switch, it always escapes that switch. Within other control structures, including the if and if-else, it escapes from the nearest enclosing loop.

The general form is

beginning of nearest enclosing loop or switch
```
{
        ...
    break;
        ...
}
```
end of nearest enclosing loop or switch

and the break takes control *out* of the nearest enclosing loop *or* switch statement.

2.6.3 return

We saw several uses of the return in the comment checker in Chapter 1. In the comment and string functions, we used return to take control back to main after we had found the end of a comment or string. We also saw it used in nextchar like this:

```
int
nextchar()
{
    int  c;

    if ((c = getchar()) == ' \n')
```

```
        lineno++;
    return c;
}
```

Note that in this function, we use return both to return control to the calling function and to return the function value. You can specify the returned value with any expression. (Many programmers enclose the returned expression in brackets; since any expression that is enclosed in brackets is also an expression, this is fine, though unnecessary.)

The general form is

return *[expression]*

where the return takes control back to the calling function. When the return is in main, control returns to the process that invoked the program (unless main is recursive!). Where the function has a type other than void, the return statement may be followed by an expression whose value is returned. In terms of syntax, the expression is optional. However, all functions that are not of type void *should* return a value of the appropriate type. We will see in Chapter 4 that lint can detect anomalies in the use of return.

2.6.4 goto

Most programs can be written conveniently using the jump statements already treated. One common class of problem where this is not so arises when you need to do a multilevel break or continue. Since the continue jumps to the end of the *nearest* enclosing loop, a jump to the next iteration of any other enclosing loop requires a goto. Similarly, the break escapes from the nearest enclosing switch or loop. Typical situations are illustrated in the code skeleton below:

```
    ...
    for ( ... )
    {   ...
        while ( ... )
        {   ...
            if ( ... )
                goto exitfor;
            ...
            switch ( ... )
            {   ...
                case ESCAPE:    goto exitwhile;
                ...
```

```
            }
            ...
        }
        exitwhile:
            ...
    }
    exitfor:
        ...
```

Note that we have chosen goto label identifiers which emphasize the fact that we are using the goto to escape the for and while loops. (Pascal programmers note that the label cannot be a number and that the label is *not* declared.)

The general form of goto is

goto *label-identifier*

where the label is any identifier (as defined in Chapter 3). The label can be written before any statement (including a null statement) and its form is

identifier:

The label can be anywhere within the same function. (If you choose to overload the goto identifier label by defining two labels with the same name, the goto jumps to the label in the nearest enclosing block. We hope you will never make use of this 'feature'.)

EXERCISE

2.9 Any for statement can be mapped to an equivalent while statement. We have given a general form of a for statement. Show how it translates to a while statement.

SUMMARY

C is a block structured language in which a *statement* may be either

- a *single statement* which is always terminated by a semicolon or
- a *block* which is a sequence of declarations and statements enclosed in curly braces { }.

Controlling expressions with a value

- zero, act as false and
- non-zero, act as true.

Selection structures:

- if
- if-else
- switch for multiway branches, where the branches are selected by constant expressions. Normally, each branch requires a break to prevent fall through. One branch may, optionally, be the default branch.
- else-if is multiway branch with variable selection expressions.

Loops:

- while, tests at beginning of loop
- do-while, tests at end of loop; controlled statement is done at least once
- for, tests at beginning of loop; control line has three components:
  - (1)   initialization expression
  - (2)   loop continuation expression, tests at beginning of loop
  - (3)   expression that is evaluated on each loop completion and is generally used as a loop increment

Jumps:

- continue, goes to the next iteration of the nearest enclosing loop
- break, escapes from the nearest enclosing loop or switch
- goto, jumps to the label specified
- return, jumps to the calling function (within main, it quits program, unless main is recursive)

Chapter 3
Simple Data Types

This chapter describes the simple types of data that C offers and the operations you can do on them. As a language that was designed for systems programming, C makes it possible to get close to the machine. It provides data types that permit you to deal with bits, bytes, words and machine addresses. The simple types in C are

- the various types of integers, **int**, **short**, **long**, and **unsigned**
- the character type, **char**
- the user specified type (or enumerated) type, **enum**
- the floating point number types, **float** and **double**
- and the pointer types.

We also deal with conversions between types, both

- explicit casts and
- implicit type conversions.

We see that C is very rich in operators.

3.1   Introduction

We describe each C data type in terms of the range of values it can take and the operations that can be performed. When we discuss each type in C, we deal first with the range of values that can be represented by the type and this includes a treatment of the representation of constants in that range. Then we discuss the operations that are appropriate for that type and some common uses.

In the earlier chapters, we have made simple use of int and char variables. In this chapter, we deal with the remainder of the simple data types in C. These are the types that are used to represent a single data element. Aggregate data types that are needed for collections of data elements are treated in Chapter 5.

C has two fundamental data types, int and double. By this, we mean that other types are best understood in terms of how they relate to one or other of these types. We treat the int type in considerable detail first. Then we discuss the types that map on to the integers. Next we consider the floating point types, which are based on the fundamental type, double. The last of the simple data types is the **pointer** which is actually a collection of types, one for each possible type to which a pointer can point. Finally we deal with the somewhat messy subject of type conversions.

3.2   Identifiers and reserved words

An identifier is a name. You have seen several examples in the preceding chapters. Identifiers must start with a letter or the underscore, '_'. The remainder of the name may be any sequence of letters or digits or the underscore. Note that upper and lower case letters are distinct. As in the examples throughout this book, it is usual practice to use purely upper case for #defined identifiers.

Depending upon your compiler, there may be a limit on the number of characters that are significant in an identifier. Generally, the first eight characters are significant. For external identifiers, to be discussed in the next chapter, the limit may be even smaller. (On some systems only six characters are significant for such identifiers.)

In addition, you cannot define identifiers that are the same as any of C's reserved words:

auto	extern	sizeof
break	float	static
case	for	struct
char	goto	switch
continue	if	typedef
default	int	union
do	long	unsigned
double	register	void
else	return	while
enum	short	

3.3 Declarations

Whenever you want to use data, you *must* declare it. A declaration associates a name and a type with some memory. Every C variable must be declared before it is used. Optionally, data can also be given an initial value in the declaration. Having defined the type of a piece of data, you should only perform operations on it that make sense for the type declared. As you may find, the range of C compilers apply different standards in the strictness with which they limit the use of operators to operands of suitable types. Older compilers generally reflect a rather laissez-faire attitude which seems to say 'C programmers should be assumed to know what they are doing and if they happen to bend the rules a bit that is fine' and 'the compiler is not supposed to be a straitjacket that prevents programmers from doing what they need to'. Newer compilers show a trend towards stricter enforcement, protecting the programmer against accidental errors. We will encourage you to be disciplined in this matter even if your compiler does not force it upon you. As in Chapter 1, we demonstrate established practice as well as good style.

Declarations appear at the beginning of a block. In the program fragment below, we illustrate the form of declarations. The first declaration is for an int variable called windows and this is initialized with a value given by a constant expression. The integer variable people is set to zero and the next int, doors, has not been initialized. The variable wall_area is declared to be real and is initialized to the value 7.2 and the character variable c is initialized to the character 'M'. We will leave the thorough treatment of initializations to Chapter 4 because it is affected by **scope.**

```
#define MINWINS ...

    int       windows = 3 * MINWINS + 1;
    int       people = 0;
    int       doors;
    float     wall__area = 7.2;
    char      c = 'M';
```

As a point of style, note that we have put each declaration on a separate line. This makes it easy to delete declarations or add them near related variables.

The general form of declarations is

type   identifier [= expression] [, ...];

where square brackets indicate that initialization is optional and the [, ...], which is often called an **ellipsis**, indicates that you can declare several identifiers of the same type if you wish.

3.4   Integers

The C type int is one of the fundamental types. This means that much of the material in this section also applies for the character and enumerated types that map on to the integers.

Essentially, integers are whole numbers. It makes sense to do arithmetic on them and to compare the value of one integer with another. C also has bit operations and several other operators that can be used with integers. The following treatment may seem quite long and it is detailed. This is partly due to the number of variants of int and partly to the large number of operators that apply to the integers.

3.4.1   Integer values

The range of values that can be represented by an int is machine dependent. It is defined by the size that is most natural for integers for the machine. So, on a machine like the PDP11, an int is 16 bits. In the case of machines like the Motorola-68000, some C compilers implement an int as 16 bits and others as 32 bits. In general, you can rely on an int being at least 16 bits on most machines (and so an int can generally be used for numbers in the range −32768 to 32767).

Table 3.1 Examples of sizeof integers.

System	short int	int	long int
DEC-VAX System V	16	32	32
DEC-PDP11 Version 7	8	16	32
MC68000 Sun	16	32	32
IBM PC Venix 2.0	8	16	32
AT&T 3B2 System V	16	32	32
Your System			

In cases where it is important to save memory space, you can define a short int. Although the size of a short int is also machine dependent, it is guaranteed to be no bigger than an int. In some C compilers, short ints are actually the same size as an ordinary int. However, a variable declared as a short int is always to be regarded as being of a *different* type from a variable type of int.

Where the size of an int is insufficient, you may be able to use a long int, which is guaranteed to be no smaller than an ordinary int. C has an operator, sizeof, which gives the number of bytes occupied by an item of a given type. Using this, we can summarize int sizes for any compiler, on any machine:

sizeof (short int) ≤ sizeof (int) ≤ sizeof (long int)

Table 3.1 shows the size of an int on various machines. We have left room for you to add values for your system. As you can see, on a machine like the PDP11, long ints may often be necessary, where on the VAX an ordinary int would suffice.

Normally, integers are signed. However, an integer type can be declared to be unsigned. The most common uses for unsigned integers are for data that are really to be considered as a bit pattern, as in the case of a mask that can be used with bitwise operators to select particular bits in a data item. You might also use them for variables that cannot have negative values and where the extra bit is required as, for example, in the case of a variable to hold an amount of time in seconds.

Some of the variety of int declarations and forms of int constants are illustrated in the following:

```
int                 thneeds = -4;
unsigned int        time = 1;
unsigned short int  maskin = 071;          /* octal 71 */
```

```
unsigned long      maskout = 0xf9;     /* hexadecimal F9 */
long               mask_1_bit = 1L;    /* long 1 */
long               mask_2_bits = 03;   /* long octal 3 */
```

Decimal constants are written as you have seen them already: an optional minus sign to indicate negative numbers and a sequence of digits where the first (leftmost) digit is *not* zero. Octal constants, like maskin above, are distinguished by a leading zero. Hexadecimal constants start with 0x (or 0X). Any constant that is written with L or l as a suffix is a long constant. Observe that the initialization of a long int does not require the L suffix as illustrated in the last example.

Whenever you **qualify** an int as unsigned, long or short, you can omit the keyword int as in the last three declarations above. In fact this is the most common practice. So the general form of integer declarations is

[qualifier list] [int] [identifier list];

where the qualifiers can be unsigned, and either of short or long and the identifiers listed may be explicitly initialized, as described in the last section. Constant values can be written as

[−][0][x or X][sequence of digits][l or L]

EXERCISES

3.1 What is the effect of the following declarations?
(a)   int n = 0170;
(b)   int m = 0810;   /* *Warning: bad style or an error* */
(c)   short int i = 0Xab;
(d)   long j = 0x172;

3.2 On a machine like the PDP11 (with a 16 bit int, 8 bit short and 32 bit long) what is the type of the following constants?
(a)   0xFFFFFF
(b)   184000
(c)   8l
(d)   13L
(e)   012L
(f)   8

3.4.2 Integer operations

Throughout this section, we use Table 3.2 on page 55. It lists all the operators that apply to ints and, in due course, we discuss each of them. The vertical layout of the table defines precedence groups. The horizontal layout shows related groups of operators. The last column of the table helps to illustrate the meaning of each operator. It shows the value of the expression where x has the value 11, y the value 4 and w the value 0.

But before we launch into a study of the vast collection of C operators that can be used with integer variables and constants, we need to deal with a number of important preliminaries.

Expression values First, you should recall the discussion of controlling expressions in Chapter 2, where we noted that C has a more generalized notion of an operator than many other languages. In particular C views = as an operator. So assignment expressions have a value that can be used. For example, one can write an expression like

    y = 3

and since this is an expression, it must have a value. This particular assignment expression has the value 3, the same as the right hand side.

Also in the earlier chapters, we saw several relational expressions used to control loops and selection statements. The program flow depended upon whether the controlling expression had a zero or non-zero value. So, for example, a loop might be controlled by an expression like

    (x = getchar()) != 'z'

which has a subexpression

    x = getchar()

which has the value that getchar returns. The value of this assignment expression is compared against 'z', using the inequality operator !=. When the test fails (meaning that getchar read a 'z'), the whole expression has the value 0. Otherwise this expression has a non-zero value.

Order of evaluation in expressions In general, the way that an expression is evaluated and, hence, its value depends upon several things.

First, the relative **precedence** of the operators defines which operations will be done first. So, when you write an expression like

a > b && c <= d

you rely upon the fact that the relational operators > and <= have higher precedence than && (the logical AND) operator. We could make the meaning of this expression clearer (for those unfamiliar with C precedence) by using parentheses thus:

(a > b) && (c <= d)

In Table 3.2, all operations between horizontal lines have equal precedence and groups of operators higher in the table have higher precedence. For example, the operators above the first line are the unary operators: as in mathematics, unary operators have very high precedence. You may think of them as being bound very tightly to the operand that is adjacent to them.

Looking now at the operators below the first line, we need to consider the way that **associativity** defines the order of evaluation where an expression has operators with the same precedence. (Associativity is also referred to as the **binding**.) Two possible rules can operate: left-to-right or right-to-left associativity. The binary arithmetic, logical, relational and bitwise operators associate from left-to-right (as in mathematics) which is why the expression

3 − 2 + 1

has the value 2 (where right-to-left associativity would give the value 0).

The assignment operators associate right-to-left and this turns out to be the natural interpretation as in a multiple assignment expression like

a = b = c = 7

which sets all three variables to 7. To do this, the rightmost assignment expression

c = 7

is done first and this expression value (7) is assigned to b and this in turn sets a to 7.

Table 3.2 Precedence levels for operators.

Integer operators	Arithmetic	Logical or relational	Bitwise	Other	when x=11, y=4, w=0
Minus	−x				−11
Increment	++x				12
	x++				11
Decrement	−−x				10
	x−−				11
Address-of				&x	‡
Size-of				sizeof x	‡
Complement			~x		‡
Logical negation		!x			0
Multiply	x * y				44
Divide	x / y				2
Modulus	x % y				3
Add	x + y				15
Subtract	x − y				7
Shift left			x << y		176
Shift right			x >> y		0
Less		x < y			0
Less or equal		x <= y			0
Greater		x > y			1
Greater or equal		x >= y			1
Equal		x == y			0
Not equal		x != y			1
AND			x & y		0
Exclusive OR			x ^ y		15
Inclusive OR			x | y		15
AND		x && y			1
OR		x || y			1
Conditional				w?x : y	4
Assignment				x = y	4
				x *= y	44
				x /= y	2
				x %= y	3
				x += y	15
				x −= y	7
				x <<= y	176
				x >>= y	0
				x &= y	0
				x |= y	15
				x ^= y	15
Comma				x, y	4

‡ machine dependent

Now consider the expression

```
x = (a * b + fnA()) + fnB();
```

The precedence rules ensure that a * b will be added to the result of fnA( ) and the result of fnB( ) will be added in. However, there is no guarantee that a * b is evaluated first: it might be that fnA( ) is evaluated first. In general, this should not matter. Indeed, it would be very poor programming practice if fnA( ) altered the values of a or b. The C compiler is also free to do a sequence of additions (+) or a sequence of multiplications (*) in any order it chooses, *regardless* even of *parentheses*. So, in the example above, fnA( ) might be added to fnB( ) first and only then added to a * b. There are rare occasions when this might matter, as in the addition of two large positive numbers with one negative number where the order of the evaluations is significant to avoid overflow. If the order of evaluation *is* critical, you need to break up the expression like this:

```
x = a * b;
x += fnA();
x += fnB();
```

One last, but critical aspect of order of evaluation concerns logical expressions. C always evaluates expressions containing && and || in the order you write them, from left to right, and *halts its evaluation* at the first sub-expression whose value guarantees the value of the whole expression. Because the continued evaluation of the expression is conditional on the result of each such logical operation, some people would describe these operators as CAND (Conditional AND) and COR. So, in the example

```
for (j=0; (j < JLIM) && (arr[j] != MARKER); j++)
    ...
```

the evaluation of the continuation condition will stop if (j < JLIM) is false since this ensures that the whole expression is false. This is just as well if arr had only JLIM elements. In practice, this frequently proves useful and it seems very natural. More formally, a statement

```
if (j = a && b) ...;
```

is equivalent to

```
if (a)
```

```
        j = b;
    else
        j = FALSE;
    if (j) ...;
```

and the statement

```
    if (k = a || b) ...;
```

is equivalent to

```
    if (a)
        k = TRUE;
    else
        k = b;
    if (k) ...;
```

where TRUE and FALSE are suitably defined.

For the most part, precedence works out pretty well as you would expect. Whenever you are in doubt, it is best to use parentheses or do the calculation in stages to ensure that an expression is evaluated as you wish. This also has the merit of making the intention of the code clearer.

For example, what does the following expression do?

```
    ch = getchar() == EOF
```

The answer is that it gets a character, compares it to EOF and depending on the result of the comparison, assigns the value 0 or 1 to ch. This is almost certainly not what the programmer intended. Misconceptions about precedence can produce bugs that are very difficult to find. Whenever in doubt, use parentheses. So, in this case, write

```
    (ch = getchar()) == EOF
```

We now consider the actual operators that can be applied to the variables of type int. We deal with operators in the groups indicated by the four columns of Table 3.2: arithmetic, logical and relational, bitwise and then the others that have been lumped together.

Arithmetic operators

First we consider the unary arithmetic operators. Unary minus should be fairly familiar. (Some C compilers also allow a unary plus operator.)

In the case of integer operands, the increment operator simply corresponds to adding 1. Similarly the decrement operator subtracts 1. As you have seen, the increment operator may either precede or follow its operand. Its position defines when the increment occurs. Using the pre-increment as in ++x will increment the value of x and then use that value, whereas the post-increment operation x++ will use the value before performing the increment. For simple statements like

```
count++;
```

the order of the increment makes no difference. However, it is significant in statements that use the value as in the following:

```
printf(" %d" , x++);
result = count++;
```

which print and assign values one smaller than the pre-incremented code below:

```
printf(" %d" , ++x);
result = ++count;
```

Pre-increment or post-increment operators are extremely useful in conjunction with arrays and structures (as we shall see in Chapter 5).

The binary arithmetic operators should look quite familiar. They all return an integer result. The divide operator / gives the value after the division, ignoring the fractional part. The modulus operator % gives the remainder. So, for non-zero y, and arbitrary x, x has the same value as the expression

$$(x / y) * y + (x \% y)$$

even for negative x and y.

Logical and relational operators

We have already seen how C deals with relational and logical expressions in the treatment in Chapter 2 of controlling expressions in loops and selection statements. We saw there that C has no special type for data that are restricted to the values 'true' and 'false'. Instead it uses integers, with the convention that zero corresponds to 'false' and all other values to 'true'.

So we read code like

```
if (scanf(" %d" , &val) != 1)
    error_exit(" expected a number − it was not there" );
```

thus: if the value that scanf returns is not equal to 1, indicating that one value was read, invoke an error handling function. We may equally interpret it as testing whether the expression

```
scanf(" %d" , &val) != 1
```

has the value zero and if so, the conditional code is executed.

By now, the relational operators $<$, $<=$, $>$, $>=$, $==$ and $!=$ should be quite familiar to you. Note that $==$ is used to test for the equality of two operands. This is quite different from the assignment operator $=$ and you need to take care of the distinction since it is common to find both together in logical expressions like the following:

```
if ((c = getch()) == SPECIAL)
    ...
```

The logical operators !, && and || should also be familiar. Given an operand, x, which has a non-zero value (corresponding to 'true') !x has the value zero (corresponding to 'false'): similarly applying ! to an expression with the value zero gives a non-zero result (actually 1).

Bitwise operators

When you want to interpret an int as a bit pattern, the sorts of operation you need to be able to do include complementing, shifting and masking. Having developed as a language for systems programming, C provides this type of bit level operation.

The best way to think about the bitwise negate, ~x, is in terms of the binary representation of the operand, x. The bitwise negate operation ~x gives the 1's complement, which is the binary sequence you get by reversing each bit in the pattern for x.

Shift operators move the binary bit pattern the specified number of places. Left shifts $<<$ get zeros pushed into the rightmost bit positions as the number is shifted. For unsigned numbers, right shifts $>>$ behave correspondingly but for **signed** numbers the situation is machine dependent. Left shifts correspond to multiplying by the specified power of two and right shifts to dividing.

The bitwise & (AND), | (OR), and ^ (exclusive OR) instructions can be used to mask selected bits in a number. Take care not to confuse them with the logical operators && and ||. In the example shown in Table 3.2, the bitwise & (AND) gives zero because different bits are set in each operand. (The values in the example of the table are x = 11, and y = 4. AND-ing bit patterns that end with 1011 and 0100 gives 0000 whilst OR-ing gives the bit pattern 1111.)

Other operators

It remains to consider the motley lot of 'other' operators.

The address-of operator & was used in Chapter 1 with the argument to the scanf function. It differs from all the operators we have discussed to date in that it does *not* result in an int result. The address of a variable is a **pointer**. We will discuss the & operator (and its inverse) in the section on pointers later in this chapter.

The sizeof operator returns the number of bytes required to store the operand. It is most often used with aggregate data types, described in Chapter 5, but may also be used with simple types as in

```
int x = sizeof (float);
```

which initializes the variable x to the size in bytes of a variable of type float. This is used to improve portability as the code will be correct for any host machine on which it is compiled.

One might also use sizeof with an expression as in the following:

```
double  z;
int  m;
...
m = sizeof z;
```

Note that we can omit the parentheses when we take the sizeof an expression. So the general form is

> sizeof (*type*)
> *or*
> sizeof *expression*

From Table 3.2 you can see that sizeof is a very high precedence operator. This means that you generally need parentheses in complex expressions following it.

As we have already noted, assignment is an operator. A classic use for it is

```
while ((x = getchar()) != SPECIAL)
```

Note that you need the parentheses around x = getchar() because the assignment operator = has lower precedence than the relational operators != and ==.

We have not used the other assignment operators yet. They permit a convenient shorthand where, for example, you wanted to increment x by the value y. The expression

```
x += y
```

is equivalent to

```
x = x + y
```

where the former is shorter, and hence less prone to typing errors as well as being clearer. (It also enables the compiler to generate more efficient code.) This shorthand way of combining a binary operator with the assignment operator may be used for all the binary arithmetic and bitwise operators.

The conditional operator corresponds to an abbreviated form of the if-else. It is convenient in cases such as

```
max = x > y ? x : y;
```

which is equivalent to

```
if (x > y)
    max = x;
else
    max = y;
```

but the operator gives more concise code that clearly illustrates how the value assigned to max depends upon the value of the expression x > y. It is also handy in cases like this

```
printf(" %d", x > y ? x : y);
```

The last operator we have to discuss is the comma operator (,). One common use is shown in the following for loop control line:

```
int        a, b;

for (
        a = b = 1;        /* loop initializations */
        not_done();       /* loop termination condition */
        a++, b++          /* statement to be done on each
                             iteration */

    )
```

```
{
    ...
}
```

where both a and b need to be initialized and both need to be in-cremented on each iteration of the loop. The comma operator causes a sequence of expressions to be evaluated from left to right and the value of the whole expression is that of the rightmost of the expressions in the sequence. In this case, the comma operator enables us to write code that clearly indicates the similar treatment of the two variables a and b.

Of course, the use of the comma operator is not restricted to for loops. The general form of a comma expression is

exp1, ..., expn

and the value of the whole expression is the value of *expn*.

EXERCISES

3.3 Given the declarations:

```
int         i = 1;
short       s = 7;
long        l = 11;
unsigned    u = 73;
```

what is the value of the following expressions (performed independently of one another)?

(a)   i++
(b)   --s
(c)   i % s
(d)   (i = 1) && (s != 3) || (s == l / 2)
(e)   u = 031
(f)   u & 017
(g)   u | 017
(h)   u ^ 017
(i)   u & ~03
(j)   u & ~0
(k)   i += 3
(l)   u /= s + l
(m)   u >>= 3
(n)   l & ~017 == 0
(o)   (l & ~017) == 0

3.4 What is the effect of the following lines?

```
x = a = 1, b = 2;
x = a = 1; b = 2;
```

3.5 What does the following statement do?

```
while (e1, e2)
    doit();
```

3.6 What do the following statements print?

```
int  x = 1;
int  y = 2;

printf(" %d", x, y);
printf(" %d", (x, y));
```

3.5 Characters

The type char is used to hold letters, punctuation marks and all the other characters. We deal with it at this point, immediately after the integers, because there is a straightforward mapping between the characters and integers.

3.5.1 Character values

Nearly all UNIX systems have ASCII as the underlying character set. Variables and characters of type char are one byte long and can hold just one character. It can be any one of the upper and lower case letters, the digits, punctuation marks, blank or the many special characters. The following code fragment shows the form of character constants, including some special characters.

```
char  Big_J      = 'J'; /* initializes to an ordinary
                               letter */
char  New_Line   = '\n'; /* initializes to new line */
char  Tab        = '\t'; /* initializes to tab */
char  Back_Sp    = '\b'; /* initializes to back space */
char  Return     = '\r'; /* initializes to carriage return */
```

```
char  FF        = ' \f' ; /* initializes to form feed */
char  Slosh     = ' \\' ;/* initializes to \ */
char  S_Quote   = ' \'' ; /* initializes to a single quote */
char  Null      = ' \0' ; /* null character */
char  Oct123    = ' \123' ; /* the character with octal
                                pattern 0123 */
```

Although the ASCII character set has a defined mapping on to the integers, it is considered better style to avoid reliance upon this where possible. There are library functions for many character manipulation operations that enable you to write code that is portable and character set independent. ASCII characters are stored in one byte, which is usually an 8 bit quantity. In ASCII, the letters of the alphabet are contiguous: so the numeric interpretation of 'a' is exactly one less than that of 'b' and so on through the alphabet. The digits '0' to '9' are also contiguous.

3.5.2 Character operations

Because the ASCII characters are mapped on to the integers 0 through 127, many but not all the integer operators are meaningful in the context of characters. For example, it is often convenient to do arithmetic on characters as in the code below which converts a lower case character ch to upper case:

```
char    ch;
...
ch += 'A' − 'a';
```

In practice, C programmers think of characters in terms of their underlying integer representation whenever it is convenient to do so.

EXERCISES

3.7 Write a code segment that reads a sequence of digits (characters '0' to '9' and converts this to the equivalent decimal number, num.

3.8 Consider the code example above for converting a lower case character to upper case. Suppose that you are sure that ch contains an alphabetic character but cannot know whether it is already in upper case. You still want to end up with it being upper case. Rewrite the code for this situation.

3.6   Enumerated types

Integers are a fundamental and very natural type on computers. Everything that is stored on a computer is represented by a binary pattern which can be interpreted as an integer. But integers are not always the most natural representation for entities that you may need to deal with in a program.

Enumerated types (like those in Pascal) allow the programmer to define a type whose elements are **identifiers**. Suppose, for example, that a program keeps track of when certain events occurred. We might need to store the time of day, the day of the week, the month and the year. Integers are fine for time and the years but not so appropriate for the day of the week or for the month. After all, the days of the week already have perfectly good names of their own and it seems reasonable to represent a day of the week as one of Sunday, Monday ... rather than some arbitrary integer. The enumerated type allows you to create your own type for situations like this by defining identifiers, like Sun, Mon ... which are the permissible values in that type.

3.6.1   enum values

When you declare an enum, *you* define the collection of legal values for that type. You enumerate the values, hence the name enum. The declaration of an enum for the type day might be

```
enum day
{
    Sun, Mon, Tues, Wed, Thur, Fri, Sat
};
```

and then you can declare variables of this type as follows:

```
enum day      today;
enum day      tomorrow;
enum day      payday;
```

Of course, enums are actually stored inside the computer as bit patterns and it is natural to think of enums as being mapped on to the integers. In the example, when the variable today has the value Sun, the binary pattern in that piece of memory corresponds to the integer zero. Indeed, each of the values for the days of the week will be mapped by the compiler on to the integers zero through to six:

Value in enum today	Sun	Mon	Tues	Wed	Thur	Fri	Sat
Integer it maps on to	0	1	2	3	4	5	6

This mapping is only a default. You can define your own mapping as in the case:

```
enum indicator
{
        dreadful = -10,
        poor = -5,
        OK = 0,
        good = 10,
        terrific = 30
} colour, texture, taste;
```

As this shows, you do not have to define the mapping on to consecutive values; they can map on to any set of int values. Observe also that we have combined the definition of indicator, with the declaration of three variables colour, texture and taste.

In general, the form of an enum declaration is

```
enum [type-identifier]
{
        value-identifier [= integer] ,
        ...
} [variable-identifier, ] ... [variable-identifier];
```

You may separate the definition of the type and the declaration of variables of that type if you wish. It is frequently better to do so. Then you can order the type definitions and variable declarations for greatest clarity.

3.6.2   enum operations

Bearing in mind that enums map on to the integers, but that the programmer may choose the mapping, there are very few operations which are generally appropriate: you can test for equality and inequality between enums and do simple assignments. Since you define an ordering on the enum identifiers, you would expect to be able to check whether one enum value is less (or greater) than another. As long as you explicitly cast the enum variables to ints, C will allow you to do so.

Most other operations make little sense; for example, it is hard to imagine why you would want to multiply two enums and most C compilers give an error message if you try.

In practice, programs exploit the mapping of the enum on to the integers as in this case:

```
if (today == Sat)
    tomorrow = Sun;
else
    tomorrow = (enum day)((int)today + 1);
```

where the else part converts the enum variable to an int and then performs the arithmetic. Finally, it converts back to an enum day.

The standard libraries do not provide functions that can do I/O on enums. So, when you want to write enums, you need code like this:

```
switch (today)
{
case Sun:      printf(" Sunday" ); break;
case Mon:      printf(" Monday" ); break;
case Tues:     printf(" Tuesday" ); break;
case Wed:      printf(" Wednesday" ); break;
case Thur:     printf(" Thursday" ); break;
case Fri:      printf(" Friday" ); break;
case Sat:      printf(" Saturday" ); break;
}
```

To read strings and interpret them as enum values, you should use standard functions (gets, fgets, scanf, fscanf and sscanf treated in Chapter 7). Since enums are most heavily used for data internal to the program, the need for input/output is not very pressing.

EXERCISES

3.9 Define a type that is suitable for representing the months.

3.10 Write code that reads an indicator value as one of the strings defined earlier in this section.

3.7 float and double

The floating point or real number types, float and double, are used to represent numbers with a fractional part. Although these types permit the representation of extremely large and extremely small numbers they bring problems too. (See a numerical analysis text for problems of floating point rounding errors.)

3.7.1 Floating point values

Floating point numbers are stored as a mantissa and an exponent. The size of each is machine dependent, with the mantissa size defining the number of significant digits that can be represented and the exponent setting a limit on the magnitude of the largest and smallest number. The type float gives a single precision floating point number and double gives a double precision type that may have more significant digits and a larger range of magnitudes.

The more fundamental type is double: *all floating point constants are handled as* double. In addition, float variables are converted to double before arithmetic operations are performed. We return to this matter in the section on implied conversions later in this chapter. Some examples of the form of floating point constants are:

```
/* a small positive number in scientific notation */
float     a = 6.419e−2;
/* a large negative floating point number */
float     b = −8495364.2;
```

3.7.2 Floating point operations

Many of the operators that apply to integers are also appropriate for the floating point number types. The arithmetic operators are applicable, except for increment and decrement where it is not clear what size increment is natural for a floating point number. (In fact, they do add or subtract 1.0 which is what you might expect.)

Of the relational operators, the ones that test whether an operand is less than or greater than are relevant. Because of floating point errors, tests for exact equality or inequality are dangerous. (But lint doesn't help here.) Similarly, the logical and bitwise operations are not normally appropriate. The other operations listed in the table of integer operators (except %) are appropriate and have essentially the same meaning.

Some examples of input and output with real numbers are shown below. Although we saw some simple I/O on floating point numbers in Chapter 1, the full range of formatting facilities is described in Chapter 7. We could print the variables a and b, that we declared in the previous section thus:

```
printf(" %e \n %f \n" ,a * b, b / a);
```

This will produce the following output:

```
-5.453174e+05
-132347160.000000
```

The same numbers could be read using a scanf with the same format string as is used in the printf.

3.8 Pointers

In Chapter 1, you saw the use of a pointer in a call to the scanf function. It looked like this:

```
scanf(" %d" ,&ftemp);
```

The scanf function requires a pointer to a memory location as its argument. The function does its work and stores the required value in the location specified by the pointer.

For the types described so far in this chapter, a declaration causes a location in memory to be reserved and a name and type to be associated with it. By contrast, you can think of a pointer as a data type which contains an address that is an indirect way to get to some other data. The declaration of a variable like

```
char    ch = '$';
```

can be depicted thus:

Now consider the effect of a declaration for a pointer variable which we write as *p and we initialize p to point to the variable ch:

```
char    ch = '$';
char    *p = &ch;
```

This can be depicted as

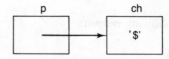

This situation can also be created with code like this:

```
char    ch;
char    *p;

p = &ch;
*p = '$';
```

Pointers often pose problems for novice programmers. This is primarily due to the need to be clear about the distinction between

- the name of a variable (its identifier)
- the value of the variable and
- the address of the variable (which may, in turn, be the value of a pointer variable).

In general, pointers are a dangerous yet powerful data type. They are also indispensable in C.

Computer addresses can be represented by integers and so it is sometimes appropriate to think of pointers in that way. However, there are many possible problems with this view: integers can correspond to addresses which are not available to your program, and on some machines pointers and ints have quite different sizes. (For example, several MC68000 C compilers.) In the past, many C programmers have ignored this and in doing so have produced code that is not portable: worse still, such programs may well run with subtle errors. You can use lint to check for many problems like this.

3.8.1 Pointer values

When you declare a pointer, you are defining an **identifier** that gives you indirect access to other data. Suppose we have the following declarations:

```
char    ch;
char    *letterp;
char    *p = &ch;
```

The pointer p is initialized to point to ch. On the other hand, letterp is uninitialized. Elsewhere in a program it may be assigned a value so that it points to a location. The value of a pointer variable can be

- the address of some variable,
- a special NULL value that indicates that the pointer does not point to anything
- or it can be undefined because no value has been assigned to it.

NULL has the value zero and is defined in stdio.h.

You can define a pointer to *any* type, including other pointers and the aggregate data types (treated in Chapter 5).

3.8.2 Pointer operations

As you would expect, it is permissible to check whether pointers are equal or not. But you may only compare pointers that point to the same type. A pointer to an integer and a pointer to a character are of *different* types. Some simple additive operations on pointers make sense when you are dealing with the aggregate data structures treated in Chapter 5. We will return to them there.

We now illustrate some simple uses of the indirection operator (*) and the address-of operator (&).

```
char    *p;          /* a pointer to a character */
char    ch = '1';    /* a character variable */
```

```
p = &ch;                /* p now points to ch */
printf(" %c" , *p);
printf(" %c" , ch);
```

Both of these printf statements have the same effect. The first finds the
value of ch going indirectly via the pointer p. The second printf prints
the value of ch directly.

Both * and & are in the group of highest precedence operators. As we
discussed on page 56, C uses short-circuit evaluation of logical expressions.
This is very convenient in cases like

```
if ((p != NULL) && (*p == VAL))
    ...
```

Should the first part of the expression be false, the rest of the expression will not be evaluated. So there is no difficulty with *p in the
second part of the expression when p is not defined.

EXERCISE

3.11 This should give you a little familiarity with the notation associated with
pointers. Assume the following declarations and work out what the code fragment prints. (You may find it helpful to draw pictures of the pointers and other
data as we have done in our introduction to pointers.)

```
int        num = 42;
int        *np = &num;
int        *ap;
char       ch = 'b';
char       *cp = &ch;
char       **ppc;

printf(" %d %c %c \n" , (*np)++, ch, *cp);
printf(" %d %d \n" , *np, (*np+7));
*np += 4;   /* observe the use of a pointer on the left hand
                side of an assignment */
ap = np;
*cp = 'k';
ppc = &cp;
printf(" %d %d \n" , *np, *ap);
printf(" %c %c %c \n" , ch, *cp, **ppc);
```

3.9   typedefs

The typedef facility allows you to define an alias (or alternative name)
for a type as in

```
typedef float      Length;
Length  height;

Length
determine__size()
{
    ...
}
```

where we have, essentially, defined Length to be a synonym for float.
This makes it clearer that the variable height represents a length and
that the function determine__size returns a length.

Note that a typedef does *not* define a new type, but rather an
alias for one of the existing types. The typedef is most useful in substantial data structures and we will see it again in Chapter 5.

However, even simple uses are valuable for improving the clarity
and portability of programs. For example, we might use the following
typedef:

```
typedef int Message__size;
```

in a program that deals with messages of a size that can be represented
by an int on our current machine. Should we port our program to a
machine with much smaller ints, we can amend this typedef to make
Message__size a long. The simple modification to this one typedef
will ensure that our whole program deals with the new definition
correctly.

3.10   Conversions

Type conversions can occur either implicitly or explicitly. You should
use explicit type conversions to make your intentions clear. This section
discusses both explicit and implicit conversions as well as the actions
that take place during a conversion.

3.10.1   Explicit type conversions—casts

There are many occasions when you need to change the type of a variable or expression. We met several in Chapter 1. Now, consider the

following example where the int expression is **coerced** or **cast** to a char.

```
int      i;
char     c;

c = (char) (4 * i + OFFSET);
```

After the expression is evaluated, it is cast to a character and then it can be assigned to a variable that is of type char. When you cast a variable, its value is adjusted according to the rules described later in this section. The general form of a cast is

(*type*) *expression*

Note that the type can be a pointer as in the following:

```
char     *p;
int  x;

p = (char *)x;
```

You can also cast an int to an enum, as in this case:

```
enum day
{
    Sun, Mon, Tue, Wed, Thu, Fri, Sat
};

day workday;
int num;

workday = (enum day) num;
```

3.10.2 Implicit type conversions

At the outset, it should be noted that this and the next section may seem rather complicated. In fact, they look worse than they really are. Most reasonable type conversions work out pretty naturally and you can skip this and the next section on a first reading of the book.

First let us consider what happens when you need to do arithmetic on variables of different types. For example, the code below uses both ints and shorts:

```
short    a, b;
int      x, y, z;
```

```
...
x = y + z * a + b;
```

Before performing the arithmetic operations, the short ints are converted to ordinary ints. This is described as **promoting** the short ints. In general, when two types are involved in an arithmetic operation, the lesser one is promoted using what are called **usual arithmetic conversions**. In addition, C performs so-called **general arithmetic conversions** that promote all short, char and float data to the fundamental data types, int and double.

General arithmetic conversions

These apply to any arithmetic expression with data types short, char or float. The conversions

$$\text{char, short} \quad \rightarrow \quad \text{int}$$
$$\text{float} \quad \rightarrow \quad \text{double}$$

ensure the same precision in all integer and all floating point arithmetic operations. We will meet the same conversions in function arguments in Chapter 4.

Conversions of operands of different types in arithmetic expressions

Once the general conversions just described have been performed, an arithmetic expression may still have operands of different types. In this case, the following rules are applied in the order shown.

(1)   If any operand is a double, the other operands and the whole expression become double; otherwise

(2)   if any operand is a long, the other operands and the whole expression become long; otherwise

(3)   if any operand is an unsigned, the other operands and the whole expression become unsigned.

So, for example, an expression that adds a long and an unsigned would see the unsigned converted to a long. (You will get an opportunity to practise these conversions in the next set of exercises.)

Conversion of types across assignment expressions

The sections above deal with arithmetic expressions. In the case of assignment expressions, the type of the left hand side dominates. So in code like this:

```
int      kk;
float    y = 1.4;
kk = y + 2.7;
```

the right hand side (the float expression y + 2.7), is evaluated as a floating point expression (giving the value 4.1) and this is converted to an int before the assignment. The whole assignment expression also has type int.

3.10.3   Actions that occur during conversions

We now consider what actually happens to values that are converted. Most of this follows logically from the way in which each type is represented on the machine and the inherent difficulty in conversion between intrinsically different types. One of the most important conclusions you should draw from this section is that type conversions, both implicit and explicit, can pose particular problems. First, let us consider some of the more obvious and safe conversions listed below.

char	→	short int, int, long int	machine dependent may sign extend or not, ASCII characters remain non-negative
short int	→	int or long int	sign extended
int	→	long int	sign extended
float	→	double	zero padding of mantissa

In general, when you want to convert a quantity of one size to some *larger* type, you would expect the sign and the value of the quantity to be preserved with the extra bits being padded appropriately to achieve this effect. In the case of integer quantities, this is referred to as **sign extension** and, as you can see, there are several conversions where this occurs. So, in those cases, the conversion should act just as you would expect. Note that the conversion from a char to any of the int types is guaranteed to be well behaved only in the case of ASCII characters, which remain non-negative. For floating point conversions to double, the sign and value are preserved by padding out the mantissa with zeros.

Now all other conversions are fraught with dangers of various sorts. Consider first the case of converting a particular quantity to a similar but smaller type:

long int	→	int, short int, char	high bits discarded
int	→	short int or char	high bits discarded
short int	→	char	may lose high bits
double	→	float	round and truncate, overflow may occur

Clearly, we are in trouble if we started with a value that does not fit in the new, smaller type. Where such conversions are between int types, the high bits of the initial commodity are discarded. For truly numeric entities this could pose a problem: in a conversion that goes to an 8-bit type from some larger one, a number like 258 would suddenly become 2. Of course the conversion can be made safe by testing the quantity before doing the conversion. The conversion from double to float also behaves as well as can be expected. The double quantity is rounded to fit a float. On machines where floats are smaller than doubles, such a conversion can cause a loss of accuracy and, even worse, if the exponent no longer fits, overflow can occur. (This may stop the program with a floating point error indication.)

Now we need to deal with conversions that pose logical problems in that they involve inherently different types:

float, double	→	*integer type*, char	machine dependent
integer type, char	→	float, double	may lose precision
unsigned	→	*signed type*	machine dependent
unsigned	→	long	zero padding

Conversion from an int to a floating point type may mean a loss of precision. In a conversion in the opposite direction, to an int, there are clearly problems with the fractional part of the number and if it exceeds the largest int. Conversions between signed and unsigned ints also pose problems. For example, the number −1 in an 8-bit quantity on a twos complement machine is represented by eight 1s which, as an unsigned quantity, would be interpreted as 255. If you were expecting the signed value −1 to become the unsigned value 1, you may be in for a shock.

The relationship between pointers and ints is clearly very close. On most machines, both are the same size and conversions between them are straightforward. So both the conversions

| *integer type* | → | *pointer type* | machine dependent |
| *pointer type* | → | int | machine dependent |

would usually be a no-op (null operation which leaves the bit pattern unchanged). Some programmers are sloppy about making any distinction between these two types. This is dangerous in machines where ints and pointers are different sizes.

Finally, we have to consider conversions involving enums.

| enum | → | int | safe: gives underlying mapping |
| int | → | enum | safe for mapped int values |

There are many instances where one may wish to cast an enum to an int. As you would expect, this simply gives the integer value that the enum maps on to. Similarly, conversions from int to an enum are straightforward provided that the int value is one for which that enum has a mapping. Any other conversions involving enums are inappropriate.

EXERCISES

3.12   Assume the following declarations:

| unsigned int | x; |

| short int | k; |
| int | kk; |

| char | ch; |
| char | *pc; |

| float | y; |
| double | yy; |

For each of the expressions below, determine any conversions that will be performed and the type of the result.

(a)   y = 1.0
(b)   y = yy * kk

(c)	yy = y
(d)	yy = (kk = 2.3)
(e)	pc = kk
(f)	y = x + 1
(g)	ch = ch − 'a' + 'A'
(h)	kk = (kk) ? k : y

SUMMARY

The fundamental types are

    int
    double

The integer type qualifiers are

    short
    long
    unsigned

Other types closely related to ints are

    char (maps on to ASCII integer range)
    enum (user may define mapping on to integers)

The floating point types are

    float
    double

Pointers

- can point to a variable of any type, including pointer types
- are the mechanism for returning parameter values from functions
- are *not* ints.

typedefs allow the programmer to define an alias for a type.
C is rich in operators. The ones we have met are

- unary − ++ −− ! ~ & sizeof *
- binary (associate left to right)

arithmetic * / % + −
shift << >>
relational test < <= > >= == !=
bitwise & | ^
logical && ||

- conditional (associates left to right) ? :
- assignment (associate right to left) = *= /= %= += −=
- comma (associate left to right)

Conversions

- can be explicit using casts
- default:

  general arithmetic conversions reduce variables to fundamental types
  mixed type arithmetic conversions reduce all variables in an arithmetic expression to the same type
  conversions across assignment expressions convert the type of the right hand side of the expression to the type of the left hand side.

Chapter 4
Functions

In this chapter, you see how to

- *use* functions
- *write* functions
- limit the *visibility* of identifiers to a block, function or file
- effect data abstraction and data hiding
- define the *storage class* of data items as **auto** (the default), **static**, **register** and **extern**
- initialize variables of each storage class
- compile and run multifile programs.

4.1   Introduction

One might view programming as building a new high level language: you write the main program in terms of statements, some of which are primitive statements in C and others are calls to functions (which may be thought of as statements in the higher level language that you create for the particular programming task).

One of the strengths of C in the UNIX environment rests on the availability of a powerful collection of functions in the standard libraries. The functions that you develop, along with those in the standard library, constitute a *tool kit* that enhances your programming productivity. The tools approach pervades the philosophy of C and UNIX. (For more on this, see *Software Tools* by Kernighan and Plauger.) There is considerable art in learning how best to define functions appropriate to a task. If you can do it skilfully, you will build up collections of functions that are useful in a range of different programs. You can then create your own special purpose libraries.

The usual C style is to write programs with many small functions and substantial C programs tend to be spread over several files. This permits separate compilation of just the parts that are under development at any stage. It also gives control over the visibility of identifiers between files. But since functions can be compiled separately, the compiler cannot always check consistency of function and argument types. You need to use lint for this.

Pascal programmers will find that program structure in C is quite different. You cannot nest functions and scope operates quite differently. Identifiers can be local to one function (or a block within it) or they can be global to the functions in a file, or global to the whole program. Global data in a file can also be explicitly imported by other files. The C programmer should be aware of the mechanisms for storing data since this defines some aspects of scope and the forms of initializations.

It is characteristic of C and UNIX that the facilities available are simple but sufficient. In keeping with this, C provides only one type of subprogram, the **function**, and only one mechanism for passing arguments, the **call by value** mechanism. So, as we saw in Chapter 1, a function that needs to return more than one value must use arguments that are pointers which simulate call by reference.

4.2   Using functions from the standard libraries

Before we plunge into the issues relevant to writing and using your own functions, we deal with the simpler matter of using the standard library functions. We illustrate important points in using C functions with the following example:

```
double  sin();
double    n;
double    x;

scanf(" %f" , &n);
x = sin(n);
```

4.2.1 Declaring functions: defining the type of the returned value

The code above invokes two functions. First is the scanf function which we have used before and, as here, we have not bothered to declare it. This is because the default function type is int and scanf returns an int (the number of items read). We could have added a declaration

```
int  scanf();
```

but it is usual to omit declarations for int functions from the standard library.

By contrast, we must declare sin because it returns a value of type double. Had we failed to declare sin, the double precision floating point value that it returned would have been interpreted as an integer! Fortunately, lint warns about this sort of mismatch between the type of a function at the point where it is defined and at each place it is used.

So, you need the function declaration to specify the type of the value returned. It has no details at all of the arguments. The general form of a function declaration is

type function-identifier ( );

where the default type for undeclared functions is int.

4.2.2 Using the value returned by a function

Let us look more closely at the following call to the scanf function:

```
scanf(" %f" , &n);
```

In this form, it seems that the only value that the function affects is the argument, n. But scanf also returns the number of input items that it succeeded in reading: if an end of file is encountered before a value can be read, the value −1 is returned. If we were writing a program in which there were some chance that scanf might not succeed in reading a number, we should use code like this:

```
if (scanf(" %f" , &n) != 1)
    error__exit(" number expected on input − not found" );
```

In fact, it was rather sloppy of us to just ignore the value returned by scanf, and lint would warn us of this. Had we been sure that there was no need to test the value that scanf returned, we should have made this clear by casting the value returned to be void, like this:

```
(void) scanf(" %f" , &n);
```

In general, the way to explicitly disregard the value returned by a function is

```
(void) function-call
```

and we recommend that you use void in cases like the scanf above. Then you can consistently write lint-free programs (at least, in this respect).

4.2.3 Invoking functions: arguments

As you might expect, a function argument may be any expression of the appropriate type. Permissible expressions include a simple constant value, a variable name or any arbitrarily complex expression that may include other function calls. The *actual* arguments, those that appear in the function call, should have the same type as the *formal* arguments (as they appear in the actual function code). So, for example, sin can be invoked with any expression that evaluates to a double.

The arguments and values returned by a function are reduced to the fundamental types. So, just as we saw in the general arithmetic conversions (page 75 of Chapter 3), char and short become int and float goes to double. So, we can call sin with a float argument because this is promoted to a double. However, int types, char, enum or pointer type expressions give incorrect results. You need to use lint to flag mismatches between the types of actual and formal arguments.

Now let us consider an example that illustrates a number of interesting function arguments. It is a call to the library sort function, qsort (quicksort):

```
#define N    100
    int  nums[N];
    int  compare();

        ...
        qsort(nums, N, sizeof (int), compare);
```

qsort requires four arguments. Our first argument, nums, is the array that is to be sorted. In fact, it is better regarded as a **pointer** to the first item to be sorted. The second argument, N, is the number of items to be sorted and its value has been set in a #define. The third argument must specify the size, in bytes, of each data item. Finally qsort requires that the user supply a function, in this case compare, to determine the relative order of any pair of the items to be sorted.

In general, a function invocation has the form

function-name (actual-argument-list);

where these actual arguments match the formal arguments defined in the function code.

EXERCISES

4.1   Are the following legal calls to the sin function?
(a)   sin(.7);
(b)   sin((double).7);
(c)   sin(0x1f1);
(d)   sin(1);
(e)   sin(x);
(f)   sin(4 * sin(3.872) − y);

4.3 Writing your own functions

To begin, let us consider a very simple example: we write a compare function to be used in conjunction with the sort function qsort. We require the function to accept two arguments, x and y, which are both pointers to ints and compare must return +1 if *x is the larger, −1 if *y is larger and 0 if *x and *y are equal. Hence:

```
    int
    compare(x, y)
```

```
int  *x;
int  *y;
{
     if (*x > *y)
          return 1;
     else if (*x == *y)
          return 0;
     else
          return −1;
}
```

This function performs a simple three-way branch on its arguments and returns the appropriate value. It is no more complex than the functions we met in Chapter 1 but we now use it to illustrate the general form of functions.

4.3.1 Function header

The first four lines of this function are the **header**. The first gives the type. If we omit it, the function defaults to type int which would make no difference in this case. It is generally better to make your intentions clear by explicitly defining the function type. Next is the function name and formal argument list: we always put this on a new line so that we can easily use a text editor to find a function definition (as it is the only place where the function name appears at the very beginning of a line). The remainder of the header declares the arguments. Any arguments that are used should be declared. If you fail to do so they too default to type int, and even when this is what you intend it is better practice to explicitly declare *all* arguments. The general form of a function is

>   *[type]*
>   *function-identifier [argument-list]*
>   *[argument-declarations]*

where *type* can be void or any type other than the array (though a pointer to an array is fine) and the default is int.

Now let us consider the header of the standard qsort library function, which illustrates several types of argument declarations:

```
void
qsort(data, number, size, compare)
int   *data;    /* pointer to the beginning of the data
                   to be sorted */
int   number;  /* number of data items */
```

```
int  size; /* size, in bytes, of each data item */
int  (*cmp__func)();/* pointer to a user-defined comparison
                         function */

{
    int  *p;
    int  *q;
    if (cmp__func(p, q) == 1)
        /* p points to the larger */
        ...

}
```

The first argument is declared as a pointer to an int. This is one way to declare an array of ints (and we return to the matter of aggregate data types as arguments in Chapter 5). The next two arguments are fairly obvious, but the last shows the form of an argument that is a function name: it is a pointer to the function. Note that you need the outer pair of parentheses because the declaration

```
int  *cmp__func();
```

declares a function that returns a pointer to an integer. We also illustrate how qsort can refer to such an argument.

4.3.2 Function body

The function body is a block: a sequence of declarations and statements enclosed in braces. So, for example, a minimal function block that does nothing looks like this:

```
{
}
```

A typical function has several declarations and statements, including at least one return statement as in our compare function. A function may return no value as in the following function (which we saw in Chapter 1):

```
void
string()
{
for (;;)
{
```

```
        switch (nextchar())
        {
        case '"':    return;
        case '\\':  nextchar(); break;
        }
    }
}
```

In this case, the function returns upon encountering a double quote. Even when there is no return statement, as in this function (also from Chapter 1):

```
void
character()
{
    if (nextchar() == '\\')
        nextchar();
    nextchar();
}
```

the function terminates and returns when the last statement has been executed. As you would expect of functions that return no value, string and character are declared as void.

The general form of the return statement is

return *[expression];*

Note that some people like to enclose the return expression in parentheses. This is fine but unnecessary.

The function return expression is converted to the function type or, in the case of char, short or float functions, it is reduced to the more fundamental types, int and double.

A function can invoke *any* function within the same program or in a library that is linked to it. A special case of this is when a function invokes itself, either directly by calling itself or indirectly by calling functions that call it. It is often possible to write simpler and more elegant code using such **recursive** calls.

4.3.3   Exiting a program

You can exit a *program* from any point within any of its functions using the standard system call function exit. Consider this example:

```
if (scanf(" %d", &n) != 1)
    exit(1);
```

where the program gives up if scanf fails to read a number. The argument to the exit system call is the **exit code** that the program returns. This value can be tested from the shell (or other invoking program), and so the exit code constitutes a limited form of communication between programs. Programs that terminate normally should return the exit code 0. The exit code can be tested as in the following sequence of UNIX commands which invoke a program and use the exit status to print an appropriate message:

```
if cmp −s tfile tfile2
then
        echo "tfile and tfile2 are identical"
else
        echo "tfile and tfile2 are different"
fi
```

The program cmp is the UNIX command that compares two files. When invoked with the −s argument cmp returns with exit code 0 to indicate that the files are identical and 1 to indicate that they are different.

You can also use the return statement within the main function to quit the program at some point other than the end of main. However, the value returned varies between systems. In the interests of portability, we recommend you use only exit to leave a program.

4.3.4 Communication between functions

Like most programming languages, C has two means of communication between functions:

- arguments and
- via data that are global.

As we saw in Chapter 1, C arguments are passed by value. On the other hand, an argument that is a pointer type permits a function to return a value as we have seen in scanf. Although a function cannot directly alter the value of one of its arguments, it can store a value at the location that the pointer argument points to.

Introductory programming texts wax lyrical on the merits of using **arguments** (also called **parameters**) for clean interfaces between the modules of a program. Arguments make function interfaces explicit and, in the case of many functions, they also give flexibility. The next section gives some background on the storage of data, and then we see how you can use global data for communication between functions.

EXERCISES

4.2 Given a function with the header

```
int
doit(a)
char    *a;
```

and the declarations

```
int     *x;
char    y;
char    *z;
```

which of the following is a correct call to the function?

```
doit(&x);
doit(&y);
doit(&z);
```

4.3 Write a header for a function that plots a function. Its arguments should be scaling factors for the x- and y-axes and the function to be plotted.

4.4 Suppose the following function has been defined:

```
void
silly(a,b,c)
int     a;
int     *b;
int     c;
{
    a += c;
    (*b) ++;
}
```

what is the effect of

```
int  x = 0;

silly(x, &x, 2);
```

4.4   Runtime stack

We will soon meet aspects of scope that are easier to understand if you appreciate the runtime stack mechanism that accommodates data for each block as it runs. To see how this storage model operates, consider the following skeleton of a program that has an input phase, followed by some processing and printing:

```
main ()
{
     int  m1, m2, m3, m4;
     ...
     Do__Input();
     Process__and__Print();
}


Do__Input()
{
     int  i1, i2;
     ...
}


Process__and__Print()
{
     int  p1, p2;
     ...
     calc(p1, p2);
}


calc(x, y)
int  x;
int  y;
{
     int  c1;
     ...
}
```

Before the main function can start to run, all the variables declared in it need to be allocated storage. Since there are just four of them, the allocation would appear as in Figure 4.1. We show the stack growing down because that is what happens in most systems.

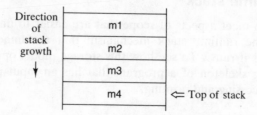

Figure 4.1 Stack when main starts.

As main runs it invokes Do__Input, which has two variables. Space is allocated for these, too, on the runtime stack, so that just before Do__Input starts to run the stack is as shown in Figure 4.2.

For the moment we will not consider the sort of housekeeping data that is required: we will stick to the simple model of how data declared in each block is allocated runtime storage. Conceptually, upon the completion of the function Do__Input, all the space for its data disappears. This means that the runtime stack reverts to the form it had immediately before this function was called (as in Figure 4.1).

A very similar set of steps takes place when Process__ and__Print is invoked. The physical storage that is allocated for this function will, in fact, be that which has just been used by Do__Input. However, Process__and__Print invokes calc, so that at the point that calc starts to run the stack will be as depicted in Figure 4.3.

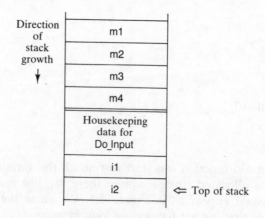

Figure 4.2 Stack when Do__Input starts

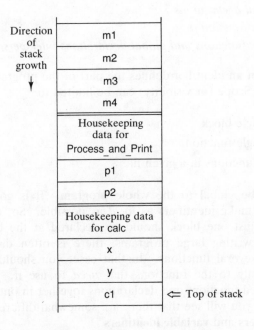

Figure 4.3 Stack when calc starts.

So the stack grows and shrinks as functions are invoked and complete execution. This has important implications: with the exception of the data associated with the first function to be invoked (main), you cannot assume that variables on the stack have some default initial value. In fact, variables that you do not explicitly initialize start out with the value that happened to be given to the last variable that occupied the same physical memory location, and this is unpredictable.

4.5 Program structure and scope

A C program is a collection of functions. The main function is like any other in all but one respect: you must have a main function because it is the point at which execution of the program starts. The functions that constitute a program may be stored in one or more files and you may arrange them in any order you choose. However, it is usual to put main first in its file so that someone reading the program will encounter an overall view of the program first. Similarly, it is usual to place functions within a file in roughly their order of execution, with high level ones first.

You *cannot* nest functions. So a typical program has the following structure:

global declarations
main function
other functions and global declarations interspersed

The **scope** of an identifier defines the part of the program where you can refer to it. Scope (or visibility) can be limited to

- a single block
- a single function
- the functions in a given file

or it may be global to the whole program. It is good programming practice to make identifiers as *local* as possible. So, a variable that is needed in just one block should be declared at the beginning of that block. In writing large programs, there is often data that must be shared by several functions. In that case, you should make that data available only to the functions that *need* to use it. To do this, you group related functions and declarations together in one file. As we discuss scope, you will see that there are somewhat different rules for **function identifiers** and **variable identifiers**.

Scope within blocks

The declarations within a block hold for the scope of the block, from the point of their declaration to the brace that closes that block. We illustrate this in Figure 4.4.

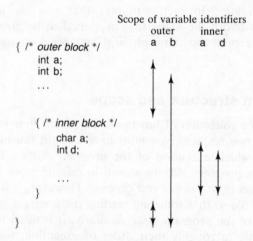

Figure 4.4   Scope in a block.

The scope rules ensure that the variable b is visible in both the inner and outer blocks. The variable d is declared in the inner block and is only visible there; the outer block cannot refer to it. The identifier a is visible in the outer block as an int, but it is declared again as a char in the inner block. So references to a in the outer block concern one variable, an int, and references to a in the inner block relate to a completely different variable, which just happens to have the same name. Re-using identifiers like this is potentially confusing and you should avoid it.

Storage class

The variables within a block are one of three storage classes, auto, static or register.

Within blocks, all three storage classes follow the scope rules above; elsewhere this is not the case. We now describe each of these storage classes.

Automatic variables This is the class of variable that is stored on the runtime stack. It includes variables like those in Figure 4.4 as well as a2 and a5 of Figure 4.5. The default storage class for variables declared within blocks is automatic (also called auto) which means that their storage is allocated as their block starts to execute. When the block finishes, this storage automatically disappears. The same storage may then be re-used by the next block that executes.

Static variables As their name suggests, static variables are persistent: they are not destroyed on completion of their block. So, for example, if we alter the declaration of a5 in Figure 4.5 to

```
static char   a5;
```

a5 retains its value between function calls. So, if a5 has the value q at the end of the first call to A, a5 retains that value until the next time A is invoked. Static variables exist for the full duration of the program execution.

Register variables You use the register storage class to give the compiler a hint that it should allocate data to a register. However, compiler writers usually devote considerable effort to ensure that the code their compiler generates makes efficient use of registers. If you know your C compiler and your machine exceedingly well, you may sometimes decide that you can make a better allocation of variables to registers than the compiler does. In that case, you can declare variables like this:

    register int   a;

Many compilers ignore the register declaration. If you try to declare more register variables than there are registers, the compiler selects some of them to be allocated to registers and the others are treated as ordinary variables.

Scope within a file

We illustrate the way that scope operates within a file in terms of the program depicted in Figure 4.5.

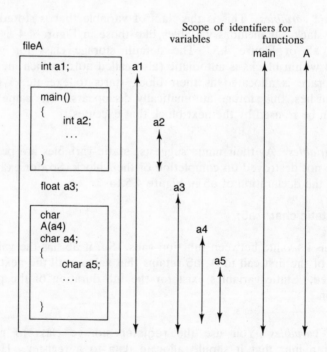

Figure 4.5 Scope within a file.

First let us consider the variable identifiers. We show each function and all of its identifiers inside a box. The walls of the box can be regarded as protecting all the variable identifiers within it, rendering them invisible to all other functions. So, for example, the identifier a2 is *local* to the main function and cannot be accessed by other functions. Similarly, the identifiers a4 and a5 are local to the function A. For the purposes of scope, you should think of a formal argument (like a4) as an identifier local to the function. It may have been initialized with the value of the *actual* argument to the function.

Now consider the identifier a1. It is **global** or **external** to all of the functions and so may be used anywhere in this sample program. The identifier a3 is also declared outside the functions but after the first one. It is visible only to the functions that appear *after* it in the file. So, the function A can use a3 but main cannot.

Now the function identifiers can be regarded as having scope that ranges over the whole file. However, this does not cover the situation completely. In many situations, C assumes the type int as the default where the programmer does not explicitly state another type. So, in the following code fragment, we need a *forward* declaration of do__this:

```
double *do__this();

do__that()
{
    double *p;
    ...
    p = do__this('m');
}

double *
do__this(a)
double a;
{
    double *p;
    ...
    p = do__that();
}
```

Had we omitted the declaration for do__this, the compiler would have assumed that it returned an int when called in do__that. It would have then complained that we assigned an int to p, which is a pointer to a double. Since each function accesses the other, we need a declaration for one of them before the other.

External identifiers

We describe variables like a1 and a3 in Figure 4.5 as **external** since this identifier is external to the functions. All function names are also external. External variables are like statics in that they exist throughout the life of the program (unlike autos).

4.5.1   Scope between files

You have already seen some aspects of scope between files in our use of functions from the standard libraries (page 83). Where we have used int functions like scanf we could assume that the function name was accessible even though it ıs in a separate file from our program. (Standard functions that are not int need a declaration only to establish their type.)

In this section, we cover the general rules of identifier scope between files. First, however, we note that the visibility of an identifier between files is determined by its *storage class*, which is one of *external*, static, auto or register. A *variable* can be any one of these storage classes and a *function identifier* can be either *external* or static.

Now we have already seen that auto variables exist only within blocks. So we have nothing new to say about their scope in multifile programs. Similarly, register variables must appear within a block.

On the other hand, function and variable identifiers that are external or static are the bases for controlling scope between files. We describe this in terms of Figure 4.6, which shows a program in two files. We see that an external identifier can be imported by other files, using an extern declaration, unless we make it static.

Importing variable identifiers

A variable like b1 which is declared in fileB is accessible throughout that file. To make it available in another file, we need an extern declaration as we have done with a1. The line

       extern int   a1;

within the function B1 in fileB *imports* the identifier a1 into B1. Had we put the extern declaration at the beginning of fileB (near the declaration of b1), then a1 would have been visible throughout fileB.

In general, extern declarations are a mechanism for importing *external* variables from other files. Note that whereas other declarations actually cause storage of the specified type to be allocated, extern declarations merely define the type of the variable and enable *access* to

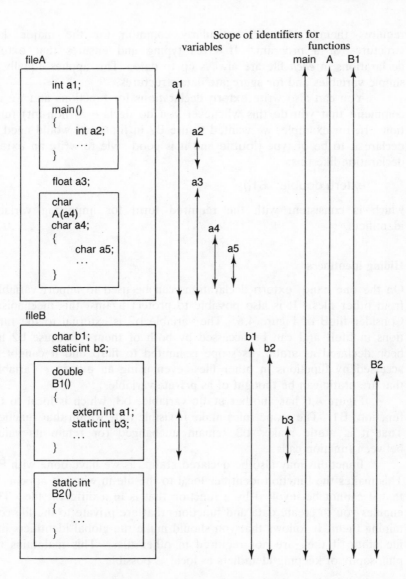

Figure 4.6   A program in two files.

data that is declared elsewhere. So, the **extern** declarations for arrays do not need to specify their size (unless they are multidimensional).

In substantial programs there may be many **externs** that are common to several files. The usual practice is to put all such declarations in a file with the suffix .h (such as **stdio.h** which has definitions used by the standard I/O functions). Then we use the preprocessor's #include facility to textually include the declarations into each file that requires them. This is particularly common for the major data structures of a program. It saves typing and ensures that **extern** declarations in *each* file are always up to date. This applies equally to simple variables and for aggregate data structures.

You can also write **extern** declarations for functions and we recommend that you do this whenever you do declare a (non-int) function. If, for example, we wanted to use B2 in fileA, we would need to declare it to be of type **double** and it is good style to write an **extern** declaration like this:

```
extern double   B1();
```

which is consistent with the required form for importing variable identifiers.

Hiding identifiers

On the one hand, **extern** declarations can be used to import variables from other files. It is also possible to protect against this mechanism. Consider fileB of Figure 4.6. The variable b2 is external to the functions in fileB and can be accessed by both of them. Because b2 has been declared as **static**, its scope is limited to fileB and it cannot be accessed by functions in other files, even using an **extern**. Variables that are **static** can be thought of as **private** variables.

Figure 4.6 has another **static** variable, b3, which is local to the function, B1. The scope rules make it visible only within that function. That it is **static** makes b3 remain unchanged (or retain its value) between function calls.

Functions may also be declared **static**, as we have done with B2. This makes the function identifier local to the file in which it appears so that it cannot be invoked by a function that is in a different file. This enables you to create data and functions that are private to the file containing them. It follows that you should make the global identifiers in a file **static** if they are not required in other files. This maintains the philosophy of keeping identifiers as local as possible.

Data abstraction

Data abstraction involves constructing your own data type, including the allowable values and operations. Although C does not support data abstraction, you can achieve something with similar effect by defining a **static** data structure and a collection of functions to manipulate it. All the functions that manipulate that data structure are put in the same file, with all of them declared **static** unless they define the allowable operations that you define for your data type. In Chapter 5 we provide an example of creating a symbol table using static declarations in this way to achieve much of the effect of an abstract data type.

4.5.2 Scope of other identifiers

The preceding discussion has dealt with variable and function identifiers. There are other types of identifiers:

- typedef
- #define
- labels

These are limited to the file in which they are declared. Since a typedef is merely a synonym for a type, it is fine to have a separate copy of it in each file as required (this is usually done with #include). We saw that a3 in fileA of Figure 4.6 is only accessible to functions that appear after it in the file. The same holds for typedef and #define identifiers.

EXERCISES

4.5 What are the situations where identifiers have default type int?

4.6 The library function strcpy copies a string. When you want to use it, you should declare it as in

```
extern char  *strcpy();
char         buf[SIZE];
char         *p;
char         *q = " arbitrary string";
...
p = strcpy(buf, q);
```

What would happen if the extern declaration line were omitted?

4.7 The following questions relate to the program depicted in Figure 4.6.

(a)   How can we make a3 accessible to main?
(b)   How can we make a3 accessible within B2?
(c)   What would happen if we added the line

```
int b1;
```

at the beginning of fileA?

(d)   What would happen if we added the line

```
int  b2;
```

at the beginning of fileA?

(e)   What is the effect of

```
extern char  b1;
```

at the beginning of fileB?

(f)   What would happen if you put the line

```
extern int    B2();
```

in fileA?

4.8

(a)   You cannot make register variables static. Why not?
(b)   You cannot use the & operator with register variables. Why not?
(c)   Given a function header,

```
char
fnA(x)
char   x;
```

how do you make the argument a register variable?

4.6   Storage classes—initializations

In view of the different storage mechanisms associated with different
storage classes, it is not surprising that initializations behave differently
for each of them. We use the following declarations to discuss the
interaction between storage class and the permitted forms of initializations as well as default initializations. However, we warn you that it is
better style to make explicit initializations whenever you need them
(and then you need never worry about which classes have default initializations and which do not).

```
#define BOUND  100
```

```
static int     a = 72 * sizeof(int);  /* constant expression */
int            b = BOUND;              /* constant expression */
extern char  x;                        /* cannot be initialized
                                          here */

int            y;                      /* defaults to zero */
fnA()
{
    static int     c = BOUND + 7;  /* constant expression */
    int            d = a + fnXX();  /* any expression */
    register int   e = b;           /* any expression */
    extern char  g;                /* cannot be initialized */
    ...
{
```

4.6.1   Initialization of auto and register variables

We show d and e initialized to arbitrary expressions. Since the space for these is allocated each time their block starts executing, it is logical that you can define their initial value with any expression. As you should expect, this expression is re-evaluated each time the block is invoked.

If you do not explicitly initialize an auto or register variable, you cannot predict its initial value. It simply inherits the last value assigned to the location that it is allocated and failure to initialize such a variable often causes insidious intermittent errors.

4.6.2   Externs

In the example we have an extern declaration for x which means that its actual declaration is elsewhere. It only makes sense to initialize a variable once and this must be at the point of its actual declaration, not in an extern statement.

4.6.3   Statics and external variables

All of these are allocated storage for the duration of the program execution. So, you can think of their initialization as happening at compile time and it follows that they can only be initialized to a *constant* expression.

The default initialization for these classes is to zero (or the appropriate type cast of zero). Even so, it is good style to make explicit initializations for *all* variables whose initial value is critical to the program's correct behaviour. It certainly makes your intent clearer and improves the chances that subsequent modifications to the program will preserve this intention.

EXERCISE

4.9 lint warns about auto and register variables that appear to be used before they are set. Why doesn't it do the same for external and static variables?

4.7   Compiling and running multifile programs

In Chapter 1 we saw how to run simple programs. We now see how to handle programs that are distributed over several files. It becomes even more important to use lint to check consistency in function arguments across files and for proper use of externs. This section shows how to use lint and also how to create your own libraries.

Figure 4.7 shows the various phases in compiling and loading a C program. You saw a similar one in Chapter 1, but here we show how the various types of files fit into the process and their naming conventions.

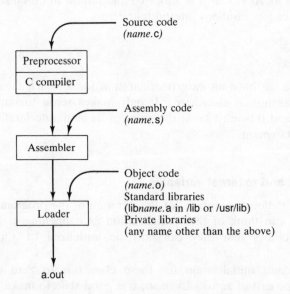

Figure 4.7   Compiling and loading a C program.

Source file names must have the suffix .c and, if they are free of syntax errors, they pass through the preprocessor, the compiler, the assembler and the loader. Your program can include files of assembly code and these must have names with the suffix .s. The compilation process generates intermediate .s and .o files which are normally removed by the end of the complete compilation. However, if you use the −c flag on the cc command, the object of each file is stored in a file with a .o suffix. If, for example, you had a program that was in three files, called doin.c, proc.c and dout.c, you might compile them with the UNIX command

    cc −c doin.c proc.c dout.c

This creates object files called doin.o, proc.o and dout.o. You can then make the loader create a binary from these using

    cc doin.o proc.o dout.o −o process_data

which gives a complete program binary called process_data. Omission of the −o flag and the file name that follows it makes for a rather unspecific binary file called a.out.

If, at some later stage, you decide to modify the code in proc.c, you recreate the program binary with the UNIX commands

    cc −c proc.c
    cc doin.o proc.o dout.o −o process_data

where the first command recompiles the single file that you have changed and the second invokes the loader to create the complete program binary. Once you have created a version of the program that can get past the compiler successfully, you should use lint to check for the multitude of problems it can find. You use the UNIX command

    lint −hpbaxc doin.c proc.c dout.c

where the flags hpbaxc ensure maximum checking.

4.7.1   Linking standard libraries

As you can see in Figure 4.7, you can link your program to **libraries**, both public and private. The C compiler presumes that an undeclared identifier (like scanf) is a function name and it tries to find the function in the file /lib/libc.a. In the case of scanf and other functions from the standard I/O library it succeeds and can link the appropriate functions.

Only the most commonly used functions are kept in /lib/libc.a and for other functions, like the mathematical functions, you need to name explicitly the library file to be searched. For example, to compile a file called calc.c that contains a call to the trigonometric function sin you use

    cc calc.c −lm

where the −l flag precedes the name of the library to be searched (in this case, m). By convention, the loader looks in directories called /lib and /usr/lib for the file with the prefix lib and suffix .a. (So, in the case of the mathematical library m, the file is called libm.a.) Libraries are searched in the order you specify to the cc command. This can pose problems and these are treated in detail in Chapter 8.

4.7.2 Creating your own libraries

A library is simply a collection of .o files. You use the UNIX ar (archive) command to put them into a single library file. So, for example, we can create a library containing three files called clear.o, move.o and curve.o using the UNIX command

    ar c drawer.a clear.o move.o curve.o

where we follow the convention that archive files have the suffix .a. If we subsequently modify move.o, we can replace the old copy of it in the library with the following command:

    ar r drawer.a move.o

Once a library has been created, you can get a list of the constituent .o files with the t flag as in this command:

    ar t drawer.a

Then you can link this library with object files, graph.o and chart.o, with this UNIX command:

    cc graph.o chart.o drawer.a −o depicter

You can choose any name you like for your own libraries, except that it should *not* have the suffixes .c, .s or .o. As Figure 4.7 indicates, the loader assumes any cc file argument which does not end in .c, .s or .o is one of your private libraries.

Once you are building programs that are large enough to be spread over several files and that use libraries, you can benefit from using make to help manage the files and ensure that they are always compiled and maintained correctly. We discuss make and the management of large programs in Chapter 8.

4.7.3   Using lint on multifile programs

We have already mentioned the role of lint in finding incorrect or poor code. It has checks for type inconsistency including:

- inconsistency between the declared function type and the type of values it returns (where we view void as a type);
- inconsistency in the use of a function's return value (including failure to use the return value of a function like scanf and an attempt to use a function return value when none was returned);
- inconsistency between actual and formal arguments (where float and double match, char, short and int match, an array name and a pointer to that array type match but all other types must match exactly).

It uses various algorithms and heuristic checks to identify problems like:

- unused variable or function identifiers
- auto or register variables that are not set before they are used
- unreachable code
- strange type casts
- other strange constructs (like the redefinition of an identifier in an inner block).

In addition, it does portability checks and identifies superseded forms of syntax.

Balanced against all the good things that lint gives is the fact that it can produce warnings about programs that work properly. For substantial programs, we have found it useful to develop a programming style that takes full advantage of lint. This means writing code that lint accepts without complaint: it is dangerous to hope that you can sort through lint warnings, ignoring only the ones that are not critical.

EXERCISE

4.10 Look in /lib and /usr/lib on your system and see what libraries are there. Explore them to see what each contains. Try using the man command to get details.

4.8 Functions with a variable number of arguments

This section deals with a machine dependent matter and may be skipped on a first reading.

You will recall that when a function is invoked, its data requirements are reserved on the runtime stack. This includes its arguments. The C compiler stores each of them as one of a small variety of storage sizes. So, for example, a char argument will generally be stored in a location that is the same size as an int (or a pointer, whichever is larger). In general, you can ignore this aspect of the implementation. However, it is important when you want to create functions with a variable number of arguments.

We use Figure 4.8 to look more closely at how the C compiler handles function arguments. Figure 4.8 depicts the runtime stack at the point when a function called fn has just been called. As is common for most C compilers, we show the function arguments on the stack *in reverse order* of their appearance in the argument list and the stack is shown as descending. So, c is stored first and the first argument, a, is the last item put on the runtime stack. In terms of this diagram, we can

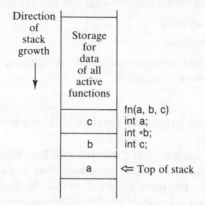

Figure 4.8 Runtime stack.

see that the value of the first argument is stored at the address &a and that the second argument, b, is at the address &b, which is also &a+1. Now we can use this approach to write a function which, like printf, can have a variable number of arguments. It starts like this:

```
fn(x)      /* BEWARE : machine dependent */
int  x;
{
      int *p;
      ...
      p = &x;/* p is the address of the first argument */
```

We only define one argument because we do not know how many there really will be on any particular call. But we do know that x will always be at the top of the stack. Now, just as we reach b in Figure 4.8 by doing arithmetic on the address of a, so we can access a second argument to fn as *(p+1) and a third as *(p+2) and so on.

In the case of printf and scanf, the first argument provides the information needed to determine the number of arguments that follow. (The format string in the first argument allows printf and scanf to work out how many arguments should follow and what types they have.) Another strategy is to require that the last of the actual arguments have some sentinel value. (The standard execl function uses this approach, with a zero as the sentinel value.)

Although this approach is typical of many C compilers, you need to check the exact mechanism for your compiler. You should also investigate whether there is a function on your system for handling variable numbers of arguments. Certainly, it is good practice to separate this sort of function and clearly document it to indicate that it may pose portability problems.

4.9 Perspectives

A number of the language aspects we have described in this chapter reflect C's history. We now discuss them.

There is a general trend towards safer C compilers with tighter function interfaces. Whereas older compilers permit the functions in one file to use the variables in other files without explicit extern declarations, newer compilers enforce the scope that we have described in this chapter.

You may have wondered why char and short arguments and

function return values are promoted to int (and similarly float to double). One very practical reason is that a single library function can service all the types that promote to its type.

By this stage you may also be surprised that so many important checks on source code are done by lint rather than the compiler. Pascal programmers will be accustomed to getting much more help from the compiler in finding errors. Some of the differences follow from the fact that C supports separate compilation. Certainly, the checks that run across files cannot be done by the compiler when it only has access to some of the files in a program. Even so, many other lint checks could be done by the compiler. For example, consider an heuristic check like finding variables that are used before they have been given a value. This can only be approximate and such checks can be very resource intensive to perform. So there is an argument based on efficiency for separating the functions of a compiler and a source code checker. A second reason is based on history and the *tools* philosophy which advocates separation of different functions into different programs. An interesting side effect of the separation between the compiler and lint is that lint is very standard across all systems, whereas the compiler may be different.

SUMMARY

A program is a collection of variable declarations and functions. It can explicitly return an exit code; the default value returned by programs that complete normally is 0.

A function has a

- header of the form

    type (can be void or any type except array, default is int)

    function identifier

    argument list

    argument declarations (can be any type other than array; can be a pointer to data of any type, including array or function; for arguments and function return values, char and short are promoted to int, float to double)

- body (block) with braces enclosing declarations and statements including zero or more return statements.

The scope of an identifier can be limited to

- a block
- a function
- a file
- several files.

Storage classes for variables are extern, static, auto and register.

Initializations of auto and register variables can be any expression; other storage classes can only be initialized to a *constant* expression.

There is no default initialization for auto and register variables; other storage classes are initialized to zero or the relevant cast of zero.

Function identifiers are *all* external but

- can be restricted to one file using a static declaration;
- require an extern declaration to ensure that their correct type is conveyed across file boundaries.

External identifiers can be imported to a file with an extern statement.

We have seen the cc command

- with the −c flag to create object files from .c files
- with the −o flag to specify the name of the executable binary file
- to load object files (.o) and library files (.a)
- with the −l flag to specify libraries to be searched.

After compiling programs you should use lint.

Chapter 5
Aggregate Data Types

The simple data types were treated in Chapter 3 and now we see how to construct aggregate data structures:

- *structures* for collections of related data of any type
- *arrays* for collections of data, all of the same type
- *strings* for character sequences
- *bitfields* for representing bit data and
- combinations of these.

We also show how to deal with arguments on the program command line. The treatment of arrays emphasizes the pointer based view of an array. One of the striking aspects of C programming idiom is the heavy use of pointers to access aggregate data structures, especially in the case of strings and arrays.

5.1 Introduction

In Chapter 1 we looked at simple uses of arrays. In this chapter we introduce the other aggregate types, the struct (which is like Pascal's record), the union (which is like Pascal's variant record) and bitfields, which look similar to a structure component and are useful for data that are viewed as a collection of bits.

We start with a simple treatment of structures, then arrays and strings. From there, we go on to discuss unions and bitfields and the more interesting and useful applications of various combinations of the aggregate data types. These include arrays of structures and structures containing arrays, strings, other structures and pointers to other types. We also show how to use information hiding to get some of the benefits of data abstraction.

Although C permits you to deal with a whole structure as one entity, in assignments, function arguments and return values, this is not the case with arrays. Arrays are consistently viewed as a sequence of items, each of the same type, with the array name being best viewed as a constant pointer to the zeroth element in the array.

We also see idiomatic code for manipulating an array in terms of pointers. So far we have used arrays in much the same way as they are used in Pascal, but here you see how C's arrays are very closely related to pointers and are commonly manipulated by pointers. The philosophical differences between Pascal and C also show strikingly in the fact that C does *not* check for out of bounds array accesses.

Strings in C are rather like those in Pascal in that they are arrays of characters. However, C has the convention that a string ends with the ASCII NUL character, \0, and the standard libraries provide a stock of functions that perform many useful string operations.

5.2 Structures

There are many situations where a program needs a data structure that is a collection of related elements, which may be of different types. In C, we call these **structures** and the components of a structure are called **members** or **fields**. A structure member can be any simple or aggregate type.

We now introduce an example of a simple structure that we use throughout this section. Consider the following declaration for representing a date:

```
enum day__name
    {
```

```
    Sun, Mon, Tue, Wed, Thu, Fri, Sat, day__undef
};
enum month__name
{
    Jan, Feb, Mar, Apr, May, Jun, Jul, Aug, Sep,
    Oct, Nov, Dec, month__undef
};
struct date
{
    enum day__name        day;
    int                   day__num;
    enum month__name      month;
    int                   year;
} Big__day =
{
    Mon, 7, Jan, 1980
};

struct date    moonlanding;
struct date    deadline = {day__undef, 1, Jan, 2000};
struct date    *completion;
```

The struct date has four components, two of which are ints and the others are enum types, day__name and month__name. The identifier date is called a **tag**. The last declaration, for completion, is an example of a pointer to a structure.

You may use the same field identifier in different structures. So the declarations above can coexist with ones like this:

```
struct car__desc
{
    enum car__cols    colour;
    enum car__make    make;
    int               year;
};
```

where we have reused the identifier year.

5.2.1 Declaration and initialization

When we declared the Big__day structure, we combined the definition of the struct date with the declaration for Big__day. The other declarations, for moonlanding, deadline and completion, use the existing definition of date. In general, it is better to separate the structure definition and declarations so that you can place each independently in your program text. The general form of a structure **definition** is

```
struct [tag]
{
        member-declarations
} [identifier-list];
```

and once a tag has been defined, data can be **declared** using this form:

```
struct tag    identifier-list;
```

The declarations for Big_day and deadline also illustrate some structure initializations. That we have initialized them indicates that they must be external or static because you *cannot* initialize auto data structures in the declaration line: these must be explicitly initialized with assignment statements.

The typedef that was introduced in Chapter 3 is widely used to create a synonym for a structure. For example, we might create a Date typedef thus:

```
typedef struct date
{
        enum day_name        day;
        int                  day_num;
        enum month_name      month;
        int                  year;
} Date;
```

and then we could have declared the structures thus:

```
Date    Big_day = {Mon, 7, Jan, 1980};
Date    moonlanding;
Date    deadline = {day_undef, 1, Jan, 2000};
Date    *completion;
```

This not only saves some typing but it can make programs clearer.

5.2.2 Structure accesses

There are two structure access operators, dot (.) to access a field within a structure and −> which gives a shorthand for accessing a field when you have a pointer to the structure. Simple accesses to our date structures might look like this:

```
moonlanding.day__num = 19;
scanf(" %d" , &(moonlanding.year));

completion = &deadline;
deadline.year++;
deadline.month = Oct;
```

where the dot operator appears between the structure name and the component name. The last three lines could equally well have been written thus:

```
completion = &deadline;
(*completion).year++;
(*completion).month = Oct;
```

where the brackets are needed because the dot operator has higher precedence than *.

In practice, it is very common to access structure members using a pointer to a structure. The −> makes this easier. It enables you to write the above code more simply like this:

```
completion = &deadline;
completion −> year++;
completion −> month = Oct;
```

Both structure operators have the same precedence, which is higher than any of the operators discussed in Chapter 3. Both are evaluated left to right.

EXERCISES

5.1 Given the declarations

```
struct A
{    int  a;
     int  *b;
     int  c[10];
};
```

```
struct A      x;
struct A      *p;
```

what does each of the following expressions do?
(a)   (*p).a
(b)   *p.b
(c)   p->c[0]
(d)   x = *p

5.2.3 Structures as function arguments and return values

Since a structure can be treated as a single entity, you can write code like this:

```
struct    mine    s1;
struct    yours   s2;
struct    mine    doit();

s1 = doit(s2);
```

where the function doit takes a structure s2 as its argument and returns a structure which is assigned to s1. The outline for doit might look like this:

```
struct mine
doit(ds)
struct yours      ds;
{
        struct mine temp__str;
        ...
        return temp__str;
}
```

5.2.4 Standard structures

In any substantial program, it is usual to define a set of structures for use in several files. By convention, these are kept with other shared declarations in a file with the suffix .h. (The h is for header.)

We have already seen some standard .h files, including stdio.h. In addition, there are several useful structures defined in UNIX systems. For example, tm holds a time with date and time of day and is defined in time.h. The file information structure called stat is defined in stat.h and passwd which contains password information for a user and is defined in pwd.h. Chapter 7 deals with their use.

There are many other standard structures that are defined for particular systems. For any application, you should try to seek out such structures so that your programs can deal with data in a standard way. For example, most systems have standard structures for I/O device control. (We discuss some of these in Chapter 7.)

5.3 Arrays

You can define arrays over any C type, including enums, pointers and any aggregate type.

C arrays are tightly linked to pointers. Indeed, the array name is actually a **constant pointer** to the zeroth element of the array and C programmers commonly access an array element using pointer arithmetic. This is illustrated in Figure 5.1.

In some respects the C view of an array is very close to the machine implementation: it is equally valid to view the array as a name with an index or as a constant pointer to the place in memory where the array begins with the facility to do pointer arithmetic to take an appropriate offset. This is why C arrays start with the index zero.

There is a sense in which C's support of pointer arithmetic allows a high level view of an array. Even if A's elements are a complex data type, the pointer arithmetic shown on the right of Figure 5.1 gives the same address as the corresponding index form.

Since you cannot have arrays as function arguments or return values, you need to use the pointer view of an array in those cases. In all, pointers are very heavily used with C arrays.

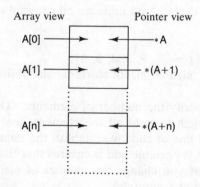

Figure 5.1 Two views of an array called A.

5.3.1 Declaration and initialization

We can initialize static and external arrays (but not auto arrays) as in this declaration:

```
int  A[10] = {1, 1, 1, 1, 1, 1, 1, 1, 1, 1};
```

where we initialize all the elements in A to one. Unfortunately, there is no shorthand form of this initialization, and had the array been much bigger, it would have been simpler to write a loop that set all the elements to one.

If you provide an initialization list that has too few elements, the remaining elements are set to zero (or the equivalent cast). So you can abbreviate

```
int  tally[10] = {0, 0, 0, 0, 0, 0, 0, 0, 0, 0};
```

to

```
int  tally[10] = {0};
```

and since all external and static data has a default initialization to zero (or the relevant cast) these are also equivalent to the following declaration:

```
int  tally[10];
```

The first of these forms is the clearest and is to be preferred when you need to rely on an initial value of zero. (Of course, auto arrays cannot be initialized in the declaration line and they have no default initialization to zero.)

We can also declare and initialize an external or static array like this:

```
int  starters[] = {1, 2, 3, 4, 5, 6};
int  Starter_size = sizeof starters / sizeof (int);
```

where we do not specify the number of elements. The compiler makes the array large enough to hold all the elements listed in the initialization. In the second line of code we establish the number of elements in starters. This form is portable and it ensures that Starter_size has the correct value even if you change the number of elements in the array (or if you cannot count accurately).

The general form of an array declaration is

> *type   array-name[[size]] [= { value, ... }];*

where the initialization is allowed only for **static** and external variables.

5.3.2 Array accesses

The array index operator [ ] has the same precedence as the structure operators, dot and −>. Its action is best described in terms of the pointer model of an array, where

> y[i] is equivalent to *(y + i)

and y is a *constant pointer* with the address of the zeroth element in the array. So, given the declarations

```
int  A[N];
int  *pa = &A[0];

struct date  B[N];
struct date  *pb = &B[0];
```

you can refer to the zeroth element of the array A as any of

```
A[0]
*pa
*A
```

and the zeroth element of B with the corresponding forms. To access the jth element of each array you can use any of the three forms

```
A[j]
*(pa + j)
*(A + j)
```

and

```
B[j]
*(pb + j)
*(B + j)
```

which works correctly because pointer arithmetic is always done in terms of the data type involved. If, for example, **sizeof date** were 27, the addition of j to p would actually involve adding 27 * j to p. The general form of an array access is

> array-name[index-expression]

or

> *(array-name + offset)

and *array-name* acts as a constant pointer.

EXERCISES

5.2   Given the following declarations

```
char    *s;
char    line[100];
char    *doit();
```

which of the following operations make sense and what do they do?

(a)   s = line;
(b)   s ++;
(c)   line ++;
(d)   s += 7;
(e)   &line[0];
(f)   *line
(g)   &(line[1]) − 1;
(h)   doit(&line[7]);

5.3   Look back at page 108 where we discussed the way the runtime stack operates. Our treatment works for int arguments. However, had the function declaration been

```
fn(a, b, c)
char    a;
int     b;
int     c;
```

how could we access b in terms of a which is at the top of the stack?

5.3.3   Out of bounds array accesses

C does *not* check that array accesses are within the array bounds. So, in code like

```
int A[100];
...
A[n] = 77;
...
```

it is your responsibility to ensure that n is in the range zero to ninety-nine. Otherwise, your program will access some arbitrary piece of memory. The resulting errors can be exceedingly difficult to find (and this is a place where lint cannot help).

One way to protect against this problem is illustrated below

```
#include <assert.h> /* contains relevant macro
                       definition */
...
int A[100];
...
assert((n >= 0) && (n < 100));
A[n] = 77;
...
```

where the library function, assert, checks the value of the index n and prints an error message if it is out of range. It must be admitted that C programmers tend to make rather little use of assert but we hope that this will change. We certainly recommend the use of assertions to improve the reliability of your code. For those situations where efficiency is critical, the assert can be made subject to conditional compilation (using the preprocessor facilities).

The other approach is to use debugging tools to find bugs due to array accesses being out of bounds.

5.3.4 Multidimensional arrays

It is not common to use a multidimensional array in C. The language idiom favours an array of pointers or a linked list. Nevertheless, let us consider a very simple function that calculates the sum of two matrices, A and B, each with three rows and five columns:

```
void
sum()
{
    int i;
    int j;

    for (i = 0; i < 3; i++)
```

```
        for (j = 0; j < 5; j++)
            AplusB[i][j] = A[i][j] + B[i][j];
}
```

To use this function, we could declare A like this:

```
int A[3][5] =
    { { 1, 0, 0, 0, 1 },
      { 1, 1, 1, 1, 1 },
      { 0, 0, 1, 0, 1 }
    };
```

where the initialization shows A as an array of row arrays, with each row initialization expressed as a separate vector initialization. The following initialization for B shows another acceptable form where the two-dimensional array is viewed as a vector or one-dimensional array:

```
int B[3][5] =
    { 1, 2, 3, 4, 5, 6, 7, 8, 9, 10, 11, 12, 13, 14, 15 };
```

Arrays are stored by rows, so that the first five elements of B are its first row of elements (the row with index 0). There is no limit on the number of array dimensions and the array is stored with the last array index changing fastest.

EXERCISES

5.4 Assuming the above declaration for B, what is the value of

```
B[2][0]
*B[2]
B[2]
```

5.5 Given the declarations

```
float    x[a][b];
float    y[c][d][e];
int      i, j, k;
```

give the pointer form for

```
x[i][j]
y[i][j][k]
```

5.3.5   Array pointers as function arguments and return values

Unlike some programming languages, C does *not* permit the manipulation of whole arrays in single operations. This means that you must use a loop to do tasks like adding a constant to each element in an array, multiplying the elements of two arrays, reading and printing a whole array. Of course, if you need to do a lot of these operations, you can build libraries of functions to do them. Indeed, C provides a collection of functions for manipulating strings, which are a particular class of array.

You can give a function access to all the elements of an array by passing a pointer to the array. We illustrate this in a revised form of the matrix addition function which accepts pointers to arbitrary arrays of the correct size and returns a pointer to their sum. This means that each time sum runs it must allocate the storage needed for the matrix sum, as shown below:

```
int *
sum(A, B)
int A[][5];
int B[][5];
{
    int *result;
    int i;
    int j;

    result = (int *)malloc(sizeof(int) * 3 * 5);

    for (i = 0; i < 3; i++)
        for (j = 0; j < 5; j++)
            result[i * 5 + j] = A[i][j] + B[i][j];
    return result;
}
```

We declare the function as int * and we have a result of the same type. The first action of the function is to call malloc to allocate space for a 3 by 5 array for the matrix sum. This is the first of many uses we make of malloc, a function that allocates space at runtime. Its argument specifies the amount of space to be allocated and it normally returns a pointer to the first location in the allocated memory. It can fail if there is not enough memory available to satisfy the request and, in that case, it returns the value (char *)0. In general, we should make it a policy to check this, and on page 128 we show you the usual way to do this. For now, we assume that malloc succeeds.

The central loop of the function is as in the earlier version. Note that the declarations for the formal arguments follow a common C convention in that we omit the size of the first index. As you can see from the last set of exercises, the compiler does not need the size of that dimension of the array to compute array indexes. (And since it does not check for out of bounds array accesses, it makes no use of the first dimension when you do provide it.)

5.3.6 Variable dimension arrays

Since we use a pointer to an array for function arguments, it is straightforward to write a function that can manipulate an array of any size. Our sum function is much more useful if we generalize it as shown below:

```
int *
sum(A, B, rows, columns)
int *A;
int *B;
int  rows;
int  columns;
{
    int *result;
    int  i;
    int  j;

    result = (int *)malloc(sizeof(int) * rows * columns);

    for (i = 0; i < rows; i++)
        for (j = 0; j < columns; j++)
            result[i * columns + j] = A[i * columns + j]
            + B[i * columns + j];

    return result;
}
```

This version of sum needs the arguments rows and columns that define the actual size of the arrays. It uses these in the call to malloc, to control the loops and in the array index calculations.

EXERCISE

5.6 What do each of the following declarations mean?

```
int *A;
```

```
int  **A;
int  *B[N];
int  C[N];
int  *D();
int  (*E)();
int  *(*F)();
int  *(*G[N])();
```

5.4   Dynamic storage allocation

We have met four classes of data: external, static, auto and register. Each has an associated storage mechanism which defines its scope rules, duration and the forms allowed for initializations. The standard functions, malloc and realloc, use yet another storage mechanism, the **heap**, which is memory that can be dynamically allocated at runtime and is accessed using pointers. (Of course, the pointers themselves can be stored by any of the mechanisms.)

We illustrate the way the heap operates in terms of the following code segment:

```
main()
{
    char    *y;
    char    *z = " arbitrary string" ;
    char    A[4];
    ...
    y = " this is a constant string" ;
    ...
    y = malloc(200);
    ...
    free(y);
    y = malloc(20);
    ...
}
```

Now the data declared in main is stored in the stack. So the pointers y and z and the array A are stored on the stack. In addition to the data on the stack, the constant strings are stored in a persistent memory area (just like external and static data.) The compiler generates code that allocates storage for constant strings and also initializes it. At the point where main does the assignment

        y = " this is a constant string" ;

all that actually happens is that y takes the value of the address of the first letter in the constant string.

You can also allocate and deallocate heap memory using the standard functions, malloc, realloc and free. We do this later in main with the statement

    y = malloc(200);

where malloc allocates space for 200 characters on the heap. After using this space, we use free to make that space available for reuse in future calls to malloc. It is quite possible that the 20 locations allocated on our second call to malloc may reuse some of the 200 that were allocated on the first call. Since malloc does not initialize the memory it allocates, you cannot rely on its initial value.

As we have noted, malloc returns the value (char *)0 if there is not enough memory available. Since you should check for this whenever you use malloc or realloc, we prefer to use our own functions salloc and srealloc which call the standard functions (malloc and realloc), check the return value and when it is (char *)0 they print an error message and exit (with an error code set). High quality software should use functions like salloc and srealloc and we use them in the remainder of this book. (We give code for these later.)

The different memory mechanisms are summarized in Figure 5.2. Now the external and static forms exist throughout the program's execution, which means that an identifier is associated with the same storage throughout the program execution. We also classify the heap as a persistent form of storage because the same locations are allocated from the time of the malloc call until the storage is explicitly freed by the programmer (using a call to free or realloc) or the program completes.

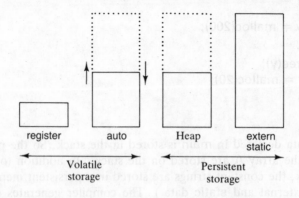

Figure 5.2 Different memory mechanisms.

By contrast, the stack grows as each function is invoked and shrinks as it completes execution. Finally, the **register** data exists only while the function in which it is declared remains active and the same registers are also heavily used by the code otherwise generated by the compiler.

EXERCISE

5.7 After the call to free, y is not set to NULL. Why is this so? What problems can it pose?

5.5 Strings

Conceptually, a C string is a sequence of zero or more characters from the ASCII character set. In fact, as a C programmer you cannot take such a pure view of them. You have to appreciate that they are implemented as a sequence of memory locations with a special sentinel value '\0' (ASCII NUL) that marks the end of the string. This means that all strings are arrays but an array of characters only represents a string if its contents is terminated by a NUL.

It is usual to view a string as a pointer to a sequence of zero or more characters, as in the example below which shows a function that accepts a string and strips any trailing white space characters:

```
/* function that strips trailing white space from a string */
char *
Detrail(s)
char    *s;
{
    char    *p;
    char    *last;  /* the last non-blank */

    last = s - 1;
    for (p = s; *p != ' \0'; p++)
        if (!isspace(*p))
            last = p;
    *++last = ' \0';
    return s;
}
```

We have used pointers to access the string. The for loop control line has a stopping condition that tests each character against \0, a very common form in string handling programs. Observe also that we increment the pointer p on each loop iteration. Once the loop has set last to be the last non-blank, we increment last and put a \0 in that position to mark the end of the string. This action may overwrite a blank character or, in the case where the function is called with a string that had no trailing blanks, the final assignment simply overwrites the \0 again.

EXERCISE

5.8 The Detrail function above deals with a string as a pointer to a character sequence. Rewrite it to treat its argument as an array of characters.

5.5.1 Declaration and initialization

Since strings are essentially character arrays, there is nothing new about string declarations. However, string *initializations* are different in that there is a shorthand form, as illustrated in the following declaration of a string containing the vowels:

```
char     *vowels = " aeiou" ;
```

Strings that are declared as char * can always be initialized. Even auto strings of this sort can be initialized where arrays cannot. This is because an auto string has only its pointer on the runtime stack and the actual **constant string** is allocated space in persistent memory.

EXERCISES

5.9 How do the two following declarations differ?

```
char     specials[] = { "!","?",":",";" };
char     *caps = " ABCD" ;
```

5.10 What does this code do?

```
int    n;
char   c;
...
c = "0123456789abcdef" [n];
```

5.5.2 Standard functions for manipulating strings

Strictly speaking, C provides little support for strings as you have to write code in terms of either the pointer to a sequence of characters model or the array of char view. However, the standard library functions do support a range of typical string operations, including

- formatted input from standard input using scanf or from other files, using fscanf, output to standard output using printf or for other files, using fprintf
- unformatted input using fgets and output using fputs
- formatted movement of strings within memory, using sscanf and sprintf
- interpreting a string as an integer, with atoi, a floating point number with atof and a long int using atol.
- string searches using strchr and strrchr
- string copying using strcpy and strncpy
- lexicographical string comparisons with strcmp and strncmp
- determining string length with strlen
- concatenating strings with strcat and strncat
- create space for strings using malloc, realloc and calloc.

This is not an exhaustive list: the complete set is treated in Chapter 7. Other useful operations, including trimming strings, deleting parts of them and using substrings are easily implemented.

We illustrate some uses of string handling functions with a program that reads a line of any length, allocating precisely the right amount of storage for it. But first, consider the following code segment that reads one line of characters from standard input:

```
#define N  256
...
char    line[N];
...
fgets(line, N, stdin);
```

The fgets function reads up to an end of line (\n) or N − 1 characters, whichever comes first. It also puts a \0 at the end of the string it returns. The usual way to use fgets is with N set large enough to safely accept any likely line of input. Although fgets is often adequate, you may need to read a line of any length and store it as a string which uses just the minimum storage. In that case you need a function like Get_line below. This uses salloc, a safer version of the standard function malloc. (It checks the value that malloc returns.)

```
extern char  *salloc();        /* safe storage allocator */
extern char  *srealloc();      /* safe storage reallocator */

#define N  10

char *
Get_line()
{
    char      *line;    /* pointer to the complete line */
    char      *cp;      /* pointer to last character put into
                           the string */
    unsigned  size;     /* current size of string buffer */
    unsigned  count;    /* count of characters read so far */
    int       c;

    size = N;
    line = salloc(size); /* allocate N bytes initially for line */
    cp = line;
    for (count = 0; (c = getchar()) != ' \n'; count++)
    {
        if (c == EOF)
            return NULL;

        if (count >= (size − 1))
        {
            line = srealloc(line, size += N); /* allow N more
                                                 chars */
            cp = line + count; /* restore cp */
        }
        *cp++ = c;
    }
    *cp = ' \0';
    count++;
    return srealloc(line, count); /* return the correct sized
                                     string */
}
```

The first call to salloc returns a pointer to a memory space N characters long. If that is insufficient we invoke srealloc which allocates space N characters bigger and ensures that the characters that were in line are also present in the bigger string. The srealloc function returns a pointer to an area of memory that contains the old contents of its first argument but with room for the number of characters specified by the second argument. Often, this pointer accesses a different physical memory area, and in that case srealloc has to copy the old line string to that new location. This means that we can no longer use any pointers that we had set up to access parts of line before the call to srealloc. Indeed, as you can see, we have redefined the pointer cp in terms of the reallocated line.

After we have read the whole line, we use srealloc again, to get a string that is just the right size for the line, and this is returned by Get__line.

5.5.3 Strings as function arguments and return values

Strings are handled in the same way as other arrays when they are function arguments or return values: they are declared as char *, a pointer to a character. For example, Get__line returns a string and it uses two such functions, salloc and srealloc. We now show you srealloc to illustrate the use of a string as a function argument:

```
#include     <stdio.h>

char     *realloc();

char *
srealloc(ptr, size)
char          *ptr; /* pointer to the block to be changed
                       in size */
unsigned      size; /* new size of block */
{
     char      *result;

     if ((result = realloc(ptr, size)) == (char *)0)
     {
          fprintf(stderr, " cannot realloc, size = %d \n" , size);
          exit(1);
     }
     return result;
}
```

As you can see, srealloc simply calls the standard function realloc and checks the value that it returns. When realloc returns the value (char *) 0 it means that it is unable to allocate the space requested (which usually means that the program has run out of memory).

EXERCISES

5.11 Given the declaration

```
char    *Bad__Data__Mess =
                " \tWARNING \n \tBad Data on Input" ;
```

what does the following print?

```
printf(" %s" , Bad__Data__Mess);
printf(" %c" , Bad__Data__Mess[4]);
printf(" %c" , Bad__Data__Mess[39]);
```

5.12 Suppose we have two strings declared thus:

```
char    s1[20];
char    s2[20] = " Hello there" ;
```

Can you set s1 to be the string "Hello there" in one assignment operation? Can you assign the whole of s1 to s2 in a single assignment operation?

5.13 What does the following call to printf do?

```
fstr = Get__line();
...
printf(fstr, a, b, c);
```

5.14 Write the salloc function (read about malloc on page 209).

5.15 What is the difference between a and "a"?

5.16 Read and store a piece of text using an array of strings (an array of pointers to characters) where each string is just the right size for the line it holds.

5.6 Program argument processing

Under UNIX, a C program can access arguments from the UNIX command line. We illustrate this in the next program, which prints its arguments. The programs in this section also demonstrate idiomatic code for manipulating strings.

Given the program binary called printargs, the command line

    printargs one "*two*" three

gives the following output:

    argument 0: printargs
    argument 1: one
    argument 2: *two*
    argument 3: three

The zeroth command line argument is always the name of the program. By convention, main is always supplied with the following:

- argc, the number of command line arguments with which the program was invoked

- argv, an array (or vector) of pointers to strings, one for each of the arguments that appeared on the command line and

- envp, a pointer to information about the program's environment (described in Chapter 7).

So we can print the command line arguments like this:

```
main(argc, argv, envp)
int     argc;        /* number of arguments, including
                        program's name */
char    *argv[];     /* array of pointers to the argument
                        strings */
char    **envp;      /* pointer to a sequence of pointers to
                        information about the program
                        environment */
{
        int  i;

        for (i=0; i < argc; i++)
            printf(" argument %d: %s \n" , i, argv[i]);
}
```

A more useful and sophisticated use of the command arguments is shown in the next code fragment which extracts the program name, excluding the full path name as necessary. So, for example, a program contained in a file called doit that resides in a directory called /usr/kim might equally well be invoked as either

      doit

or

      /usr/kim/doit

and the following code extracts the filename, doit, in either case:

```
char     *prog__name; /* pointer to filename */

if ((prog__name = strrchr(argv[0], '/')) == (char *)0)
    prog__name = argv[0];
else
    prog__name++;
```

The first line uses strrchr to scan backwards through the zeroth program argument string for the first occurrence of a slash. If none is found, strrchr returns (char *)0 and we need simply to set prog__name to the zeroth argument. However, if a pathname was specified in the command line that started the program, strrchr returns a pointer to the last slash in that pathname. So, to make prog__name the actual filename, we need to increment that pointer (making it the first character past the slash).

Note that this example also illustrates the use of a **substring**, as prog__name is a string with just the required part of the complete string argv[0]. In general, you can set a pointer to any character within a string so that the characters from that point to the terminating \0 constitute a substring.

EXERCISE

5.17 Some C programs may declare the argument vector like this:

```
char     **argv;
```

Rewrite the code samples of this section to match this definition.

5.7 Combining arrays, strings and structures

In typical programs, you need to combine arrays and structures in more complex forms than we have shown so far. Consider the following declaration for a structure that a library catalogue might need to keep for the information about a library book.

First, we have a **typedef** for the structure that holds the information about an individual book:

```
enum lib {childrens, central, reference, stack};
typedef struct
{
    char    *title;            /* Book's title */
    char    *author;           /* Author(s) or Editor(s) */
    char    *classification;   /* Dewey or F code */
    enum lib heldin;           /* Sub-library of holding */
    int     quantity;          /* Number of copies held */
} Book_Info;

Book_info  Ubook =
{
    "The UNIX System",
    "S. Bourne",
    "FBou 32",
    central,
    7
};

Book_info  Abook;
Book_info  *bookptr;
```

Here we have defined a structure with five components and we have established the synonym **Book_info** for that structure. We have declared two structures of this type, **Ubook** and **Abook**, and **bookptr** is a pointer to a **Book_info** structure. We have also initialized **Ubook** (which is only allowed for external and static data).

We can establish a title like this:

Abook.title = " Introduction to Data Structures" ;

If you do not know the string at compile time, you have to allocate storage for it at runtime, as we did in the **Get_line** function. Indeed, you can use **Get_line** (on page 132) to allocate storage for

strings within a structure as in the following example that reads the title
of a book from input:

```
if ((Abook.title = Get__line()) != NULL)
    ... ;
```

where we check whether Get__line reached an end of file.

Since a library has a large number of books, we might decide to
store the information about the whole catalogue as an array of
structures like this:

```
#define BOOK_COUNT 1000
Book__info Books[BOOK_COUNT];
```

We extend this example in the following sections to illustrate unions
and recursive data structures.

EXERCISE

5.18 Use the library function qsort to sort an array of Book__info structures
on the author field.

5.8 Unions

A union is used for data structures that hold any one of several different types (it is like Pascal's variant record). For example, we might
need to alter the Book__info definition if the library were to hold items
other than books. Suppose we wanted to keep a catalogue with, say,
films and toys. It would then make sense to define a catalogue entry
like this:

```
enum lib {childrens, central, reference, stack};
enum holding__type  {book, film, toy};
struct catalog
    {
    char                    *title;    /* Book's title */
    enum holding__type holding;
    union
        {
        struct                  /* used for books */
            {
```

```
            char     *author;
            char     *classification; /* Dewey or F code */
        } book_info;

        struct                              /* used for films */
        {
            char     *director;
            char     *producer;
        } film_info;

            char     *brand;                /* used for toys */
        } info;
        enum lib     held_in; /* Sub-library of holding */
        int          quantity; /* Number of copies held */
    };
    struct catalog  x;
    struct catalog  y;
```

where it is your responsibility to be consistent in the view taken of the
union. If you are sloppy in the use of unions using, say, x as a book at
some points in the code and interpreting the same value as a film in
others, the program may behave unpredictably.

5.8.1 Declaration and initialization

As the declaration for info shows, union declarations have a similar
form to struct declarations. We could have separated the union definition from that of the catalog structure like this:

```
    enum lib {childrens, central, reference, stack};
    enum holding_type {book, film, toy};
    union holding_info
    {
        struct                              /* used for books */
        {
            char     *author;
            char     *classification; /* Dewey or F code */
        } book_info;

        struct                              /* used for films */
        {
            char     *director;
            char     *producer;
        } film_info;
```

```
        char    *brand;                /* used for toys */
};
struct catalog
{
        char                    *title;
        enum holding__type      holding;
        union holding__info     info;
        enum lib    held__in;   /* Sub-library of holding */
        int         quantity;   /* Number of copies held */
};
struct catalog  x;
struct catalog  y;
```

A union is usually a substructure of a struct and there is generally a field in the structure to specify the appropriate view of the union: in our example, the value of holding indicates whether the struct is for a book, in which case we *should* use the book__info structure in the union.

5.8.2 Union accesses

You access union fields in exactly the same way as struct fields. So, for example, the following code prints the information about the item x in the library collection:

```
switch ((int)x.holding)
{
case (int)book:
    fprintf(stdout, " author: %s \n",
                x.info.book__info.author);
    break;
case (int)film:
    fprintf(stdout, " producer: %s \n",
                x.info.film__info.producer);
    break;
case (int)toy:
    fprintf(stdout, " brand: %s \n", x.info.brand);
    break;
}
```

Since a union data structure is one area of storage, large enough for the largest form of the union, you must take great care to be consistent in your interpretation of a union data structure: there are no checks or warnings on this.

EXERCISE

5.19 Declare a data structure that holds a string and one value which can be any of the types, int, double or char.

5.9 Recursive data structures

It is beyond the scope of this book to discuss the selection of data structures and representations for a particular situation. However, we illustrate the form of some data structures in terms of information about a library's collection. The array of Book_info structures has severe limitations if we need to delete books from our records or if we need to preserve some sort of order to facilitate efficient searching of the catalogue.

One approach is to keep the information as a linked list, using a data structure like this:

```
struct clist
{
    char        *title;          /* Book's title */
    char        *author;         /* Author(s) or
                                    Editor(s) */
    char        *classification; /* Dewey or F
                                    code */
    enum libs   heldin;          /* Sub-library of
                                    holding */
    int         quantity;        /* Number of copies
                                    held */
    struct clist *next;          /* Pointer to next
                                    book in list */
};
```

We have one extra field, next, which is a pointer to another clist structure that has information on the next book. We can create a new clist structure with a function like this:

```
struct clist *
create(cl)
struct clist    *cl;
{
```

```
        struct clist        *ncl;

        ncl = (struct clist *)salloc(sizeof (struct clist));
        ncl->next = cl;
        return ncl;
}
```

where the last item has its next field set to a null pointer.

Then we can use the following function to search for all books by a given author:

```
    struct clist *
    find(author)
    char     *author;
    {
        struct   clist   *t;

        for (t = first__book; t != (struct clist *)0; t = t->next )
            if (strcmp(t->author, author) == 0)
                break;
        return t;
    }
```

An alternative approach is to keep the books in a sorted **binary tree** using this structure where the sort key is the author field:

```
    struct ctree
    {
        char          *title;          /* Book's title */
        char          *author;         /* Author(s) or Editor(s) */
        char          *classification; /* Dewey or F code */
        enum libs     heldin;          /* Sub-library of holding */
        int           quantity;        /* Number of copies held */
        struct catalog   *left;        /* Left subtree */
        struct catalog   *right;       /* Right subtree */
    };
```

In a real library application you would probably allow many search keys and you may use database techniques.

5.10   Bitfields

You can specify the size, in bits, of a structure field. These so-called **bitfields**, can be useful where you want to regard a data entity as a collection of bits, as in the following:

```
struct IOdev
{
    unsigned    R_W : 1;
    unsigned    Dirn : 8;
    unsigned    mode : 3;
};

struct IOdev    dev1 = {01, 0, 07};
struct IOdev    dev2;
```

This declaration establishes a bitfield that is to be used in driving an I/O device. The component fields are all unsigned.

This makes for a quite convenient way to do **bit-picking**, as in the following code:

```
if (dev1.mode == 03)
    ...
dev1.R_W = 1;
dev1.Dirn = 01;
```

The alternative is to set up an unsigned int and use masks with the logical and shift operators we saw in Chapter 3. Bitfields pose some problems for portability: the order in which the fields are stored is left to right within a word on some machines, and in other machines fields are stored right to left.

Bitfields can be mixed with other structure fields, as in the following example:

```
struct devIOT
{
    char        *description;
    unsigned    R_W : 1;
    unsigned    :0;        /* alignment */
    unsigned    Dirn0 : 1;
    unsigned    Dirn1 : 1;
    unsigned    Dirn2 : 1;
    unsigned    :4;        /* padding */
    unsigned    mode : 3;
} dev3 =
{
    "first device",
    1,
    0,
    1,
```

```
        0,
        2
};
```

Unfortunately, you cannot have an array of bitfields; so we cannot simplify the rather unwieldy definitions for the three Dirn bits. You can align a bitfield as shown in the example where we want to be sure that Dirn0 is on a word boundary regardless of whether R_W ends on a word boundary. You can also pad over bits in the word that you want to ignore as we do for the four bits between Dirn2 and mode. On the matter of initializations, bitfields are like other structure fields. So you can initialize them only if the struct is external or static.

No single bitfield may overlap a word boundary; so the maximum size of a bitfield is machine dependent. Bitfields are further limited in that they are generally unsigned ints. (There is no requirement that other bitfield types be supported: it is up to the compiler writer.)

In addition to using bitfields for the interface to hardware devices, they can be convenient when you need to pack several structure fields into one word, either to save space or to meet the requirements of some other software. However, the portability problems of bitfields mean that they are not heavily used in practice.

All of the int operations apply to bitfields except the address-of & operator.

5.11   Data abstraction

In describing each of C's types, we have defined the values that each type can represent and the operations that may be performed on those data entities. There are many situations where you need to define a complex data structure and the permissible operations on it. Some modern languages allow you to define a new type in terms of the forms it can represent and all the permissible operations. Then you can declare any number of instances of data of that type. C does *not* have this facility but it does allow information hiding which gives some of the main benefits of data abstraction. You can write a collection of functions that manipulate a data structure and you can ensure that the only way in which other functions can use the data structure is via the functions you provide for the task. This means that a programmer may use the data structure without needing to know the details of its representation and, even more importantly, users cannot inadvertently corrupt the data structure because the only interface is via the functions you provide.

For example, suppose you are writing a program that needs a symbol table. The program should be able to put symbols into the table and extract details associated with symbols already entered. However, the details of the data structure used to hold the symbol table and the exact mechanism used to find or insert entries is irrelevant to the rest of the program. So, the essential aspects of a symbol table might be:

find(x)	returns the entry for x in the symbol table
add(x)	adds x to the symbol table
delete(x)	deletes the x entry

When you write the functions to manipulate the symbol table, you need to select a representation for the symbol table. To ensure the *integrity* of the symbol table, you would probably want to be able to ensure that *all* accesses and modifications to it be performed exclusively by your utility functions. For this you need to define an interface like that summarized above as the sole means of communication between the symbol table and the rest of the program. You can achieve what is needed using C's scope rules. In the case of the symbol table, you create a file that looks like this:

```
/*
** Global symbols available in this file and included in other
** files which use the symbol table.
*/
struct  Entry { ... };
typedef ... Key__type;

/*
** The symbol table is a hashed array of structures but this
** is a detail that is kept private to this file.
*/
static struct    tableitem
{  ...
} table[N];

static int
hash(key) /* returns the hashed index for the item */
Key__type key;

/*
** 'find' returns a pointer to an 'Entry' structure with a copy
** of the symbol table information associated with 'key'
```

```
** or NULL if 'key' is not in the symbol table.
*/
struct    Entry *
find(key)
Key_type key;
    ...
/*
** 'add' adds the 'new_entry' to the symbol table.
** returns 0 if successful
** returns 1 if it fails because there is not enough room
** returns 2 if there is already an entry with the same key as
** 'new-entry'.
*/
int
add(new_entry)
struct Entry new_entry;
    ...
/*
** 'delete' removes the information associated with 'key'
** returns 0 if successful
** returns 1 if there is no match for the key
*/
int
delete(key) ...
Key_type key;
```

The actual data structure that is used to implement the symbol table is hidden from functions in all other files. In addition, functions like hash are hidden. Only the find, add and delete functions are accessible outside this file. This interface makes it easy to alter the way in which the symbol table is implemented quite independently of functions that use the symbol table. So, for example, we might find that an array of structures was less efficient than a tree structure. By altering the static structures and functions, as well as the dependent functions within this file, we could effect the change of data structures. Yet all functions that make use of the symbol table would behave correctly without modification.

5.12 A complete program

We now discuss a program which uses several of the data structures we have discussed. It takes the current time on the machine and gives the time at various locations around the world. So, if you run the program in Sydney at 19 minutes past one o'clock in the afternoon with the UNIX command

wt london

it prints

At 13:19 here, it is 03:19 (today) in london

The code for the program is given below. The preprocessor commands are similar to ones we have used in the past. We need to include stdio.h in order to use the standard I/O functions and time.h for the definition of tm and for localtime. We have defined the symbols HOUR and OURZONE so that we can make the compiler do arithmetic for us, and for clarity.

We use one structure t for the time zone of the host machine. The structure time_diff represents a place name and its time difference from Greenwich Mean Time (GMT), and places is an array of time_diff structures.

The program starts, like many C programs, by checking the program arguments. First we check if the wrong number of arguments has been supplied and, if so, we give a message in a form that is common in UNIX. It gives a brief indication of the proper usage form for the program. Note that we have followed the usual practice of totally ignoring the third program parameter, envp, because we do not need it here.

Next we call the time function, which returns the current time in clock (in seconds since 1st January 1970). We use clock in the call to localtime to set t (a tm structure as defined in time.h) with the full date and time that corresponds to the value in clock. We use the local time in hours and minutes to calculate lmins, the local time in minutes past midnight.

The loop scans through the places array, looking for an element with a place name that matches the command line argument. If we reach the sentinel element of the array, we quit the program with the exit code of 1 to indicate an error.

If we find the place name, we calculate the time of day there, in minutes past midnight. Next, we make an adjustment to the day as necessary.

```
/*
**    world times
**
**    Usage is:
**       wt location
```

```
**
*/

#include <stdio.h>
#include <time.h>

#define HOUR    60
#define OURZONE (10 * HOUR)  /* parentheses are customary
                               here to avoid precedence problems */

extern long  time();
extern void  exit();

struct tm   *t;

struct time__diff
{
    char    *name;  /* name of place */
    int     zone;   /* minutes ahead (+) or behind (−)
                       GMT */
};

struct time__diff places[] =
{
    { "la",     −8 * HOUR },
    { "chicago", −6 * HOUR },
    { "nyc",    −5 * HOUR },
    { "london", 0 },
    { "perth",  8 * HOUR },
    { (char *)0, 0 }        /* sentinel value */
};

main(argc, argv)
int  argc;
char  *argv[];
{
    long    clock;
    int     lmins;  /* local minutes */
    int     rmins;  /* remote minutes */
    char    *day;
    int     i;

    if (argc != 2)
    {
```

```
                fprintf(stderr, " usage: %s location \n" , argv[0]);
                exit(1);
        }


        (void)time(&clock);
        t = localtime(&clock);
        lmins = (t->tm_hour * HOUR) + t->tm_min;


        for (i = 0; ; i++)
                if (places[i].name == (char *)0)
                {
                        fprintf(stderr, " %s: don't know about %s \n" ,
                                argv[0], argv[1]);
                        exit(1);
                }
                else if (strcmp(argv[1], places[i].name) == 0)
                        break;


        rmins = lmins + places[i].zone - OURZONE;
        if (rmins < 0)
        {
                day = " (yesterday)" ;
                rmins += 24 * HOUR;
        }
        else if (rmins > (24 * HOUR))
        {
                day = " (tomorrow)" ;
                rmins -= 24 * HOUR;
        }
        else
                day = " (today)" ;


        printf
        (" At %02d:%02d here, it is %02d:%02d%s in %s \n" ,
        lmins/HOUR, lmins%HOUR, rmins/HOUR,
        rmins%HOUR, day, places[i].name);

        exit (0);
}
```

EXERCISES

5.20 Modify the program so that it takes the information about world times from a file called world_times in the directory /usr/pub rather than having this data built into the program. This version of the program can direct users to the world_times file if they enter a place name that the program cannot find. (You will need to use functions that read from files other than standard input: see page 179 in Chapter 7.)

5.21 Amend the program so that it can take account of daylight saving.

SUMMARY

An aggregate data structure can be

- a **struct**, which has fields (members) that can be of different types and it is possible to specify the field size in bits
- a **union**, which can hold one of several different types and is usually part of a structure that also has a field to specify its type in a particular instance
- an array, which is a collection of items, each of which is the same type
- a string, which is an array of characters with the sentinel \0 to mark the end of the string.

Structure fields and array elements can themselves be any aggregate data type.

A structure is viewed as a single entity and a whole structure can be assigned, passed as an argument or returned by a function. An array is viewed as a collection of items and cannot do any of these. The norm is to use a pointer to an array for function arguments and function return values.

An array name can be viewed as a constant pointer. Pointer arithmetic is commonly used to access array elements.

Initialization is allowed for:

- external and **static** arrays
- external and **static** structures
- all strings.

The operators for aggregate data type accesses are

- . for accessing structure fields
- -> for accessing structure fields using a pointer to the structure
- [] for accessing array elements, where A[i] is the same as *(A + i).

These three operators have higher precedence than the other operators and they associate from left to right.

Chapter 6
The C Preprocessor

This chapter covers the full range of facilities provided by the preprocessor. Like the C language itself, as described in the preceding chapters, the preprocessor supports programming at various levels including the construction of large systems. Two uses of the preprocessor that you have already seen are

- **#include** for including files of text into a program
- **#define** for defining constants

Others that you meet here are

- **#define** for defining powerful in-line macros
- **#if**, **#ifdef**, **#ifndef** and **#undef** for managing conditional compilation

and #line, a C command that looks like a preprocessor command and preserves line numbers in language pre-processors.

6.1 Introduction

We have already made simple uses of #include and #define. These are so fundamental to C that it is unusual to write a program that uses neither of them. This makes the preprocessor an essential part of C.

Indeed, it is easy to think of the preprocessor as a first pass of the compiler. But you can equally see it as a separate **filter** that transforms C programs before they reach the compiler.

Preprocessor commands have a different syntax from most C code. They start with a # in the first character position in the line and they have no semicolon terminator.

6.2 Text inclusion

The #include incorporates text of one file into another. It is widely used to include

- #defines,
- externs,
- typedefs,
- struct definitions and
- nested #includes.

So #include is generally used to include various types of declarations. It is most unusual to have other code because C supports separate compilation, which means that you should not need to include a whole function text in another file of source code. Nor should you need to include other executable code in several parts of a program: it is better to encapsulate the code in a function that is called at each point it is needed.

The #include can take two forms:

#include *"filename"*

or

#include *<filename>*

In either case, the preprocessor inserts a copy of **filename** at that point in the code. The difference between the two forms is in the place that the preprocessor looks for the file. In the first, it looks for the named file in the current directory unless a full UNIX path name is given. So, for example, the lines

```
#include  "/usr/kim/defs.h"
```

and

```
#include  "defs.h"
```

include the same file when the current directory is /usr/kim.

We have seen the second form of the #include in cases like this:

```
#include  <stdio.h>
```

which includes standard I/O definitions, such as EOF. With this form, where the file name is enclosed in angled brackets, the preprocessor searches a particular library directory, typically /usr/include, for the file to be included. Additional directories are searched when you use –I*directory-name* parameter on the cc command.

By convention, files that are to be #included have the suffix .h. This makes it easy to distinguish #include files from other C source code. The convention probably originated from the term **header file** since most #included files belong at the head of a file.

6.3 Defined symbols

To this point we have used #defines to create constants (sometimes called **manifest** or **symbolic** constants). However, this is just the simplest use of the preprocessor's macro facility. We now discuss the full range of macros you can write using #define, from the simple but important definition of a constant value or expression to macros that can be called like C functions.

Parameterless macros

It is good programming practice to avoid using 'magic numbers' directly. For example, in a program that produces text for a device that has 60 characters per line, you can use #define to define an identifier LINESIZE with the value 60. This has two advantages over using 60 directly: it makes the meaning of the code much clearer since there may be many other uses for the number 60. But even more important in a program that is really going to be used, it is inevitable that there will be changes: a new output device might accept 110 characters. If the magic number 60 is embedded in the text, it could be a very tedious and risky business to change every relevant occurrence of the string 60 and no other. (Careless editing might produce a program that used 110 second minutes!)

Having convinced yourself that your program should represent the line length with a suitable identifier, you use a preprocessor command of the following form:

```
#define LINESIZE        60
```

Then you can use LINESIZE, as necessary throughout the program text. The preprocessor replaces each occurrence of the identifier, LINESIZE, with the **token**, 60. When a new output device appears, it is a safe and easy operation to alter the #define appropriately.

A common use for defined symbols is in declarations, especially in array declarations where the size of the array is specified by a defined symbol, as in this example:

```
#define NUMLINES      66
#define LINESIZE      80

char     page[LINESIZE * NUMLINES]; /* space for a whole
                                              page */
```

The preprocessor deals with a #define as follows: upon finding each occurrence of the identifier, it does a textual replacement, substituting the token for the identifier. The replacement string can be a series of tokens, as in this example where DAYSECS is the number of seconds in a day:

```
#define DAYSECS (24*60*60)
```

We use parentheses to prevent precedence problems.

Some programmers avoid using defined symbols out of misplaced concerned for efficiency: the overhead for a defined symbol like DAYSECS is small and, since constant expressions are calculated by the compiler, it incurs no runtime penalty. The advantages far outweigh the small overhead: the program becomes more readable and maintainable and you avoid error-prone hand calculation.

The expression may be arbitrarily complex but it is a good idea to enclose it in parentheses. Since the preprocessor simply replaces the defined identifier with the token string, you can get problems in cases like this:

```
#define SUM      3 + 4   /* DANGEROUS */
...
x = SUM * 3;
```

After preprocessing the assignment statement becomes

```
x = 3 + 4 * 3;
```

and precedence rules make the expression value 15, not 21. This problem can be completely avoided if you routinely use parentheses, like this:

```
#define SUM      (3 + 4)
```

The scope of a #define is confined to its file. To make a definition available in several files, you use #includes.

The usual style is to make #defined identifiers upper case. This makes it easier for someone reading the code to see which identifiers are defined symbols.

The general form of the command is

```
#define identifier token-string
```

where the token string can span several lines, using a backslash (\) at the end of each but the last line.

6.3.1 Macros with parameters

In its full generality, the #define can define **macros** with parameters (sometimes called **inline** functions). Calls to these look just like a call to an ordinary C function. Indeed, you have seen some standard macros, including isupper, isalpha and isdigit. We followed the usual practice of calling these functions. In fact, they are usually implemented as macros for efficiency but the programmer using them may not be aware of this. These are invoked in the same way as a C function, including parameters.

Consider the following example of a macro that finds the smaller of two values:

```
#define min(a,b)     ((a) > (b) ? (a) : (b))
```

We can use it like this:

```
y = min(stsize, 132)
```

which the preprocessor translates to this:

```
y = ((stsize) > (132) ? (stsize) : (132))
```

which is the form that is presented to the compiler. The arguments in these macros are *called by name*, which means that the actual arguments textually replace the formal arguments in the macro. This means that you can get nasty side effects, as in the following use of min:

```
y = min(a++, b);
```

which becomes

```
y = ((a++) > (b) ? (a++) : (b))
```

which is almost certainly not what was intended.

The primary benefit of a macro over a true function is in terms of runtime efficiency: a function call incurs some overhead where a macro involves replacing the call by the full code text before compilation. (The tradeoff for the gain in runtime efficiency is that it may take up more code space.)

The general form of a macro definition is

#define *identifier(identifier, ..., identifier) token-string*

and macro definitions can extend over several lines in the same way as other #defines, with a backslash at the end of all but the last line of the definition. However, the convention for macro identifiers is that they may be lower case. This means that they may look like function calls, which can be confusing. We return to this matter in Chapter 7 when we discuss some of the standard macros.

EXERCISES

6.1   Write macros to select bits from an integer:

(a)   bit0(x) returns the least significant bit of x

(b)   bit(x,n) returns the *n*th bit (counting the least significant bit as 0)

6.2   What does the following program look like after preprocessing?

```
#define NUMBER 50

/* print NUMBER squares */
main()
{
    int     i;

    printf(" NUMBER = %d \n" , NUMBER);

    for (i = 1; i < NUMBER; i++)
        printf(" %d \t%d \n" , i, i*i);
}
```

6.3   Why are the formal parameters parenthesized in the following example?

```
#define min(a,b)     (a)<(b)?(a):(b)
```

6.4   Conditional compilation

Since the early days of computing, assemblers have allowed programmers to specify lines of a program that are to be compiled under
certain conditions. This facility is not often found in higher level
languages. C has a flexible facility for conditional compilation using the
commands #define, #ifdef, #ifndef, #if-#else, and #undef.

One common use for conditional compilation is to selectively
compile debug output statements. For example, the following printf is
compiled and executed because DEBUG has been defined:

```
#define DEBUG
...
#ifdef     DEBUG
    printf(" loop counter = %d \n" , i);
#endif
```

The #ifdef and #endif commands delimit code for conditional compilation.

To prevent execution of this debug printf, simply remove the
#define statement or add

```
#undef DEBUG
```

before the #ifdef. (You can also set DEBUG from the cc command line: see page 162.)

The #undef is most useful in complex systems that are configured to a form that is fairly typical. For example, you may have a program you want to run on a machine that does not have a device corresponding to FASTPRINTER in this code:

```
#ifndef FASTPRINTER
      ... /* code that you need compiled */
#endif
```

Now you might expect that most machines do have a FASTPRINTER and the program might have an #include file with a definition for the identifier. You can insert the statement

```
#undef identifier
```

before the #ifndef to make FASTPRINTER undefined from that point (until a #define is encountered).

The preprocessor also allows you to test whether an identifier has *not* been defined, like this:

```
#ifndef   DEBUG
     printf(" MyProg Version 1.0 (production)" );
#endif
```

You can use the #if–#else where you want to compile one section of code if an identifier is defined and another if not:

```
#ifdef    DEBUG
     printf(" MyProg Version 1.0 (debug) \n" );
#else
     printf(" MyProg Version 1.0 (production) \n" );
#endif
```

You can use expressions to select the code to be compiled, as in the following case where we need one set of code for line printers with more than 132 columns and different code for smaller printers:

```
#if COLUMNS > 132
...code for wide printers...
#else
...code for narrow...
#endif
```

If the expression is true (non-zero), the first piece of code is passed to the compiler (the lines between the #if and the #else); otherwise, the second piece of code is compiled (after the #else to the #endif).

These commands can be nested just like if–else statements in C itself. The preprocessor handles the dangling #else in the same way as C: #else always belongs to the closest #if that has not been closed by #endif.

The combination of #ifdef, #ifndef, #if, #else and #endif enable you to keep a single program text which contains different versions of the program for different purposes. Common uses for this are in programs being distributed to sites with different devices or device parameters and different machine characteristics, as well as for debugging versions. A very common use is for different versions of UNIX with different #defined symbols denoting the different versions.

On the other hand, overuse of conditional compilation can make a program unnecessarily hard to read. Like most language features, these need to be used with discretion.

EXERCISES

6.4 Given a case like this:

```
#if A
    ...code A...
#   if B
    ...code AB...
#   else
    ...code C...
#   endif
#endif
```

the #else belongs to #if B. If you want the opposite interpretation, what do you do?

6.5 What if you want different code for five variants of a device?

6.5 Line numbers on preprocessed text

Suppose you are writing a program that translates Pascal into C. Once a Pascal program has been translated to C, you would like the C compiler to report any errors in terms of the original Pascal source text.

Your translator generates one or more lines of C for each Pascal line. If it also generates a line of the form

#line *line-number file-name*

before the C statements that correspond to the *line-number* line of the Pascal program in *file-name*, the C compiler produces diagnostics in terms of the original Pascal line number and file.

In this type of application, you would probably use the two pre-defined symbols ___FILE___ and ___LINE___ which have the current source code file name and line number. (We have a macro that uses these symbols on page 164 of this chapter.)

Although the #line command has the same syntax as pre-processor commands, it is actually handled by the compiler. Its use is normally restricted to programs that produce C programs.

6.6 Preprocessor control from the cc command

We showed in Chapter 4 how to use cc to run programs. In Figure 4.7 we depicted the preprocessor as tightly coupled to the compiler. In fact, you can get the form of a program after it has been through the preprocessor and before it reaches the compiler. The actual flag used for this can vary but it is often −E.

In addition, you can set the values of defined symbols on the cc command line, using the −D flag as in this example:

cc −DLINELENGTH=80 prog.c

which has the same effect as the command

#define LINELENGTH 80

at the very beginning of the program. Any #define or #undef within the program overrides the command line setting.

There is also a shorthand form which looks like this:

cc −D*identifier*

and is equivalent to

#define *identifier*

You may need to use quotes to avoid the shell interpreting special characters inside the token string, as in:

cc −D"VERSION=6(1984)" prog.c

where we need to protect the parentheses from the shell. To put a double quote in the token string, use a backslash:

cc -Dnamestring=\"MyProg\" prog.c

The −D flag may also be repeated allowing several identifiers to be defined. This is very useful for switching debug code on and off using the #if commands without having to modify program code. For example:

cc −DTEST=3 −DLINESIZE=80 −DVERSION=1.2 myprog.c\
                                        −o myprog

may enable level 3 debug output, determine the line size and version number.

The general form is

cc -D*identifier[=token-string]*

EXERCISE

6.6 Use the appropriate flag on your cc to get the preprocessed form of a program so that you can see what the preprocessor produces.

6.7 Perspectives

The facilities provided by the C preprocessor are an integral part of the C language. However, it is possible to use another program in place of the standard C preprocessor. Some implementations of the cc command allow you to specify alternative preprocessors or, indeed, alternative passes of the C compiler. You may use a more powerful macro processor such as m4 as the preprocessor.

The preprocessor provides powerful facilities for modifying your program before it reaches the C compiler. The macro facility is especially useful for improving the efficiency of code and as a debugging aid. Consider the following example of a macro that processes assertions when the symbol CAUTIOUS is defined (it is similar to the standard assert):

```
#ifdef CAUTIOUS
#define assert(expr) \
    if(!(expr)) \
    { \
        printf(" assertion \"(expr)\" failed\n"); \
        printf(" (line %d, file %s)\n", __LINE__, __FILE__); \
    }
#else
#define assert(expr)    /* null statement */
#endif
```

This can be used as in

```
assert(charcnt < 100);
```

which is handed to the C compiler as

```
if(!(charcnt < 100))
{
    printf(" assertion \"(charcnt < 100)\" failed\n");
    printf(" (line %d, file %s)\n", 18, "myprog.c");
};
```

If we remove the #define for CAUTIOUS, the preprocessor removes all asserts.

The preprocessor can also be misused, making your C program almost unreadable through the use of too many defined symbols and macros or complicated conditional compilation. For example, it is possible to make C look like an entirely different language. The definitions:

```
#define IF      if(
#define THEN    )
#define BEGIN   {
#define END     }
#define ELSE    else
```

enable you to write your C to look like this:

```
IF a == 1 THEN
BEGIN
    tryone();
    trytwo();
END
```

Each C preprocessor typically has its own predefined symbols. These may be related to the machine type or UNIX version. For example, a preprocessor on a VAX UNIX System V may have the symbols 'vax' and 'sysV' predefined. These symbols are useful in controlling the compilation of different versions of a program for different machines or systems.

EXERCISE

6.7   What happens to our **assert** macro in code like:

```
if ( ... )
    assert( ...);
else
    ...
```

and how can you fix the problem?

SUMMARY

To include text you use #include in the forms

> #include *"filename"*

> #include *<filename>*

Macros can be defined using

> #define *identifier token-string*

> #define *identifier(identifier,...) token-string*

and it is safer to put parentheses around the *token-string*.

Conditional compilation is controlled with selection commands #ifdef, #ifndef, #if, #if−#else, #define and #undef.

Source code line numbers in preprocessed text can be preserved using

> #line *line-number file-name*

Chapter 7
C Libraries

We have already met some of the large collection of standard functions which are grouped into various libraries. The standard library is automatically searched by the loader and includes functions for:

- standard I/O on
     standard I/O files
     any file
- system call I/O
- storage allocation

- string handling
- character types
- sorting and searching
- assertions
- non-local **goto**
- system interface
- user information
- time of day handling

Other libraries need to be explicitly searched and contain functions for:

- mathematics
- plotting
- terminal handling

We also describe several standard #include files.

7.1   Introduction

The standard C function library is a very important resource. Its functions have been written by experts and well tested over many years and you can save a great deal of effort by exploiting them to the full. The library helps you avoid re-inventing the wheel. So, for example, there is an efficient and flexible sort function: C programmers rarely write their own sorts, preferring to use the supplied one. Most of the functions in the standard libraries are written in C and are designed with efficiency and portability in mind. (The remainder are written in assembler and are implemented anew for each machine.) You should think very carefully before writing your own version of a library function.

The large function library fits very well into the UNIX **tools** philosophy (as described by Kernighan and Plauger in their 'Software Tools' books) where many prewritten components are supplied. The basis of this approach is the observation that many programming problems can be reduced to the simple task of assembling the necessary function calls.

To take full advantage of the tools approach, you need to know what functions are available. In this chapter, we give descriptions of most, but not all, the functions in the standard C library. We aim to give you an understanding of the most widespread and important functions and a feeling for the classes of functions you should be able to find in the libraries. These libraries include a wide range of functions, from simple but indispensable ones that open, close, read and write files, to sophisticated functions that allow you to initiate and control other programs. An expert UNIX C programmer has a detailed knowledge of most of the functions in the standard library but this takes some time and effort.

Do not be afraid to skim quickly through some sections of this chapter and refer back to them when you need the information. Also, there are sections which assume some knowledge of the UNIX file system. You may need to refer to one of the many books about UNIX. (See our bibliography for a few.)

We illustrate the use of functions with code fragments and programs and we include many hints and programming techniques that we have learned over years of experience (some of it hard earned and bitter). We do not cover every tiny detail of every function but rather we give a thorough treatment of the major ideas. Once you have mastered this fundamental material, you can dip into Volume 1 of the *UNIX Programmer's Manual*: it is *the* reference for the detailed description of UNIX commands and functions and it is an essential resource for any serious C programmer working in the UNIX environment. (Most systems keep a copy of these manual entries on-line.) Your system documentation should have exhaustive documentation for all the functions you can use, including ones that have been written locally. The latter are likely to have been tailored to the particular programming tasks common in your area.

When we refer to manual entries, we follow the usual convention of writing the function name followed by its section in the manual. For example, the manual entry for printf which appears in the third section of the manual is referred to as printf(3). The sections of the manual group functions as shown in Table 7.1. All of these are in Volume 1 of

Table 7.1 Contents of the *Unix Programmer's Manual*.

Section	Description of contents	Examples
1	Utility programs	who
2	System calls	exit
3	Functions from libraries	printf
4	Special files	tty
5	File formats	passwd
6	Games	
7	Miscellaneous	
8	Maintenance	

the *UNIX Programmer's Manual*. Volume 2 has documents with tutorials and descriptions of major programs for a range of tasks including text manipulation and program management.

What are standard libraries?

At this point, we need to clarify just what is meant by *standard functions*. After all, if you write programs in terms of functions that are not widely available, you should at least be aware of the implications for portability. Unfortunately, there are a number of *de facto* standards. For example, the IEEE P1003 standard (commonly called POSIX) defines a set of 170 functions and most of these are very widely available on all flavours of UNIX. By contrast, System V and Berkeley 4.2BSD have many more 'standard' functions.

This chapter covers a safe subset of functions that are generally provided with UNIX. Certainly this chapter does not give an exhaustive coverage for any of the standards but it does give a solid overview of the standard libraries. More important, it gives advice on common pitfalls in using an important core of standard functions. However, it does not replace your system manual, which gives terse but complete coverage of all that *your* system has to offer.

Linking functions

In our outline at the beginning of this chapter, we distinguished between functions that are automatically searched by the loader and those you need to link explicitly. The C compiler automatically searches the standard function library whenever symbols (usually functions) remain undefined after linking together each of the functions in the files given as arguments to the cc command. Sometimes you refer to functions that are not found in the standard library but are available on your system in a standard directory (usually /lib or /usr/lib). You can direct the loader to search one of these libraries by compiling the program with the option −lX on your cc command line, where X is the name of the library. We discussed this in detail in Chapter 4.

Accessing standard identifiers and linking functions

Right from Chapter 1, we have used standard predefined symbols like EOF which is defined in stdio.h. As you can see, in many of our programs, we have to use the preprocessor's #include facility to make such symbols available. In this chapter, we introduce many more files of standard symbols and state the file that must be #included to make them accessible to your program.

Format for standard function descriptions

For each function, we give the form of its header, including a brief comment on the behaviour of the function in terms of its arguments and return value. This is enclosed in a box for easy reference. The main text discusses other aspects of the functions, giving advice on their appropriate use, common problems and examples.

We use the same format for 'functions' that are actually implemented as macros.

7.2 Input and output

As we noted in Chapter 1, there are no I/O statements in C. Instead, all I/O is done by functions that execute system calls. This approach gives considerable flexibility since you can write your own special purpose I/O functions.

The lowest level of I/O is provided by UNIX system calls. These allow you to read and write blocks of memory but provide no formatting or buffering. Although this level of I/O is the most basic, it is not as convenient for general applications programming as the standard I/O library. We illustrate the relationship between the system call I/O functions, the standard I/O functions and a typical applications program in Figure 7.1.

There are functions in the standard I/O package to carry out character-at-a-time I/O or formatted I/O operations on any file. You have already seen several of these in earlier chapters.

Before we pursue the details of the I/O functions, we observe that the UNIX files have a very simple structure. In fact, they have

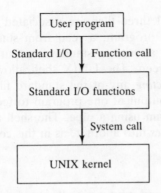

Figure 7.1 Relationship between a user program and I/O functions.

almost no structure at all! All UNIX files consist of a variable length sequence of bytes. There is no record or block structure imposed. You may read a single byte or a million bytes from a file and, assuming the file is big enough, exactly one or a million bytes are returned. So you do not have to manipulate a complex entity—you simply do I/O on streams of characters.

Of course, you may impose your own record structure on the file if you wish. It may be appropriate, for example, to construct a file consisting of fixed length records. The UNIX file system itself imposes a structure on **directory** files.

7.3 I/O on the standard files

In this section, we treat I/O on the standard files which are automatically available to your program. These are the **standard input**, **standard output** and **standard error message** files, also commonly referred to as stdin, stdout and stderr because these are the names of the file pointers associated with them (as we discuss at greater length in the section that introduces file pointers on page 179). In this section, we discuss functions that read from standard input and write to standard output. Before we deal with the functions for I/O on the standard files, we show how useful this is in the UNIX environment:

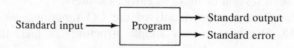

By default, all three files are associated with a user's terminal. So, in an interactive program, a read from standard input takes what the user types, while a write to standard output or standard error puts characters on the screen. The UNIX shell allows the user to override this default by *redirecting* any of the standard files. In addition, UNIX allows the standard output of one program to feed into the standard input of another program using a **pipe**. The shell allows a user to specify that one program *pipes* into another, as in this command:

    who | lpr

which runs the command **who** piping its standard output to the standard input of the program **lpr**. The **who** command normally produces a list of currently logged-on users on its standard output file and **lpr** reads data from its standard input and sends it to a printer. So the combined command gets a list of logged-on users and prints it on a printer.

Because pipelines are so useful, programs that read data from standard input, modify it and write it to output, are important building blocks. They are called **filters**. For example we can use the sort command as a filter in an extended pipeline like this:

> who | sort | lpr

which sends a *sorted* list of logged-on users to a printer.

Many of the functions in the standard I/O library are implemented as C preprocessor macros. The definitions of these macros along with a number of useful typedefs and other definitions are in the file stdio.h. You need the preprocessor command

> #include   <stdio.h>

to incorporate these definitions into any program that uses standard I/O functions.

7.3.1 Character I/O

An elementary form of I/O is the reading and writing of characters to or from the standard input and output files. In Chapter 1 we used getchar and putchar to read and write single characters.

```
/*
**   'getchar' returns the next character from input.
**   If at end of file, it returns the predefined value EOF.
*/
int
getchar()
/*
**   'putchar' writes the character 'c' to the standard output
**   file.
**   The value of 'c' is returned.
*/
int
putchar(c)
```

Note that getchar returns an int. This is because the integer value -1 is returned when end of file is found. Characters read from a UNIX file may take any unsigned value that can be represented in 8 bits (0 to 255). If getchar were to return a char there would be no way to distinguish a legal value from the special end of file indicator value. One solution would be to use one of the 256 possible values. But this would be unacceptable because a binary file, such as a program object code file, would almost certainly contain all possible values within it. The alternative is to enlarge the set of values that can be returned by getchar so that there is an extra value to represent end of file, and this is what UNIX does in making −1 the end of file indicator value.

The include file **stdio.h** has the definition

```
#define EOF   −1
```

so the result of getchar may be compared with EOF to detect end of file.

The putchar function writes a character to the standard output file. Both getchar and putchar are commonly implemented as macros. We use them in the following program which copies its standard input file to its standard output file using getchar and putchar:

```
/*
** copy standard input to standard output using 'getchar'
** and 'putchar'.
*/

#include   <stdio.h>

main()
{
    int  c;

    while ((c = getchar()) != EOF)
        putchar(c);
}
```

In addition to I/O that operates on a character at a time, there is a pair of functions that read and write **lines** of ASCII characters, where a *line* is a sequence of characters terminated by a newline character \n.

```
/*
** 'gets' reads a string, terminated by a newline from
** standard input into the area pointed to by 's'.
** The trailing newline is replaced by ' \0'.
** If at end of file, it returns NULL.
*/
char
*gets(s)
char      *s;
```

```
/*
**   'puts' writes the string 's' on to standard output
**   appending a newline.
**   The predefined value EOF is returned on error.
*/
int
puts(s)
char     *s;
```

Here is another version of the program that copies standard input to standard output, this time using gets and puts:

```
/*
**   copy standard input to standard output using 'gets' and
**   'puts'.
*/
#include    <stdio.h>
#define LINESIZE        512 /* This defines the maximum line
                                length the program can handle */
main()
{
      char    line[LINESIZE];

      while (gets(line) != NULL)
            puts(line);
}
```

Note that you must make LINESIZE large enough for the longest line expected.

7.3.2 Formatted I/O

As you saw in Chapter 1, scanf interprets characters from standard input according to a format that you supply. The declaration of scanf is

```
/*
**   'scanf' reads characters from standard input according
**   to 'format'
**   returns the number of items found and assigned.
*/
int
scanf(format/*[, pointer] ...*/)
char     *format;
```

and **scanf** reads characters from the standard input file, matching them with the supplied format, performing conversions and assigning results as needed. The parameters to **scanf** are a pointer to a character string specifying the format and a variable number of pointers to be used for the results.

The format string may contain white space (blanks or tabs), printing characters or conversion specifications. White space is matched with white space on input. Printing characters specify that the same characters must be found on input at that point. Conversion specifications consist of the percent character (%) followed by a character that determines the conversion to attempt. For example:

```
scanf(" age   %d" , &age);
```

attempts to match the characters **age** followed by white space, followed by a decimal integer. That integer value is assigned to the integer variable **age**.

The allowable conversions include those shown in Table 7.2. The codes **d**, **o**, **x** may be preceded by an **l** to indicate that a **long** integer is expected, in which case a pointer to a **long int** must be provided. Similarly, **h** preceding **d**, **o**, or **x** indicates a **short** integer. The codes **e** or **f** preceded by **l** (lower case L) indicates a **double** precision number expected and a pointer to a **double** must be provided. The conversion specification code may also be preceded by a * indicating that a field is to be matched but not assigned to a result pointer. For example:

```
scanf(" %s %*d %d" , name, &age);
```

Table 7.2 Permitted conversions.

Conversion character	Input field	Result pointer type
d	Decimal integer	int
o	Octal integer	int
x	Hexadecimal integer	int
s	Character string	char
c	Single character	char
e, f	Floating point	float
l [e, f]	Double precision	double
h [d, o, x]	Short decimal, octal or hex	short int
l [d, o, x]	Long decimal, octal or hex	long int

reads a string into name, skips a number and then assigns the next number to age.

scanf returns the number of input items that it successfully matched and assigned. If end of file is encountered, the value EOF is returned in the same way as the getchar function described above. A return value of 0 indicates that no items were assigned. You should normally check that the value scanf returns is as expected. In general, if there is a mismatch between a literal string in the format specification and the actual text read, the only indication is the count of items that scanf returns. This often makes scanf unsuitable for writing really robust I/O.

If you want complicated matching of the input lines with some pattern, a single call to scanf is not recommended. Instead, you should consider using a series of scanf calls, checking the result of each call. Alternatively, you can write your own input function using getc or read a whole line at a time and use functions like sscanf (which we discuss soon) to analyse each line. The scanf(3) manual entry has more esoteric details and examples.

The output function printf is similar to scanf. Its first argument is a pointer to a string argument that specifies the output format and then it accepts expressions that are to be written.

```
/*
**    'printf' prints the 'arg' values according to the 'format'
**    specified
**    It returns the number of characters it printed.
*/
int
printf(format/*[, arg] ...*/)
char    *format;
```

For example, the following program prints the value of pi:

```
#include   <math.h>
main()
{
        double  pi = 4.0 * atan(1.0);
        printf(" The value of PI is %f \n", pi);
}
```

giving this output:

The value of PI is 3.141593

As with scanf, the format string includes ordinary characters which are printed directly and sequences beginning with a percent (%) character specify that the next printf argument is to be printed according to the given format.

As well as free format output, printf provides facilities for finer control over the formatting of items. Integer items can be left or right justified in a given field width and may be padded with blanks or zeros. The field width can be specified in the format string or can be taken from an argument to printf. Strings may also be left or right justified in a given field. For example, the program fragment

```
hour = 12;
min = 5;
printf(">%20.20s %02d:%02d \n", "lunch", hour, min);
hour = 16;
printf(">%20.20s %02d:%02d \n", "important meeting",
     hour, min);
```

gives the output

```
>                   lunch    12:05
>       important meeting    16:05
```

The general form of a conversion specification can have the following elements:

```
%-f.plc
```

The % introduces a conversion specification. The − indicates left justification in the field. A digit string f gives the total field width. A dot followed by a digit string p gives the precision or number of digits after the decimal point for float or double types or the maximum number of characters to be printed from a character string. Finally, the particular conversion is indicated by a character as in scanf which may be preceded by l indicating a long type. Short integers may be printed with the formats for ordinary integers.

The p or f may be replaced by an asterisk to indicate that the next printf argument to be processed contains the field width or specification. This allows some format changes to occur at runtime as a consequence of some aspect of the data. This is particularly useful to indicate the field width for printing a string or whether the output of the string should be suppressed (by using a zero precision value).

Table 7.3 Abbreviations of control characters.

Sequence	Octal code	Description
\t	011	Tab
\n	012	Newline
\f	014	Form feed
\r	015	Carriage return

You may be wondering how to print the percent sign itself. Since % normally introduces a format conversion, you use another percent sign as the conversion code as in

```
printf(" %% is a percent sign! \n" );
```

which prints

```
% is a percent sign!
```

Ordinary characters can be printed by simply including them in the format string but non-printing control characters are often required. We have seen one such character in most of our uses of printf where we have the character \n at the end of the format string. This indicates that the newline control character, ASCII code 012 (octal), is to be printed. There are other useful abbreviations of control characters, as shown in Table 7.3. You can use any of the character constants in any of their forms. (See page 63 in Chapter 3.) These may include characters that are specified by their ASCII codes.

7.4 Files other than standard input and output

We now introduce functions that can act on any file. When a program accesses a file other than the standard input, output and error files it must first *open* the file (using a standard function): the standard files are automatically open when a program begins execution. You also need to use a **file pointer** which is declared in terms of a predefined type FILE *. For example:

```
FILE     *accfile;
```

declares the variable accfile as a pointer to a file. You can associate any file with the pointer **accfile** using one of the file **opening functions** described below. The standard files have predeclared file pointers:

stdin   standard input
stdout   standard output
stderr   standard error

The declarations of FILE, stdin, stdout and stderr are in stdio.h. In the answer to Exercise 5.20 we illustrated the use of functions that open a file, read data and close the file. We now discuss the general forms of the functions that do these tasks.

7.4.1 Opening files

The usual way to open a file (and associate a file pointer with a particular file) is with fopen.

```
/*
**  'fopen' opens the file 'filename' for reading or writing
**  as defined by 'type'.
**  On failure, it returns NULL.
*/
FILE *
fopen(filename, type)
char    *filename;
char    *type;
```

The type argument can take the values:

"r"   open for reading
"w"   create for writing
         (existing files are truncated)
"a"   open for append
         (existing files are opened for writing at end of file)
"r+"   open for reading and writing
         (existing files are positioned at the beginning and
         both reading and writing allowed)
"w+"   create for reading and writing

If the file does not exist or the user does not have the appropriate read or write permission, fopen fails to open the specified file, and returns the value NULL.

When your program no longer needs a file, you should **close** it with the matching fclose function.

```
/*
** 'fclose' closes a file with pointer 'filep', flushing and
** freeing buffers.
** On error, it returns non-zero.
*/
int
fclose(filep)
FILE    *filep;
```

All files are automatically closed when your program terminates. However, it is clearer if you explicitly call the fclose function for each file.

Sometimes you may want to close a file and then open another using the same file pointer. You can do this with an fclose, fopen sequence, or with freopen.

```
/*
** 'freopen' closes the file with pointer 'filep', and opens
** the file 'filename' with 'type' as for 'fopen'.
** It is equivalent to a call to 'fclose' followed by one to
** 'fopen'.
** The value of 'filep' is returned on success and NULL
** on failure.
*/
FILE *
freopen(filename, type, filep)
char    *filename;
char    *type;    /* as for 'fopen' */
FILE    *filep;
```

In practice, freopen is most often used to associate a file with the standard input, output or error file pointers. For example, this code

```
if (freopen("outfile", "w", stdout) == NULL)
{
    fprintf(stderr, "cannot reopen stdout as outfile\n");
    exit(1);
}
```

tries to close stdout and then reopen it as the file called outfile in write mode. freopen can fail for the same reasons as fopen.

7.4.2 Character I/O on files

We now show how to read and write characters from an arbitrary file. First, we give the usual (and preferred) method which uses the macros getc and putc (in stdio.h). Then we show you the equivalent functions fgetc and fputc. The principal advantage of using macros is that you save the runtime overhead associated with function calls.

```
/*
**    'getc' is a macro that reads a character from 'filep'.
**    On success, it returns the character read.
**    On error or end of file, it returns EOF.
*/
int
getc(filep)
FILE      *filep;

/*
**    'putc' is a macro that writes the character 'c' on
**    to 'filep'.
**    On success, it returns the character written.
**    On failure, it returns EOF.
*/
int
putc(c, filep)
int c;
FILE      *filep
```

The disadvantage of using macros is that you must be careful of side effects (as we discussed on page 157 of Chapter 6). So code like

```
result = putc(*c++, filep);    /* WRONG */
```

should be avoided and this is no hardship in normal uses you are likely to want to make of getc and putc. You should make it a rule to use only simple arguments for macros and, with that proviso, it is generally better to use macros. Note that you cannot tell that getc and putc are macros rather than true functions by examining programs in which they are used; you simply have to know it.

Here is the program that copies standard input to standard output, this time using getc and putc:

```
/*
**    copy standard input to standard output using 'getc'
**    and 'putc'.
*/
```

```
#include    <stdio.h>

main()
{
    int  c;
    while ((c = getc(stdin)) != EOF)
        putc(c, stdout);
}
```

The true functions which do the same task are fgetc and fputc.

```
/*   'fgetc' reads a character from 'filep'.
**   On success, it returns the character read.
**   On error or end of file, it returns EOF.
*/
int
fgetc(filep)
FILE    *filep;


/*   'fputc' writes the character 'c' on to 'filep'.
**   On success, it returns the character written.
**   On failure, it returns EOF.
*/
int
fputc(c, filep)
int  c;
FILE      *filep;
```

Because input is automatically buffered, it is possible to reread a character by using the function ungetc followed by getc or fgetc.

```
/*
**   'ungetc' places the character 'c' on to 'filep'.
**   If 'c' was the last character read from 'filep',
**   'ungetc' effectively "unreads" the last character
**   it read and the same character will be returned
**   by the next call to 'getc'.
**   On success, it returns the character.
**   On failure, it returns EOF.
*/
int
ungetc(c, filep)
int  c;
FILE      *filep;
```

Additional calls to ungetc take you further back in the buffer. However, you cannot go back beyond the current buffer. So, if you have just read from a stream, you can only be certain of making one successful call to ungetc.

7.4.3   Other I/O on files

Now we see two functions that are similar to gets and puts but these can deal with any open file.

```
/*
**    'fgets' is a function that reads a string from 'filep' into
**    'string'.
**    Normally, 'fgets' reads one line; this, including the '\n'
**    is placed in 'string' (unlike 'gets').
**    The numbers of characters read is at most 'n' − 1.
**    On success, it returns it argument ( 'string').
**    On error or end of file, it returns NULL.
*/
char *
fgets(string, n, filep)
char    *string;
int     n;
FILE    *filep;

/*
**    'fputs' is a function that writes 'string' on to 'filep'.
**    Unlike 'puts', it does not append a newline.
**    EOF is returned on error.
*/
int
fputs(string, filep)
char    *string;
FILE    *filep;
```

Note that the string size n needs to be large enough to accommodate the \0 at the end of the string.

There are some important differences between gets and fgets. First, and most obvious, is the fact that fgets allows you to specify both the maximum number of characters and the name of the file pointer. Another important difference is that gets removes the newline at the end of the string that it reads, while fgets keeps it. This is easy to forget and it can be annoying. (The reason for this inconsistency is compatibility with old versions of the standard I/O function library!)

A corresponding relationship applies to fputs and puts: fputs writes a string to a nominated file, but unlike puts it does not append a newline character.

The fscanf and fprintf functions correspond exactly to scanf and printf: the only difference is that a stream can be specified for the I/O operation.

```
/*
**   see descriptions of 'scanf' and 'printf'
*/
int
fscanf(filep, format/*[, pointer] ...*/)
FILE    *filep;
char    *format;

int
fprintf(filep, format/*[, arg] ...*/)
FILE    *filep;
char    *format;
```

7.4.4 Formatting data to or from a memory area

The functions in this section allow you to reformat strings. These are not really I/O functions but each has a matching I/O function that performs the same formatting task. So, for example, sscanf interprets a string in a way that corresponds to scanf's interpretation of a string of characters on input. You will find sscanf particularly useful where you want to read from input but cannot know the exact format until you have analysed some of it: sscanf allows you to effectively reread parts of a line that have been read into a string.

```
/*
**   'sscanf' interprets the string according to the
**   'format' specification.
**   On success, it returns the number of items matched
**   and assigned (like 'scanf').
**   On error or a string too short to match the 'format',
**   it returns EOF.
*/
int
sscanf(string, format/*[, pointer] ...*/)
char    *string;
char    *format;
```

```
/*
** 'sprintf' formats data in a similar way to 'printf'
** except that the output is placed in the memory area
** pointed to by 'buffer'.
** For System V UNIX 'sprintf' returns the number of
** characters of output (excluding the ' \0' character
** at the end).
** Other versions of 'sprintf' may be of type char and
** return 'buffer'.
*/
int
sprintf(buffer, format/*[, arg] ...*/)
char    *buffer;
char    *format;
```

Unfortunately the value returned by the sprintf function varies according to the particular version of UNIX being used. On UNIX System V the number of characters stored in the area is returned, which is like printf, except that sprintf puts a \0 character at the end of the string and does *not* include it in the count. On some other versions of UNIX the first argument is returned.

Sometimes it is convenient to interpret a string as a single integer or floating point number. The following functions enable you to do this.

```
/*
** 'atoi' converts ASCII characters in 'string' to an int.
** It returns the integer interpretation of the string.
** It stops analysing the string on the first non-digit
** character.
*/
int
atoi(string)
char    *string;


/*
** 'atof' is similar to 'atoi' except that it converts
** characters to a float.
*/
float
atof(string)
char    *string;


/*
** 'atol' is similar to 'atoi' except that it converts
** characters to a long.
```

```
*/
long
atol(string)
char    *string;
```

The argument to each of these functions is a pointer to an ASCII string. The string is scanned and the result (int, float or long) returned as the result of the function. The first unrecognized character terminates the scan.

We can view the functions treated in this section as doing string manipulation operations or we can view them as doing I/O-like operations on strings that are in memory rather than on an I/O stream.

7.4.5 Binary I/O

Binary I/O means I/O (either on memory or a file) without interpreting the bit pattern as an ASCII character sequence. A common use for binary I/O is in reading or writing files of structures (especially when reading or writing more than one structure at a time).

```
/*
**   'fread' reads 'number' items of 'size' bytes into 'area'
**   from 'filep'.
**   It returns the number of items read.
**   On error or end of file, it returns zero.
*/
int
fread(area, size, number, filep)
char    *area;
int     size;
int     number;
FILE    *filep;

/*
**   'fwrite' writes 'number' items of 'size' bytes
**   from 'area' to 'filep'.
**   It returns the number of bytes written.
**   On error or end of file, it returns zero.
*/
int
fwrite(area, size, number, filep)
char    *area;
int     size;
int     number;
FILE    *filep;
```

Note that the first argument must be a char * since we think of these functions as dealing with bytes of data. Where you are actually dealing with structures or some other type, you need to cast them to char *. We illustrate how to use fread and fwrite to read and write a file of structures on page 218.

7.4.6 File positioning

All the preceding sections have presumed that you read a file strictly in sequential order. You can also read or write a file by *seeking* a particular position in it and doing I/O from that point. The fseek function positions a file at the specified number of bytes from the beginning, the current position or the end. It is generally used in conjunction with ftell which returns the current position in a file in terms of the number of bytes from the beginning. Typically, you might scan through a file, keeping a collection of values, each of which corresponds to some point of interest. Then you use fseek to move to any one of these points as required.

So a typical form for code that reads a file in other than sequential order is like this:

```
fseek(dbfile, (long)myrec, 0); /* position 'dbfile' at 'myrec' */
fread(data, RECSIZE, 1, dbfile);
    ...
fseek(dbfile, 0L, 0); /* position 'dbfile' at the beginning */
```

We move to the point in the file, myrec bytes from the beginning. Since this argument must be a long, we needed the cast in our code. With the third argument set to zero, the offset is myrec bytes from the *beginning* of the file. Having reached that position, we read the record at that point in the file using fread. Then we position dbfile at its beginning. In general you can also specify positions as offsets from the current position or the end of the file, but always with a long argument.

```
/*
**    'fseek' moves to 'position' bytes offset in 'filep'.
**    'from' indicates 'position' is offset from
**         0   beginning
**         1   current position
**         2   end of file
**    On error, it returns −1.
```

```
*/
int
fseek(filep, position, from)
FILE    *filep;
long    position;
int     from;
```

You can seek the end of a file with

```
...
fseek(dbfile, 0L, 2);              /* position 'dbfile' at end of file */
...
```

Once you have reached a position to which you may need to return, you can use ftell.

```
/*
**   'ftell' returns the current file position, in bytes from
**   the beginning of 'filep'.
*/
long
ftell(filep)
FILE    *filep;
```

It returns the position as a long that can be used later in a call to fseek.

7.4.7 File status

Many of the I/O functions described so far can return an end of file or error indication. You can check for these conditions independently with the following tests (which are actually macros).

```
/*
**   'feof' returns non-zero (true) when end of file
**   has been read on 'filep'.
**   Otherwise, it returns zero.
*/
int
feof(filep)
FILE    *filep;
```

```
/*
** 'ferror' returns non−zero (true) when there has been
** an error while reading or writing on 'filep'.
** Otherwise, it returns zero.
*/
int
ferror(filep)
FILE    *filep;

/*
** 'clearerr' resets the error indicators.
*/
void
clearerr(filep)    /* reset error condition */
FILE    *filep;
```

The clearerr function is the only way to clear an error condition.
You use it when you want to continue in spite of an error. If you do
not use it, the error condition remains set for subsequent I/O operations
and future calls to ferror are meaningless.

7.4.8 Pipes

As we noted in the introductory section on I/O, the pipe is one of the
most powerful features of UNIX. From the point of view of a program,
a pipe looks like any other file except that the functions used to open
and close it are different. For example, the following code fragment
reads and processes lines containing the string unix from all the files in
the current directory:

```
FILE    *p;    /* pipe stream */
char    line[MAXLINE];/* lines read */

if ((p = popen(" grep unix *" , " r" )) == NULL)
{
    fprintf(stderr, " cannot create pipe \n" );
    exit(1);
}

while (fgets(line, sizeof line, p) != EOF)
    /* do something with 'line' */
    ...

pclose(p);  /* close the pipe */
```

In the while loop, we read from the pipe with file pointer p just as we read from any file. The popen call differs from a call to fopen in that its first argument is a string containing a normal shell command. The ouput of this command is the input to the pipe.

In general, popen invokes a program and creates a pipe to the standard input or output of that program.

```
/*
**   'popen' opens a pipe to the shell command pointed to
**   by 'command' in the mode specified by 'type' where:
**      "r" is for read mode
**      "w" is for write mode.
**   It returns a file pointer to the pipe.
**   If the shell cannot be accessed or the files or processes
**   cannot be created, it returns −1.
*/
FILE *
popen(command, type)
char    *command;
char    *type;
```

The corresponding function to close a pipe is pclose.

```
/*
**   'pclose' closes the pipe file 'filep'.
**   On success, it returns the exit status of the
**   shell command.
**   If the file was not opened by 'popen', it returns −1.
*/
int
pclose(filep)
FILE    *filep;
```

A normal shell command is used to specify the program to be invoked and the command can have any of the usual shell metacharacters. Your program can pipe data into a file (in which case it must be open for writing) or you can use the pipe to get input as we did in our sample program.

7.4.9 Buffer control

In general, it is more efficient to buffer I/O so that data are read or written in a smaller number of large blocks. This is because each I/O operation requires one system call. Our getchar version of the copy program on page 174 is inefficient because every character requires one system call to read and another one to write. Had we buffered stdin and stdout, the standard I/O functions would have used one system call per buffer read and one for each buffer written. Given a typical buffer of 512 characters this could mean a 512 to 1 reduction in system calls.

Some file streams are not buffered. These are normally the ones associated with your terminal. So when stdin, stdout and stderr are attached to your terminal, it would be irritating and impractical to buffer them: output on stdout or stderr should appear immediately and if they were buffered, output would not appear until the buffer was full. Similarly, you normally want input on stdin to be available immediately rather than having to wait until a complete buffer is available.

The standard I/O functions do buffering on your behalf in an almost transparent manner. They check (using the stat function) if the file is attached to a terminal and, if so, the file is not buffered.

It is important to close files (using fclose) as this ensures that any data left in the buffers is written to the file.

Here is an example program with setbuf used to indicate buffering on stdout:

```
/*
**   copy standard input to standard output using 'getc'
**   and 'putc'.
**   'stdout' is buffered.
*/
#include    <stdio.h>

char    outbuf[BUFSIZ];

main()
{
    int  c;
    setbuf(stdout, outbuf);
    while ((c = getc(stdin)) != EOF)
        putc(c, stdout);
}
```

We have declared a global buffer area outbuf and set its size with the defined constant BUFSIZ. Our call to setbuf establishes outbuf as the buffer to be used for stdout. You will generally make buffers global: if you declare one within a function other than main, you should close the file before the function completes because the stack space that the buffer occupies will typically be reused.

The functions setbuf and fflush enable you to override the default buffering, setbuf specifying that buffering is to occur even for a stream that is normally unbuffered.

```
/*
** 'setbuf' indicates buffering is to occur on 'filep'
** using the buffer 'buf'.
** When 'buf' is NULL, it indicates no buffering.
*/
void
setbuf(filep, buf)
FILE    *filep;
char    *buf;
```

The buffer pointed to by buf can be set to BUFSIZ, a constant in stdio.h.

Even when you use setbuf to establish buffered I/O, you may want to **flush** the buffer. For example, if your program writes some control characters to a screen to make some parts appear as flashing text, you need to use fflush on the output stream to ensure that the screen change is effected immediately.

```
/*
** 'fflush' flushes the buffer for 'filep' (which remains
** open).
** Where 'filep' is not opened for writing or the flush
** otherwise fails, it returns EOF.
*/
int
fflush(filep)
FILE    *filep;
```

7.5 System call I/O

In this section, we treat the system call level of I/O functions. You should have read about the standard I/O functions in the last section and you will observe the similarity in behaviour between some of the standard I/O functions and system call I/O.

The relationship between the two is illustrated in Figure 7.2. It shows what happens when a program calls a function like fopen from the standard I/O library. First fopen arranges buffering and the like

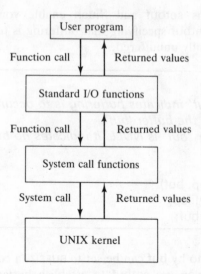

Figure 7.2   How standard I/O and system call I/O functions interact.

and then calls the system call I/O function open which sets up arguments appropriately and does a system call. Finally, the system manages the primitive disk functions required to open a file. There is also a flow of status information back up to the calling program.

In general, you should not intersperse standard I/O and system call I/O functions for, say, reading from a single file. Each has different ways of dealing with the file and if you are not careful you could create a dreadful mess. For example, the standard I/O function may do buffering, and so a standard I/O read followed by a system call I/O read could make it seem as though you have jumped through the file.

In general, system call functions are written in assembler and massage their parameters before executing a system call instruction that causes the UNIX operating system *kernel* to perform the actual I/O operation. (The kernel is the essential core of code in the UNIX operating system and it does tasks like managing memory, I/O devices and the file system.) The kernel returns control to the function which returns status information to the calling C program as illustrated in Figure 7.2. At the system call level, there are typically 100s of UNIX calls. The actual number depends on the version of UNIX.

Because the functions treated in this section are low level, we rely more heavily on your knowledge of UNIX. You might just skim the whole of this section on a first reading. Some of the functions in this section are lower level or primitive forms on which standard functions are built. However, others, including most of the file status and control commands, are used in their own right.

Overview of UNIX concepts used in this section

In this section, we give a very brief overview of the organization of the UNIX file system and the access modes associated with a file. This overview is terse and you may want to read a book on UNIX (see the Bibliography) for more information.

The UNIX file system is organized in a hierarchy, with the top node or root of the tree having a number of directories that are common to most UNIX systems. These include /bin and /usr/bin where many command binaries are kept. Directories can contain files or other directories. You can specify a file name in terms of its **full pathname**, starting from the root directory. Alternatively, you can use a shorter form of file name by stating it relative to the **current directory**, which is set to your HOME directory when you log in and can be altered with the cd shell command.

When you create a new file, the system creates a link to it. You can create additional links which act as aliases for the file. To remove a file, you have to remove all the links to it.

An important aspect of the file system is the control of file access. UNIX defines three forms of access to a file: **read**, **write** and **execute**. Read access to a file or directory means being allowed to see its contents. Write access allows modifications to it and execute permission allows the execution of the file as a program or, in the case of a directory, access to files within it. There are also three classes of users whose access to a file is defined as an attribute of the file: the **owner**, the **group** and **others**. Each file has a user identifier, **uid**, associated with it and that uid defines the user who owns the file. Similarly, a file has a group identifier, **gid**, and all the members of that group have the group access privileges for the file. The file access allowed for everyone else is defined by the 'others' access mode.

The access mode is generally viewed as a sequence of bits as follows:

ttttsssuuugggooo

where the *tttt* bits give the type of the file, the *sss* bits indicate if the file is *setuid* (which means that when this file is executed, the effective uid becomes the uid of the user that owns the file), *setgid* (similar to setuid but for the group of the owner) and the *sticky bit* (indicating that the executable image of the program should be saved in the swap area for rapid execution in the future). The permission bits (*uuugggooo*) consist of three fields each of three bits. These indicate the three access permissions for each of the following: the owner of the file; users within the group that owns the file; and finally, all users. The three bits within each field indicate if the file can be read, written or executed.

Overview of process ownership in UNIX

Processes, like files, each have an individual owner and a group owner. This means that UNIX associates a user *id* (uid) and a group *id* (gid) with each process and the process can act with the privileges associated with that user and group. So, for example, a process that you own can access files that you are entitled to access. When you start a program (or process), it is associated with your uid and gid.

Now, some programs are described as *setuid*, which means that no matter who starts them running, they take on a different *effective* uid. There are many setuid programs you can run where the program has a *real* uid (yours) and a different effective uid that enables the program to do operations allowed for that uid but not for yours. For example, as an ordinary user, you cannot create a directory but you can run mkdir which sets its effective uid to that of the **superuser** (also called **root**) who is able to create a directory. We concentrate on the C to UNIX interface as most programmers use it: superusers need considerable knowledge about system maintenance and other UNIX matters that are not related particularly to C programming.

7.5.1 Error handling and system calls

When an error occurs in a system call, the UNIX system call functions usually return a value of -1. A more useful error code number is also returned in the external variable errno, which is used by perror as in the following code:

```
if ((fd = open(" datafile" , 0)) == −1)
{
        perror(" datafile" );
        exit(1);
}
```

which might cause the following error message to be printed:

> datafile: No such file or directory

In general, this code deals with an error on using open by printing an error message of this form:

> *file-name: error-message-text*

The argument to perror, in this case the file name, is printed first and then perror prints one of the standard error message strings. The defined values that make all this work are:

sys__errlist	an array of pointers to error message strings
sys__nerr	the number of values in sys__errlist
errno	error value that is used as an index into sys__errlist (in errno.h)

The full range of values that errno can take is documented in the UNIX manual entry intro(2).

The function perror prints on the standard error file.

```
/*
** 'perror' prints 'message' followed by a text describing
** the error as set in 'errno'.
*/
void
perror(message)
char    *message;
```

7.5.2 Primitive I/O

The primitive I/O system calls can open, close, read and write files. Unlike the standard I/O functions, they do not format or buffer the data for you. They also manipulate directories, get file status, change permission information and perform device-specific control operations.

Like the standard I/O package, I/O system calls require that a file be open before it is used. Where the standard I/O package uses **file pointers**, I/O system calls use small integer **file descriptors**.

```
/*
** 'open' opens 'filename' in the 'mode' defined where:
**      0 = read
**      1 = write
**      2 = read/write
** On success, it returns file descriptor.
** On failure, it returns −1.
```

```
    */
    int
    open(filename, mode)
    char    *filename;
    int     mode;
```

Normally your program begins execution with standard input, output and error files open and available for use. Their file descriptors are always

standard input	0
standard output	1
standard error	2

Once you have a file descriptor for a file, either from open or from one of the standard files, you can read or write data using the read or write functions.

```
    /*
    **   'read' reads 'count' bytes into 'buffer' from file with
    **   descriptor 'filedesc'
    **   On success, it returns the number of bytes actually read.
    **   On end of file, it returns 0.
    **   On error, it returns −1.
    */
    int
    read(filedesc, buffer, count)
    int     filedesc;
    char    *buffer;
    int     count;

    /*
    **   'write' writes 'count' bytes from 'buffer' on to file with
    **   descriptor 'filedesc'
    **   On success, it returns the number of bytes actually
    **   written.
    **   On error, it returns −1.
    */
    int
    write(filedesc, buffer, count)
    int     filedesc;
    char    *buffer;
    int     count;
```

Here is our familiar file copy program again, this time using the read and write system calls:

```
/*
**   copy standard input to standard output
**   using 'read' and 'write' system calls
*/

main()
{
    char   buf[BUFSIZ];
    int  count;

    while ((count = read(0, buf, BUFSIZ)) > 0)
        write(1, buf, count);
}
```

This is a very efficient way to copy standard input to standard output because it uses the standard sized buffer, BUFSIZ, and avoids the extra function call overhead of the standard I/O functions.

When a file is no longer needed it should be closed using close.

```
/*
**   'close' closes the file with descriptor 'filedesc'.
**   On success, it returns 0.
**   If the file descriptor is unknown, it returns -1.
*/
int
close(filedesc)
int      filedesc;
```

Although the open function opens an *existing* file for I/O, to create a *new* file you need to use the creat (sic) function.

```
/*
**   'creat' creates a file with the name 'filename' with the
**   'access_mode' specified where the 'access_mode'
**   defines user, group or public access.
**   On success, it returns a file descriptor.
**   On failure, it returns -1.
*/
int
creat(filename, access_mode)
char      *filename;
int       access_mode;
```

The file is created and opened for writing. (It would make no sense to open a new file for reading.)

As well as creating files, you can remove them using unlink. This function removes a single named **link** to the file. Of course, the file does not disappear if there are other links to it.

```
/*
**    'unlink' removes a link to a file called 'filename'.
**    On success, it returns 0.
**    On failure, it returns −1.
*/
int
unlink(filename)
char      *filename;
```

7.5.3 Temporary file names

Programs often need files just for the life of the program. In general purpose programs you normally create such temporary files in /tmp, but since many users create temporary files in this directory, you can fail in an attempt to create a file there because its name already exists. You can avoid this by using mktemp to create unique names for temporary files, as in this example:

```
char      *tmpname = "/tmp/mineXXXXXX";
...
if ((tmpf = creat(mktemp(tmpname),mode)) == −1)
{
      perror(progname);
      exit(1);
}
```

This generates a file in /tmp with a name that starts with mine and has a generated end. Our test covers the unlikely situation that the file name created is not unique (because someone happened to choose the same name as mktemp generated). It is very unlikely (but not impossible) that another file of that name exists in the /tmp directory.

```
/*
**    'mktemp' takes a string, 'template', that ends in six X's
**    and returns it with the X's replaced by the program's
**    process number and a unique letter.
```

```
*/
char *
mktemp(template)
char    *template;
```

7.5.4 Positioning

You can alter the point in the file at which the next read or write operation takes effect, using the lseek system call.

```
/*
**    'lseek' sets the read/write position of the file with
**    descriptor 'fd'.
**    The position is defined by the 'from':
**        0 'offset' bytes from the start of the file.
**        1 'offset' bytes from the current position.
**        2 'offset' bytes from the end of the file.
**    On success, it returns the new position value.
**    On failure, it returns −1.
*/
long
lseek(fd, offset, from)
int     fd;
long    offset;
int     from;
```

As with the standard I/O function, fseek, the position can be set relative to the current position, the beginning of the file or the end of the file and the offset is a long integer, as this code illustrates:

```
lseek(fd, 0, 0); /* WRONG way to seek to beginning of file */

lseek(fd, 0L, 0);/* CORRECT */
```

7.5.5 Interface with the standard I/O package

Although there are dangers in mixing system call I/O with calls to the standard I/O functions, it is sometimes unavoidable. In that case, you need to use fileno to get the file descriptor used by a particular file pointer and fdopen to associate a new file pointer with a given file descriptor.

```
/*
**   'fileno' is a macro that returns a file descriptor for a file
**   with file pointer 'filep'
*/
int
fileno(filep)
FILE     *filep;

/*
**   'fdopen' returns a file pointer for an existing, open file
**   with descriptor 'filedesc'
**   The 'mode' must agree precisely with that used to
**   open the file.
*/
FILE *
fdopen(filedesc, mode)
int      filedesc;
char     *mode;
```

7.5.6 Pipes

We have already met the standard I/O function, popen. A pipe may be thought of as a file that is created by a program and disappears when it is closed. Although pipes are managed by the UNIX file system, they do not have a directory entry like proper files and they are never saved on disk: they are used purely for communication between programs.

A pipe has two ends and so the pipe system call returns two file descriptors, one for each end. One file descriptor is used for writing data into the pipe and the other for reading data from the pipe.

```
/*
**   'pipe' creates a pipe with file descriptors 'fd[0]'
**   and 'fd[1]'.
**   Data written into 'fd[1]' can be read from 'fd[0]'.
**   'pipe' returns 0 if the pipe was created, - 1 if not.
*/
int
pipe(fd)
int      fd[2];
```

You may wonder why a program should need a pipe to talk to itself. In fact, one program can start another one running using the fork and exec system calls (described later) and the pipe file descriptors are inherited by the new program. Data can then be sent between the parent and child programs.

7.5.7 File status and control

The UNIX file system has a consistent structure that allows ordinary files, directories and device files to be handled in the same way. Each entry in the file system has a data structure associated with it and this is called an **information node** or **inode**. This contains information about its type, owner, size and location on disk. If the inode refers to a file that has an I/O device driver associated with it, the field normally used for the disk location is used to indicate which device driver is used when accessing the file. Information from the inode for a particular file is given by the stat system call.

```
#include     <sys/types.h>
#include     <sys/stat.h>
/*
**   'stat' places information about 'filename' in area
**   pointed to by 'status'.
**   On success, it returns 0.
**   If the file cannot be found, it returns −1.
*/
int
stat(filename, status)
char *filename;
struct stat *status;
```

The fstat function can be used when the file name is unknown but the file is open. The file descriptor is the number returned from an open, creat, pipe or fileno operation.

```
/*
**   'fstat' places information about an open file with
**   descriptor 'filedesc'
**   in the area ponted to by 'status'.
**   On success, it returns 0.
**   If the file cannot be found, it returns −1.
*/
int
fstat(filedesc, status)
int     filedesc;
struct stat *status;
```

The user must provide a pointer to an area into which the information about the file is placed. This structure is declared in sys/stat.h and this declaration in turn requires declarations of a number of types, which are in sys/types.h. The #include lines shown above in the description of stat ensure inclusion of the necessary declarations in your program. Here is the declaration of the structure stat:

```
struct  stat
{
    dev_t   st_dev;     /* device numbers         */
    ino_t   st_ino;     /* inode number           */
    ushort  st_mode;    /* type and permission    */
    short   st_nlink;   /* number of links        */
    ushort  st_uid;     /* owner's user ID        */
    ushort  st_gid;     /* owner's group ID       */
    dev_t   st_rdev;    /* device numbers         */
    off_t   st_size;    /* size in bytes          */
    time_t  st_atime;   /* last accessed time     */
    time_t  st_mtime;   /* last modified time     */
    time_t  st_ctime;   /* time created           */
};
```

The definitions of the types are machine dependent, which is why they are in a separate include file (sys/types.h). We now discuss fields of stat that need elaboration.

The st_mode element of the structure contains information about the file type and access permissions. The individual parts of st_mode can be extracted using shifting and masking operations and appropriate masks are usually defined in sys/stat.h.

The st_ctime, st_atime and st_mtime elements give the time of creation, last access and modification of the file as the number of seconds past 00:00 GMT 1st January 1970. This is the base time that is used throughout UNIX and you can manipulate it easily using the local-time or ctime functions described in Section 7.14.

The st_nlink element gives the number of *links* to this file. UNIX directory files contain a list of file names and their associated *inode* numbers. One file can have several links which means that it has entries in several directories. Since each call to unlink removes only one directory entry (link), a file does not actually disappear until all links have been removed and the link count in the inode is reduced to zero.

A new link to an existing file can be created using link.

```
/*
** 'link' creates a new link name, 'newfile', for a file
** named 'origfile'.
** On success, it returns 0.
** On failure, it returns −1.
*/
int
link(origfile, newfile)
char       *origfile;
char       *newfile;
```

After creating a new link (using link), the link count in the inode for the file increases.

A normal unprivileged user program cannot directly create or alter directories and inodes. File access permissions can be changed with chmod (for change mode).

```
/*
** 'chmod' changes the 'access_mode' bits for the
** file 'filename'.
** On success, it returns 0.
** On failure, it returns −1.
*/
int
chmod(filename, access_mode)
char       *filename;
int        access_mode;
```

You can alter some of the access mode bits (and others can be altered only by root). You would normally only be interested in changing the permission bits to allow or deny access to the file. You do this in much the same way that you use the UNIX command chmod. A typical set of permissions can be established with the following code:

```
...
chmod("myprog", 0751);
...
```

which sets the access modes for myprog with the octal constant 0751. The octal digit 7 has all three bits set and so it defines the owner's access as readable, writable and executable. The next set of three access mode bits is set to 101 (5 octal), making myprog readable and executable for members of its group. Finally, the lowest digit has only the execute bit set so that the file is only executable by everyone else.

The creat function also has an access_mode argument. The actual access_mode value used when creating the file is the logical AND of the supplied mode with the negation of the mask that the system maintains for each user. This mask is initially set to zero when a user logs on to the system but may be changed with the command umask or from within a C program using the umask function.

```
/*
**    'umask' sets 'mask' as the user's new mask and
**    returns the previous mask value.
**    The initial mask value is 0 for root.
*/
int
umask(mask)
int     mask;
```

To determine if a given file is accessible to your program you can use stat and examine the mode bits. (With knowledge of the uid and gid of the program at that point in execution you can tell if the file in question can be read, written or executed by your program.) Or you can simply use the access function.

```
/*
**    'access' checks for 'access_mode'
**    specified on 'filename'.
**    When that access is allowed, it returns 0.
**    When that access is denied, it returns −1.
*/
int
access(filename, access_mode)
char    *filename;
int     access_mode;
```

The three least significant bits of the mode argument indicate the access permission required. As in the case of chmod's access modes the binary value 100 indicates read access, 10 write access and 1 execute access and combinations of these values are allowed.

The access function is particularly useful when the *effective* uid and gid are not the same as the *real* uid and gid because access checks for accessibility using the real uid or gid. (Note that, normally, both the effective and real id are the same. However, a file can have its *setuid* bit set. Then, any user who invokes it has an effective uid set to that of the file's owner, whilst their real uid remains unchanged.)

Each executing program in a UNIX system has a **current directory**. File names that do not begin with a / are interpreted relative to this directory. This is equivalent to prepending file names used within your program with the full path name for the current directory and a /. For example, if your current directory was /usr/kim, then an attempt to open the file mydata actually opens the file /usr/kim/mydata. When a user first logs in, the current directory is set to their HOME or log-in directory. The current directory can be changed with the cd command to the shell or the chdir function within a C program.

```
/*
** 'chdir' change current directory to 'dirname'.
** If the change is successful, it returns 0.
** Otherwise, it returns −1.
*/
int
chdir(dirname)
char    *dirname;
```

When a file is created or opened by a program, the system internally allocates a data structure and returns the associated file descriptor. The data structure maintains the current position within the file. This can cause some problems if the program forks (see page 227) since there would then be two programs each using the same file descriptor and this could cause confusion about the position of the file. The problem is avoided by the creation of another copy of the data structure and a new file descriptor. So the two programs can be at different positions within the same file. The dup function creates a new copy of the data structure and associated file descriptor.

```
/*
** 'dup' duplicates the file descriptor, 'filedesc'.
** On success, it returns the new file descriptor.
** On failure, it returns −1.
*/
int
dup(filedesc)
int     filedesc;
```

7.5.8 Device control

So far we have described operations on files without reference to physical devices. This has been possible because the UNIX file system presents a consistent view of a file as a linear stream of bytes. There is no record structure and files are independent of the physical device used to store them. So files may be stored on a range of disk storage devices of different sizes and physical structures and users need not be aware of how or where the system keeps their files.

In addition, the UNIX file is the interface to physical devices such as tape drives and terminals. From the point of view of your program these devices are accessed in exactly the same way as normal files: they have an entry in a directory, permission bits like any other file and the system calls open, close, read and write are used to access them. However, some devices may require additional control. For example, a tape drive may need rewinding or a terminal may require a particular communication baud rate. The ioctl system call permits this.

```
/*
** 'ioctl' performs a device specific operation with code
** 'request' on the device with file descriptor 'fd' and with
** a pointer to the required parameters, 'reqparams'.
** 'request' and 'reqparams' depend on the device
** being controlled.
** If an error occurs the value −1 is returned.
*/
int
ioctl(fd, request, reqparams)
int fd;
int request;
struct   req *reqparams;
```

For example, communication lines have a number of changeable parameters including line speed, line parity, type of delay needed for certain control characters, upper to lower case character mapping and character echo. A set of useful definitions of requests and of the reqparams structure is found in a system include file. (On some systems it is sgtty.h, on others termio.h) The following example changes the speed of a communication line to 1200 baud:

```
#include    <sgtty.h>

    struct sgttyb tty;
    ...
    ioctl(fd, TIOCGETP, &tty); /* get the line parameters */
    tty.sg_ispeed = tty.sg_ospeed = B1200; /* change
                            speed to 1200 baud */
    ioctl(fd, TIOCSETP, &tty); /* set the new parameters */
    ...
```

The declaration of the structure sgttyb and definitions of the symbols TIOCGETP, TIOCSETP and B1200 are all in sgtty.h. A complete description of these is in tty(4).

7.6   Storage allocation

We have already described the heap, a storage space that is dynamically allocated at runtime (page 127 in Chapter 5).   It is managed by the standard functions, malloc, calloc, realloc and free. Typically, the allocation uses a **first fit** algorithm. Although these functions reallocate blocks that have been freed and merge adjacent free blocks, they do no garbage collection or compaction.

```
/*
**   'malloc' allocates 'size' bytes on the heap.
**   On success, it returns a pointer to the allocated memory.
**   If there is insufficient memory available,
**   it returns (char *)0.
*/
char *
malloc(size)
unsigned int        size;
/*
**   'calloc' allocates 'number' elements each of 'size' bytes
**   on the heap and initializes the memory to zero.
**   On success, it returns a pointer to the allocated memory.
**   If there is insufficient memory available,
**   it returns (char *)0.
*/
char *
calloc(number, size)
unsigned int        number;
unsigned int        size;
```

There are two differences between malloc and calloc. Firstly, malloc is called with a single argument giving the size of the data area in *bytes* to be allocated, whereas calloc accepts a count of the number of elements to be allocated storage and the size of each. Secondly, calloc clears the memory that it allocates, whereas malloc does not. Typically, calloc is used where memory is to be allocated for structures or when it is important for memory to be initialized to zero.

```
/*
**   'realloc' allocates space on the heap for the data in 'ptr'
**   in 'size' bytes.
**   On success, it returns a pointer to the allocated area.
**   If necessary, it copies the data in the relocation process,
**   and in that case, the old pointer 'ptr' is no longer useful.
**   If there is insufficient memory available,
**   it returns (char *)0.
*/
```

```
char *
realloc(ptr, size)
char            *ptr;
unsigned int    size;
```

To deallocate an area previously allocated with these functions, free is called with a pointer to the area to be freed.

```
/*
** 'free' deallocates the memory accessed by 'ptr'.
** This memory must have been previously allocated by
** 'malloc', 'calloc' or 'realloc'.
*/
void
free(ptr)
char    *ptr;
```

As we noted in Chapter 5, it is critical that you check the value returned by the allocation functions. Failure to do so can produce insidious errors. If available memory is exceeded, a zero pointer is returned by the allocation functions and using a zero pointer gives unpredictable results. So we use **salloc** and **srealloc**, safer versions of **malloc** and **realloc** as shown on pages 321 and 133.

Also, you commonly need to allocate space for structures. Since **malloc** and **salloc** return a pointer to a character, you must cast their result to a pointer to your structure. The following preprocessor macro is very convenient for this:

```
#define talloc(type)    (type *)salloc(sizeof (type))
```

Then, to allocate space for a structure you need only invoke **talloc** with the type of the structure, as in this example.

```
struct datanode
{
...
} *oldptr, *newptr;
...
newptr = talloc(struct datanode);
...
```

A common bug involves exceeding the space allocated for a block. In particular, you should take care to allow for the terminating \0 character when allocating space for a string. Otherwise, a string that is copied to the allocated area overwrites the first byte past the end of the block. The allocation technique used by malloc and calloc places pointers to other blocks just after and just before each block. If a block is overfilled these pointers are overwritten and further allocation or deallocation causes havoc.

The storage allocation algorithm used by these functions may not make the best use of memory for particular applications. Many other algorithms exist, one of which may be more appropriate for your program. (If you are interested in this area, see the paper by D.G. Korn and K.P. Vo in the Bibliography.)

7.7   String handling

In our treatment of strings in Chapter 5, we observed that C does not have a string data type. However, using a pointer to an area of memory containing ASCII characters and the appropriate library functions, you can do powerful string handling. By convention, a C string is a sequence of characters terminated by a null character (\0). A string is manipulated using a pointer to the first character of the sequence.

We have already described, (in the section on formatted I/O) some of the string handling functions: sscanf and sprintf can be used to scan and generate strings in a memory area. Here we describe a toolkit of string functions including those that find the length of a string, concatenate, copy or compare strings. These functions do *not* allocate storage for the parameter strings or the result string; they operate on preallocated areas only.

7.7.1   String length

A function that gives the length of a string is simple but very useful.

```
/*
** 'strlen' returns the length of 'string'
*/
int
strlen(string)
char    *string;
```

Note that the length value returned is the number of characters in the string *excluding* the terminating \0.

7.7.2 Copying strings

The functions strncpy and strcpy copy a string from a **source** area to a **destination** area (which must have already been allocated).

```
/*
**    'strncpy' copies at most 'count' characters from 'src'
**    to 'dest'.
**    The characters counted include the terminating ' \0'.
**    It returns a pointer to 'dest'.
*/
char *
strncpy(dest, src, count)
char     *dest;
char     *src;
int      count;/* This should not exceed size of
                      destination area */

/*
**    'strcpy' copies 'src' string to 'dest'.
**    It returns a pointer to 'dest'.
*/
char *
strcpy(dest, src)
char     *dest;
char     *src;
```

In general, strncpy is safer because it uses count as the *maximum* number of characters to be copied. (By contrast, strcpy makes no check that the string has exceeded the size of the destination area and it may overwrite memory causing insidious bugs.) Note that if the src string length exceeds count, the new string is *not* \0 terminated. Some examples of the use of strncpy appear in the next section.

7.7.3 Concatenating strings

There are two string concatenation functions with forms that correspond to the copy functions.

```
/*
**   'strcat' concatenates 'src' on to the end of 'dest'.
**   It returns a pointer to 'dest'.
*/
char *
strcat(dest, src)
char      *dest;
char      *src;


/*
**   'strncat' concatenates 'src' on to the end of 'dest'.
**   It allows the new string to be 'count' characters at most.
**   It returns a pointer to 'dest'.
*/
char *
strncat(dest, src, count)
char      *dest;
char      *src;
```

Strcat takes two character pointer arguments. It copies the src
string into the area of memory beginning at the terminating \0 of the
dest string. You need to take care to allow enough storage in the first
string to hold the concatenation. The only difference between strncat
and strcat is that the additional integer argument limits the number of
characters copied. Unlike strncpy, strncat always makes the final
string \0 terminated, even if the final string length exceeds count.

The following code fragment copies constant strings into two
areas, concatenates them along with a newline and finally prints the resulting string, "good luck":

```
#define STR_SIZE      50

        char      s1[STR_SIZE];
        char      s2[STR_SIZE];
        char      *s;

        strncpy(s1, " good ", STR_SIZE);
        strncpy(s2, " luck", STR_SIZE);
        s = strncat(s1, strncat(s2, " \n", STR_SIZE), STR_SIZE);
        printf(" %s", s);
```

Note that strncpy and strncat have been used to avoid potential overflow. Also, we have found it convenient to use the result returned by
one string function as an argument of another.

7.7.4 Comparison and scanning

There is a similar pair of functions that do string comparisons.

```
/*
**    'strcmp' compares 'string1' and 'string2'.
**    It returns
**         -1 if string1 <  string2
**          0 if string1== string2
**         +1 if string1 >  string2
*/
int *
strcmp(string1, string2)
char    *string1;
char    *string2;


/*
**    'strncmp' is like 'strcmp' except that it compares at
**    most 'count' characters
*/
int *
strncmp(string1, string2, count)
char    *string1;
char    *string2;
int     count;
```

Here, too, the difference is that strcmp compares two arbitrary length strings and strncmp compares strings up to a specified size. Both functions return +1, 0 or −1 if string1 is greater than, equal to or less than string2 when compared lexicographically. For example:

    strcmp(" ant" , " bee");

returns −1 since "ant" is alphabetically before "bee" and

    strncmp(" ant" , " another" , 2);

returns 0 because the first two characters of both parameters are identical. (Of course, a general alphabetic comparison has to take account of case.)

The strchr function scans a string for a given character, returning a pointer to the first occurrence of that character and strrchr is similar but scans *backwards* from the end of the string, returning the last occurrence of the character.

```
/*
**    'strchr' searches forward through 'string' for
**    the character 'ch'.
**    If it finds 'ch', it returns a pointer to it.
**    If not, it returns (char *)0.
*/
char *
strchr(string, ch)
char    *string;
char    ch;

/*
**    'strrchr' searches backward through 'string' for
**    the character 'ch'.
**    If it finds 'ch', it returns a pointer to it.
**    If not, it returns (char *)0.
*/
char *
strrchr(string, ch)
char    *string;
char    ch;
```

The following example illustrates the use of strchr to find the second occurrence of the character X:

```
if ((firstX = strchr(s, 'X')) != NULL)
    secondX = strchr(firstX, 'X');
```

Some UNIX systems have functions index and rindex that correspond to strchr and strnchr.

7.7.5 Common uses and errors

The most common errors in string manipulation programs are due to strings overflowing their allocated destination area. To help avoid this, you should use strncat and strncpy where possible. A particularly common and nasty variant of this error can occur when you allocate string storage (using either malloc or an array declaration) and forget to allocate space for the complete string *including* the terminating \0 character. The correct code to make a copy of a string in a dynamically allocated area is as follows:

```
/* make a copy of 'oldstring' */
newstring = strcpy(salloc(strlen(oldstring)+1), oldstring);
```

You might well define this form in a macro or a function in your own library of utilities. Another use for the functions strchr and strrchr is to check if a character is a member of a particular set, as in this example:

```
/* check if 'ch' is one of dot, question mark or exclamation */
if (strchr(".?!" , ch) != (char *)0)
```

The string functions can be used on the left hand side of assignments. For example, the function fgets reads a string from a file and leaves a newline character before the terminating \0. To remove the newline from a string s we can use this code:

```
/* remove newline left by 'fgets' */
*(s+strlen(s)−1) = ' \0' ;
```

which overwrites the newline with the string terminator.

7.8 Character types

It is common for programs that manipulate text to test if a character is a member of a particular class. For example, you may wish to test whether a character is a digit or an upper case letter. Although you could easily write simple functions to do these tests, you do better to use those provided. In fact, they are not true functions but **macros**. Each is called with a character argument and each returns TRUE (non-zero) on success or FALSE (zero) on failure of the test. To use them, you must include ctype.h.

Several examples of the use of these macros appeared in Chapter 1 and they are also used in Chapter 8.

```
#include        <ctype.h>

                /* true if c is: */
isalpha(c)      /*     a letter */
isupper(c)      /*     an upper case letter */
islower(c)      /*     an lower case letter */
isdigit(c)      /*     a digit */
```

```
isalnum(c)   /*    alphanumeric */
isspace(c)   /*    space, tab, form feed, CR or NL */
ispunct(c)   /*    neither alphanumeric or control */
isprint(c)   /*    a printing character */
iscntrl(c)   /*    a control character */
isascii(c)   /*    an ASCII character (less than 0200) */
```

There is also a pair of somewhat less useful macros for converting characters from upper case to lower case and lower case to upper case.

```
toupper(c)   /* converts from lower case to upper case */
tolower(c)   /* converts from upper case to lower case */
```

You should be warned that most implementations of these macros require that the character being converted is not already in the target case. If you try to convert an upper case letter to upper case, the toupper function may not give the correct result. We recommend that you either write your own macro or test each character before calling toupper or tolower.

7.9 Sorting and searching

The qsort function uses the quickersort algorithm to sort items of data.

```
/*
**   'qsort' uses the quickersort algorithm to sort the array
**   'data' containing 'number' elements, each 'size' bytes.
**   'comp_func' is a pointer to a user supplied
**   comparison function.
*/
void
qsort(data, number, size, comp_func)
char    *data;
int     number;
int     size;
int     (*comp_func)();
```

You must provide qsort with the name of a function which compares two of your data items. This should return −1 if the first item is less than the second, 0 if they are equal and 1 if the first is greater than the second. qsort calls your function with pointers to the data items as arguments. The program below illustrates the use of qsort:

218   C PROGRAMMING IN A UNIX ENVIRONMENT

```
/*
**   read a file of records, sort them and write them out
*/
#include    <stdio.h>
#define MAXRECS    200

struct  rec
{
    char    name[30];
    char    address[100];
} recs[MAXRECS];

int compare();

main()
{
    int  i;
    int  numrecs;

    for (i = 0; i < MAXRECS; i++)
    {
        if (fread(&recs[i], sizeof (struct rec), 1, stdin) == 0)
            break;
    }
    if (i == MAXRECS)
    {
        fprintf(stderr, "too many records on input\n");
        return 1;
    }
    numrecs = i;

    qsort(recs, numrecs, sizeof (struct rec), compare);

    for (i = 0; i < numrecs; i++)
        if (write(&recs[i], sizeof (struct rec), 1, stdout) == 0)
        {
            fprintf(stderr, "cannot write output\n");
            return 1;
        }
}

compare(a, b)
struct   rec *a;
```

```
struct rec    *b;
{
    return strcmp(a->name, b->name);
}
```

It reads a file of rec structures into the array recs, sorts them on the name field and writes the sorted structures on to stdout.

Useful search functions are bsearch, regex and regcmp: bsearch searches for a string in a table using a binary chop algorithm; regex and regcmp match a regular expression with a string. The regular expressions are similar in form to those accepted by the UNIX text editor ed. Descriptions of these functions are in the *UNIX Programmer's Manual*. Their use is illustrated in the next chapter where they allow the flexible selection of an item from a mailing list file.

7.10 Assertions

It is said that there are two ways in which a program can be wrong. The first way is for it to fail dramatically and obviously, as with a memory dump message. This is the better mode of failure. The second, far worse, form of error is when a program runs to completion and produces plausible but incorrect results. Appropriate uses of assertions can improve the chance that programs, which might be wrong in the second way, produce error messages.

The assert function is useful in program debugging as well as helping you produce correct programs. It simply prints an error message if its argument is zero and does nothing otherwise. It should be used when you *know* something should be true at some point in your program. Then if this condition fails to hold, the problem is brought to your attention by assert's error message. In fact, assert is a macro defined in the file assert.h.

```
/*
** 'assert' prints an error message if 'expression'
** is non-zero
*/
assert(expression)
int  expression;
```

The following code fragment illustrates a use of assert:

```
#include    <assert.h>

/* copy name to next record in list */
```

```
update(pname, list, index)
char        *pname;
struct prec *list[ ];
int         index;
{
    assert(strlen(pname) < NAMESIZE);
    assert((index >= 0) && (index < MAX));
    strcpy(list[index]->name, pname);
}
```

It ensures that we know about an overlength string or an out of bounds array index before the call to strcpy. Note that the program continues to run even if the assertion prints an error message.

7.11 Non-local goto—long jump

The functions setjmp and longjmp can jump from deep within nested function calls to another location in your program. This facility may sound very primitive, unstructured and error-prone but it does have important uses: in particular, it is useful in a large and complex program which may encounter serious error conditions in a deeply nested portion of the code. It may not be acceptable to simply print an error message and quit. Nor is it desirable to take the approach of unravelling the nested function calls by passing back an error indicator which then needs to be tested at several points. In such cases, you can use a longjmp to jump to a location previously marked with a setjmp.

The setjmp function saves the current local variable state and the longjmp function restores that state and returns control as if the first call on setjmp were returning. When first called, setjmp returns the value 0 and saves the state. On returning as the result of a longjmp it returns a user specified value. The buffer used to hold a state is declared in longjmp.h.

```
#include        <setjmp.h>

/*
**   'setjmp' saves the function call state in 'state'
**   it returns 0 when first called and a user specified value
**   when returning as the result of a 'longjmp'
*/
int
setjmp(state)
jmp_buf state;
```

```
/*
**   'longjmp' restores the function state to the value stored
**   in 'state' as the result of a 'setjmp' call.
**   The corresponding 'setjmp' call will return 'value'
*/
void
longjmp(state, value)
jmp__buf state;
int     value;
```

You should be aware that the state saved by setjmp includes local variables from the stack but *excludes* register variables. Also you cannot jump to a function that has returned and is no longer on the stack.

7.12   System interface

Like most operating systems, UNIX provides a way for one program to initiate the execution of another. This facility is used by the shell to start the appropriate program after it has analysed a command line. It can also be very useful to the ordinary C programmer.

This section deals with the interface between your program and its operating environment. This includes communication between your program and another program, where this may be the shell, some other process that initiated your program, a process that is initiated by your program or various other processes that run in parallel with your program. Much of this section requires more sophisticated understanding of UNIX than most other parts of the book, so you may wish to skim it on a first reading.

7.12.1   Environment information

We saw in Chapter 5 (page 135) that when a program starts, the main function is called with three arguments, as shown in the following declaration:

```
/* declaration of main function for any program */
int main(argc, argv, envp)
int     argc;    /* number of arguments in argv */
char    *argv[]; /* array of pointers to argument strings */
char    *envp[]; /* array of pointers to environment
                    variables */
```

Although we discussed argc and argv in Chapter 5, we ignored envp which is a pointer to an array of strings with a range of useful information about the program's environment, including environment variables which are character strings in this form:

variable__name = value

You can set them using the shell and they are passed to a program that is started from the shell. For example, the name of the log-in directory of a user is usually kept in the environment variable HOME and the type of terminal currently in use is kept in the variable TERM. We can set these with shell commands like these:

```
HOME=/usr/kim
TERM=5620
```

To make environment variables easier to use, the value of envp is also available in the global variable environ which must be declared like this:

```
extern char *environ[];
```

Unlike envp, this can be used anywhere in your program. Also, the getenv function scans the environment list and returns the value of a specified variable. So, for example, you can find the type of terminal being used thus:

```
if ((terminal = getenv(" TERM" )) == (char*)0)
{
    fprintf(stderr, " %s: TERM variable not set \n" , argv[0]);
    exit(1);
}
```

The actual details of the environment variables tend to differ across systems, but the type of information you can expect includes the default set of directories that the shell searches for command names, called the search path (PATH), the prompt strings used by the shell (PS1, PS2) and the user's home directory (HOME).

```
/*
**   'getenv' gets the value of the environment variable
**   'name'.
**   On success, it returns a pointer to the value string.
**   If 'name' is not found, it returns (char *)0.
*/
```

```
char *
getenv(name)
char    *name;
```

7.12.2 Initiating processes

The system call that starts another process is called exec. It operates by suspending the current process and handing control to a new process. If you want your program to initiate another program and continue execution itself, you need to use the fork system call which we describe later.

As well as starting another process, exec can pass arguments to it. There are several forms of the exec function, with each processing its arguments differently before invoking the exec system call to start another process. The differences relate to the type of file that is executed, the places the file can be and the number of arguments and the environment passed to the program that is invoked.

The first of the exec functions that we consider is execve, which hands control to another process and explicitly passes both the program arguments and the environment.

```
/*
**   'execve' starts the program in 'filename' with
**   arguments 'argv' and the environment in 'envp'.
**   On failure, it returns −1 (and any return indicates failure).
*/
int
execve(filename, argv, envp)
char    *filename;
char    *argv[];
char    *envp[];
```

The last string pointer in argv and the last environment variable pointer in envp must be followed by NULL pointers ((char *)0) to indicate the end of the list. The execve function is useful if the number of arguments or environment variables cannot be determined until runtime. The file-name argument specifies the file that contains the program to be run. This is interpreted relative to the current directory unless an absolute path name is given. (An absolute path name starts with a slash.) The file must contain an executable binary program and cannot be a command file (but see the execlp and execvp functions later).

When you do not want to explicitly pass environment variables to the new process, use the execv function so that the environment of the invoking process is passed to the new process.

```
/*
** 'execv' starts the program in 'filename' with
** arguments 'argv'.
** On failure, it returns −1 (and any return indicates
** failure).
*/
int
execv(filename, argv)
char    *filename;
char    *argv[];
```

The more commonly used function of this pair is execv because you usually do not need to provide an explicit environment for a new process. The usual reason for using execve is for security, particularly in the situation where you want the new process to run in a restricted environment.

Where the number of arguments to be passed to the new process is known in advance, you can use execl or execle.

```
/*
** 'execl' starts the program in 'filename' with
** the arguments 'arg0' to 'argn'.
** On failure, it returns −1 (and any return indicates
** failure).
*/
int
execl(filename, arg0/*, ..., argn, (char *)0*/)
char    *filename;
char    *arg0;
     ...
char    *argn;

/*
** 'execle' is identical to 'execl' except that it explicitly
** passes the environment in 'envp'.
** On failure, it returns −1 (and any return indicates
** failure).
*/
int
execle(filename, arg0, /*..., argn, (char *)0,*/ envp)
char    *filename;
```

```
char    *arg0;
        ...
char    *argn;
char    *envp[];
```

The last argument pointer must be NULL ((char *)0) to indicate the end of the argument list.

For example, the following code segment passes control to the UNIX sort utility program:

```
    ...
if (execl("/bin/sort", "sort", "in", "-o", "out", (char *)0)
        == -1)
{
    perror(argv[0]);
    exit(1);
}
/* program can never reach this point unless 'execl' fails */
```

Note that the full path name of the file containing the sort program has to be specified. The remaining arguments in the execl call are the arguments we want for the sort utility, the program name sort being argv[0], and the other arguments ensure that the input data is taken from the file called in and the sorted output goes to the file out. Notice also the use of the perror function to print an error message on the standard error file.

When you type a UNIX command, the shell searches one or more directories looking for a file of that name. On finding it, the shell uses the exec system call to invoke it. The sequence of directories that is searched is described by the environment variable PATH and you can redefine this to change the directories searched or their search order. The same facility is available with execvp and execlp which are identical to execv and execl except that they search the directories given in the PATH environment variable looking for the specified program.

```
/*
**  'execvp' searches PATH for 'filename' and starts the
**  program or, if 'filename' contains shell commands,
**  it invokes a shell.
**  It passes the arguments 'argv'.
```

```
**   On failure, it returns −1 (and any return indicates
**   failure).
*/
int
execvp(filename, argv)
char    *filename;
char    *argv[];
/*
**   'execlp' is identical to 'execvp' except that
**   it passes the arguments 'arg0' to 'argn'.
*/
int
execlp(filename, arg0/*, ..., argn, (char *)0*/)
char    *filename;
char    *arg0;
   ...
char    *argn;
```

These functions have an added bonus: if the file found contains commands rather than an executable binary, they invoke a shell to interpret the commands. The name of the particular shell to be used is taken from the environment variable SHELL, and if SHELL is not set then /bin/sh is used. Security issues are particularly important in the situation where a shell could be invoked. The shell will search directories specified in PATH for commands to be executed. If this is set to a user's directory, programs other than the ones you may have intended could be executed.

7.12.3 Parallel execution

Whereas exec allows a process to hand over control to another program, fork duplicates a process and sets both executing in parallel. By combining fork and exec, one program may start a second program and continue execution itself.

When a program uses the fork system call, a copy is made of its code, data space and attributes such as environment variables, current working directory, nice value and many others. The original is then called the **parent** process, the copy is called the **child** process and both execute in parallel. Both processes are identical with one important exception: the value returned by the fork call in the parent process is the **process ID** of the child process, while the value returned in the child process is zero. If an error occurs, no duplication takes place and the call returns the usual −1 error code.

```
/*
**    'fork' duplicates the current process
**    On success, it returns:
**        0 to child process
**        pid of child to parent process
**    On error, it returns −1
*/
int
fork()
```

The companion system call for fork is wait. This allows a parent process to wait for the completion of a child process. A call on the wait function returns immediately if the child process has already terminated or if the calling program is interrupted by a signal (described later in this chapter).

```
/*
**    'wait' waits for termination of the child process with
**    'status' value.
**    On success, it returns process id of terminating process.
**    If there is no child process to wait for the value −1
**    is returned.
*/
int
wait(status)
int *status;          /* pointer to integer containing
                         status returned by child process */
```

When a process returns or uses the exit system call it passes back a small integer value which is made available to the parent process in the location pointed to by status. In fact the least significant eight bits of the value returned by the child process is shifted left eight places and placed in *status. A termination code is placed in the least significant eight bits. (These codes are described in the UNIX manual entry for signal(2).)

Here is an example of the use of fork and exec to start another program and wait for it to terminate:

```
switch(pid = fork())
{
case 0: /* child exec's new process */
        execv("newproc", argv);
        /* fall through if exec fails */
case -1:/* could not fork */
        /* print appropriate error message */
        perror(myname);
        exit(1);

default:/* parent waits for child to finish */
        while ((wval = wait(&status)) != pid)
            if (wval == -1)
            {
                perror(myname);
                exit(1);
            }
}
```

Note that this example uses execv to initiate a program and so cannot be used to run any arbitrary shell command. To do that, we need to exec the shell with the −c option and the command as arguments as in the following function (which has the disadvantage of using an extra process):

```
/*
**    Execute a shell command.
**    This is similar to the standard 'system' function
*/
system(command)
char    *command; /* command to execute */
{
    int  status; /* status returned by command */
    int  pid;    /* process id of command */
    int  wval;   /* value returned by wait */

    switch(pid = fork())
    {
    case 0: /* child exec's shell */
            execl("/bin/sh", "sh", "−c", command, 0);
            /* fall through if exec fails */
    case -1:/* could not fork */
            /* print appropriate error message */
```

```
                    perror(myname);
                    exit(1);

        default:/* parent waits for child to finish */
                while ((wval = wait(&status)) != pid)
                    if (wval == -1)
                        return -1;
        }
        return status;
}
```

Note that this example has been given purely to illustrate the use of exec. It mimics the standard function system and you would be better to use that than to write your own.

7.12.4 Controlling a process

Once you get a process started using fork or exec there are several actions it can take to control its own execution. For example, it can terminate, pause for a given time, change its priority, change the size of its data area or change its uid or gid. (Some of these operations require appropriate permission). Now we see the functions that give such control.

The most basic action a process can take is to terminate itself using exit.

```
/*
** 'exit' stops execution of the process with the least
** significant 8 bits of 'status' being passed to the
** parent process.
** It never returns!
*/
exit(status)
int  status;
```

A process can suspend itself or *go to sleep* using pause.

```
/*
** 'pause' waits indefinitely for a signal from 'kill'
** or 'alarm'.
** After a signal, 'pause' returns the value -1.
*/
int
pause()
```

This may seem as drastic as the exit system call. In fact, after execution of pause, the process is still **alive** but suspended and may be reactivated upon receipt of a signal (described on page 234 in the section on inter-process control).

Processes can also change some aspects of their execution environment. For example, each process in a UNIX system has a scheduling priority value. This value can be increased (i.e. made worse) by any process and decreased (made better) by processes whose user id is zero (this is the superuser uid).

```
/*
** 'nice' alters the scheduling priority by 'increment'.
*/
void
nice(increment)
int  increment;
```

This is called nice because you typically use it to be nice to others by lowering the priority of long running compute bound programs.

The uid and gid of a process can be changed using the setuid and setgid system calls. These calls are normally used by programs executing with the superuser uid.

One last aspect of a process's environment that it can modify is the extent of its data area. This area occupies a contiguous set of memory addresses, the last available address being called the **break**. You can change the break (to allocate more or less memory) with the brk or sbrk functions.

```
/*
** 'brk' sets the last address in the data area (the break)
** to 'address'.
** On success, it returns 0.
** On failure, it returns −1.
*/
char *
brk(address)
char *address;

/*
** 'sbrk' increases the program data area by 'increment'.
** On success, it returns a pointer to the beginning of the
** new area.
** On failure, it returns −1.
*/
```

```
    char *
    sbrk(increment)
    int  increment;
```

These functions are used by the storage allocation functions (malloc and realloc).

7.12.5 Process information

Every process has an identifying number or **process id**. As each process is run by a particular user and group, it also has a **uid** and **gid**. These three values are given by the following functions.

```
/*
** 'getpid' returns the process number  of this process
*/
int
getpid()

/*
** 'getuid' returns the user identification number
** of this process
*/
int
getuid()

/*
** 'getgid' returns the group identification number of this
** process
*/
int
getgid()
```

There are corresponding functions geteuid and getegid that give the effective uid and gid.

The process id can be used to generate unique names within a program since at any one point in time all process numbers are different. As we saw, mktemp generates the names of temporary files using the process id.

The uid and gid can be used to find the log-in and group names of the process and also to determine other user information as described in Section 7.13.

The execution time of a process and its child processes is available from the times function.

```
/*
** 'times' places the execution time for this process and its
** child processes in 'buffer'.
** On error, the value −1 is returned.
*/
long
times(buffer)
struct
{
    long    user;          /* user time of process */
    long    system;        /* system time of process */
    long    child__user;   /* user time of child procs */
    long    child__system; /* system time of child procs */
} *buffer;
```

The times are given in **clock ticks** where the length of a clock tick depends on your system.

The **user time** is the amount of time spent executing the user's process, while the **system time** is the time spent in the system on behalf of the user's process. The times for child processes are calculated as the sum of the times for all children (and other descendants) of the current process.

7.12.6 Process monitoring

UNIX has powerful facilities for monitoring and controlling process execution. The ptrace function allows a program to control the execution of a child process. It also allows the memory containing the child process to be examined and modified. This function is commonly used by debugging programs such as adb. Another system call function, profil, allows statistics to be gathered on the frequency of execution of parts of your program. This system call is supported by the function monitor and the program prof. A detailed description of these functions is in prof(1), ptace(2), profil(2) and monitor(3).

7.12.7 Standard Interprocess communication

UNIX has only a simple mechanism for interprocess communication, the **signal**, which is something like a software interrupt that can be initiated by some external event or another process. When a signal arrives at a process it can cause the program to be terminated, it can be ignored (except for the **kill** signal) or it can be **caught**. Catching a signal means invoking a user specified function that carries out an appropriate action. The user's process is often unaware that a signal has arrived since execution is interrupted, the catching function invoked and execution resumed when the function returns.

Signals can occur as a result of some external action such as the user typing the interrupt or quit characters on the keyboard of the controlling terminal. They can happen when the program fails because it executed an illegal instruction or tried to reference memory that it did not own. A complete list of signals and their description is in signal(2).

For example, the following function uses signals to put a process to sleep for a given number of seconds:

```
/*
** Suspend the current process for 'time' seconds.
** Similar in purpose to the standard 'sleep' function.
*/
#include <signal.h>

sleep(time)
unsigned time;
{
        unsigned    alarm();
        int      (*alrm_func)();
        int      wakeup();

        if(time == 0)
                return(0);

        /* set pointer to alarm signal catching function */
        alrm_func = signal(SIGALRM, wakeup);
        /* set the alarm clock */
        alarm(time);
        /* wait for it to ring */
        pause();
        /* restore previous alarm catcher */
        signal(SIGALRM, alrm_func);
        /* return amount of time unslept (if any) */
        return alarm(0);
}
```

```
static
wakeup()
{
    /* nothing to do except return */
}
```

Our function starts by checking its argument. If this is all right, it proceeds to call signal which establishes an association between the signal SIGALRM and the function wakeup: when the SIGALRM signal occurs, the wakeup function will be invoked. We also keep in alrm__func a pointer to the function that would have been called on the occurrence of SIGALRM. Next it calls alarm which evokes the signal SIGALRM after time seconds. Then the program pauses until a signal occurs. In general, this signal will be SIGALRM and our wakeup function executes. The sleep function is restarted after the call to pause and then we use signal again to re-establish the previous association between SIGALRM and the function it previously would have invoked. The alarm function returns the amount of time remaining in the alarm clock, so if any other signal ended our pause, the amount of time remaining will be returned by the alarm(0) call.

Before we discuss the signal management functions, we emphasize that our sleep function is only to illustrate the use of signals. A more sophisticated version of the sleep function is already available in the C library. The library version takes care of the situation where the alarm facility is already being used by your program and it also handles wakeups from signals other than SIGALRM. This situation is typical: standard functions are generally better than you would be likely to write.

Each signal has a number. Names are associated with these numbers in a set of #defines in signal.h. To catch a signal the system must be given the signal number and the address of a function to execute when the signal occurs. This is done by signal.

```
    #include    <signal.h>

/*
**    'signal' establishes an association between 'sig' and
**    'func' so that when the signal number 'sig' occurs, the
**    function 'func' is invoked. When 'func' is SIG__IGN
**    the signal is ignored.
**    When 'func' is SIG__DFL the process is terminated.
**    'signal' returns a pointer to previous signal catching
**    function or −1 (you have to cast the result to int before
**    testing it) if an illegal signal number is specified
*/
```

```
int
(*signal(sig, func))()
int  sig;
int  (*func)();
```

As well as external events or internal error conditions, signals can be generated by other processes, using the kill function.

```
/*
**   'kill' sends the signal 'sig' to the process with id 'pid'.
**   On success, it returns 0.
**   On failure, it returns -1.
*/
int
kill(pid, sig)
int  pid;
int  sig;
```

Although this could be used to set up a primitive interprocess communication system, it is more often used for one process to terminate another, in which case sig is normally set to SIGTERM.

Except in the case of the superuser, a process sending a signal must have the same effective uid as the process receiving the signal (and a process may send a signal to itself). A process may also specify that the SIGALRM signal is to be sent to it after a given time has elapsed, using the alarm function.

```
/*
**   'alarm' requests the signal 'SIGALRM' after 'time'
**   seconds.
**   It returns the amount of time remaining from the
**   last call to it.
**   If there has been no previous alarm call, it returns 0.
*/
int
alarm(time)
unsigned time;
```

In most situations, execution of a process is interrupted by a signal and then resumed at the point after the signal catching function returns. However, when the process is executing certain system calls, the system call returns prematurely with an error indication and errno is set to the value EINTR (defined in errno.h). For example, SIGALRM can be used to terminate a **read** system call that is taking too long. This can be used in interactive systems where you may want to give the user help if he or she takes too long in replying to a question. It is also a way of implementing similar **timeouts** in programs that handle communication lines. The following code fragment gives users help if they take too long to respond:

```c
#include    <signal.h>

int  toolong;
int  count = 0;
int  wakeup();
int  number;

main()
{
    for (;;)
    {
        printf(" What is your number? " );
        toolong = 0;
        signal(SIGALRM, wakeup);
        alarm(10);
        scanf(" %d" , &number);
        if (toolong == 0)
            break;

        if (count == 1)  /* First timeout response */
            printf(" \nYour number is on your ID card. \n" );
        else    /* Second timeout response */
        {
            printf(" \nPlease report to your supervisor " );
            printf(" if you have lost your ID card. \n" );
            exit(1);
        }
    }

    alarm(0);

    printf(" Number: %d \n" , number);
}

wakeup()
{
    toolong = 1;
```

```
        count++;
    }
```

The central for loop starts by printing a message to the user. Then it sets up a signal and an alarm so that the program waits no more than ten seconds for the user to respond: it calls signal so that the function wakeup will be called if the SIGALRM signal occurs and then it calls alarm to send the signal (SIGALRM) in ten seconds. Next we have a scanf which reads the user's reponse. Now, if the user does repond within ten seconds, toolong will still be zero in the tests immediately after the scanf and we break out of the for loop. On the other hand, if the user takes more than ten seconds to respond, the SIGALRM signal will be sent by alarm and wakeup will execute, setting toolong and incrementing count and terminating the scanf function so that the user gets the first help message. If the user takes more than ten seconds the next time the input is requested, he or she gets the second message. Note that the signal is reset to SIG_DFL after being caught, and so we need to call signal before each call to alarm.

7.13   User information

Utility programs often need information about the user running the program. This is typically the user's account name or home directory. While it is usually possible to get this information from environment variables (see Section 7.12.1), it is better and more secure to get it from the system password file (because the user may have changed the environment variables.)

The getuid function (page 231) returns the identification number of the user running the program. This can be used in getpwuid to search for that user's entry in the password file and getpwnam finds the entry, given a user name.

```
/*
** 'getpwuid' returns to a pointer to the password
** information for the user with id 'uid'.
*/
struct passwd *
getpwuid(uid)
int   uid;

/*
** 'getpwnam' returns a pointer to the password
** information for the user with log-in name 'username'.
```

```
*/
struct passwd *
getpwnam(username)
char    *username;
```

Both functions return a pointer to a structure containing all the fields of a password file entry, a structure defined in **pwd.h**:

```
struct passwd
{
    char    *pw_name;       /* user name */
    char    *pw_passwd;     /* encrypted password */
    int     pw_uid;         /* user ID number */
    int     pw_gid;         /* group ID number */
    int     pw_quota;       /* unused */
    char    *pw_comment;    /* unused */
    char    *pw_gecos;      /* unused */
    char    *pw_dir;        /* HOME directory */
    char    *pw_shell;      /* program to use as shell */
};
```

The fields that are most used are the user name, user/group ID, HOME directory and shell program.

We illustrate how you access a user's HOME directory in the following code from a program that maintains diaries. It opens the file **monday** in the directory **Diary** in the user's HOME directory:

```
struct passwd    *pwent;
char             fname[NAMESIZE];

pwent = getpwuid(getuid());
strncpy(fname, pwent->pw_dir, NAMESIZE);
strncat(fname, "/Diary/monday", NAMESIZE);

if ((mon = fopen(fname, "r")) == NULL)
{
    fprintf(stderr, "%s: cannot open file %s\n",
        myname, fname);
    exit(1);
}
```

Strictly speaking we should have checked the result of the getpwuid function. Since it would be very unusual and probably a system error to have a uid without a corresponding password file entry, it is normally safe to omit the test.

7.14 Time of day

You can get the actual time of day, as opposed to the amount of time used by a process, with a collection of functions of which we met two (time and localtime) in the program that printed times at different locations in the world on page 146 of Chapter 5. This section covers these and the other functions for dealing with the time and date.

```
/*
**    'time' returns the time in seconds since 00:00:00 GMT,
**    1st January 1970. It also sets 'resultp' to access the
**    same value
**    Note: 'time' itself returns a value
**    'resultp' is a pointer to the value.
*/
long
time(resultp)
long    *resultp;
```

Beware! There is a very common error in using time: you must remember that its argument must be a *pointer*. The time is returned both as a function value and through the argument pointer. You can call the function with a null pointer ((long*)0) to indicate that the time is to be returned only as the value of the function. You usually use time in association with other time and date functions, and since these take a *pointer* argument you usually need the pointer argument to time rather than the value returned.

Now the value returned by time is expressed as the number of seconds past the beginning of 1970. This is not directly useful! There is a set of library functions that convert it into something more meaningful. The ctime function takes a pointer to a time as returned by time and returns a pointer to a string that gives the date and time in a standard fixed format string.

```
/*
**    'ctime' sets the value pointed to by 'timeptr' to a
**    date/time string.
*/
char *
ctime(timeptr)
long    *timeptr;
```

For example, for the corresponding time value, ctime returns this string:

"Mon Jan 7 11:20:00 1980\n"

The string returned always occupies 26 characters including a newline and \0 at the end. Each field (day of the week, month, date, time and year) occupies a constant space. So, for example, in the date above, the number 7 has an extra space in front of it, allowing for two digit dates. The fixed format means that the string can be used either for direct output or parts can be extracted. Note that you cannot write an expression like

```
ctime(time(x))   /* WRONG */
```

because time returns a *value* and ctime requires a *pointer* to the value. You should also be aware that ctime uses a **static** area for the result string: subsequent calls on ctime overwrite this area.

If you need individual parts of the date/time it can be more convenient to use the localtime function.

```
/*
** 'localtime' returns a pointer to a 'tm' structure with
** time information corresponding to the time in seconds
** pointed to by 'timeptr'.
*/
struct tm *
localtime(timeptr)
long *timeptr;
```

The structure tm is defined in time.h as follows:

```
struct tm
{
        int  tm__sec;    /* seconds */
        int  tm__min;    /* minutes */
        int  tm__hour;   /* hours (0-23)*/
        int  tm__mday;   /* day of month (1-31)*/
        int  tm__mon;    /* month of year (0-11)*/
        int  tm__year;   /* year (1900-?)*/
        int  tm__wday;   /* day of week (0-7)*/
        int  tm__yday;   /* day of year (0-365)*/
        int  tm__isdst;  /* daylight saving */
};
```

The function gmtime is similar to localtime except that the values returned in the tm structure are Greenwich Mean Time (GMT).

Where localtime or gmtime is used, asctime can convert the time components into a standard ctime string.

```
/*
**   'asctime' returns a 'ctime' -style string from the 'tm'
**   structure pointed to be 'tmptr'.
*/
char *
asctime(tmptr)
struct tm      *tmptr;
```

The last function in this group gives the standard name for a time zone.

```
/*
**   'timezone' returns the name for the timezone
**   'minutes' west of Greenwich, with daylight
**   saving as defined by 'dst'.
**   If no name can be found for that time zone, it returns
**   a string describing the zone relative to GMT.
*/
char *
timezone(minutes, dst)
int   minutes;
int   dst;
```

The first argument gives the number of minutes west of Greenwich of the location for the time-zone named: for zones ahead of GMT, this is a negative number. The second argument is non-zero if daylight saving is in effect. If the time zone name is not available, the string returned has this form:

GMT+hh:mm

7.15   Other libraries

There are several other general purpose library functions, including the mathematical, plotting and terminal capabilities libraries. These libraries are *not* automatically searched by the loader: you need to explicitly name them, using the −l flag on the cc command. For example, a program that uses mathematical functions such as sin must have the mathematical library called m linked to it. So you compile it with a command like:

        cc myprog.c −lm

The general form is:

        cc *program-name*.c −l*library-name*

We described the complete process associated with the cc command in Chapter 4.

7.15.1 Mathematical

As you would expect, there is a considerable range of mathematical functions. Most of them are in the mathematical library m.

They include trigonometric and hyperbolic functions which accept **double** arguments and return a **double**. The trigonometric functions accept angles expressed in radians and, as always, you need to be aware of potential overflow in using badly behaved functions like tangent. These functions have largely self-explanatory names: sin, cos, asin, acos, atan, atan2 (which returns the tangent of its first argument divided by its second), sinh, cosh, and tanh.

The exponential functions are all of type **float** and have the following actions.

```
exp(x)              /* e raised to the power x */
float   x;

log(x)              /* natural log of x */
float   x;

log10(x)            /* log to the base 10 of x */
float   x;

pow(x, y)           /* returns x raised to the power y */
float   x, y;

sqrt(x)             /* returns the square root of x */
float   x;
```

There is also a collection of functions for getting absolute values and conversions to integers.

```
int abs(x)     /* returns the absolute value of x */
int     x;

float fabs(x) /* as 'abs' but operates on floating point x */
float   x;

int floor(x)   /* gives the largest integer smaller than x */
float   x;

int ceil(x)    /* gives the smallest integer larger than x */
float   x;
```

There are several others, including hypot and cabs which give the Euclidean distance between two double arguments, various forms of Bessel functions, multiple precision arithmetic functions as well as rand and srand which give sequences of random numbers. These all appear in Section 3 of Volume 1 of the *UNIX Programmer's Manual*.

7.15.2 Plotting

The plot library has functions for graphical output. It is searched if you have the −lplot option on the cc command line. It has the following functions.

```
openpl()         /* initialize plotting functions */

erase()          /* erase the display screen */

label(string)    /* plot "string" at the current position */
char   *string;

line(x1, y1, x2, y2)  /* draw a line from x1,y1 to x2,y2 */
int   x1, y1, x2, y2;

circle(x, y, radius)  /* draw a circle of radius "radius" */
int   x, y, radius;    /* centred on x,y */

arc(x, y, x1, y1, x2, y2)  /* draw an arc from x1,y2 to x2,y2 */
int   x, y, x1, y1, x2, y2;  /* centred on x,y */
```

```
move(x, y)        /* make the current position x, y */
int  x, y;

cont(x, y)        /* draw a line from the current position */
int  x, y;        /* to point x,y */

point(x, y)       /* plot point x,y */
int  x, y;

linemod(style)    /* select line style: dotted, solid, */
char  *style;     /* longdashed, shortdashed, dotdashed */

space(x1, y1, x2, y2) /* specify the size of the drawing */
int  x1, y1, x2, y2; /* drawing is scaled to fit the device */

closepl()         /* finish plotting */
```

A very useful feature of the functions is that they send device-independent plotting commands to standard output and these can be interpreted by the plot **filter** for any one of a range of devices. For example, the following command line plots a graph on an HP7220 plotter:

      myprog | plot -THP7220

7.15.3 Terminal capabilities

There is a vast range of asynchronous video terminals that can be connected to a UNIX system. For any one operation, each type of terminal requires a different set of control codes. So, for example, there is no standard character sequence for common operations like clearing the screen or moving the cursor to the upper left corner. This poses problems when you want to write programs that can work on a number of different terminals.

The **termcap** package overcomes this problem by creating a uniform interface between a program and any terminal. It uses a database of terminal capabilities and functions. It also gives a program access to properties of terminals such as the number of characters per line or lines per screen. The database has descriptions of a large number of different terminals and you can easily add new ones as you acquire terminals.

Termcap's capability database is simply an ASCII file that can be modified with a normal text editor. The entry for each terminal consists of a series of colon separated fields. These may be spread over several lines, using a backslash at the end of each line except the last. The first field is the name, or names, for the type of terminal. It consists of one or more words separated by vertical bars. The second and subsequent fields can be one of three types:

- a word alone indicates that the terminal has a particular named property
- a word followed by a hash sign (#) and a number indicates that the property has the numeric value
- a word followed by an equals sign (=) and a sequence of characters associates that character sequence with the named property. The character sequence extends from the equals sign to the colon that marks the beginning of the next field.

A large number of capabilities have been given standard names. For a complete list and more details of the format of fields see termcap(5).

Here is an example of a termcap entry:

```
ADM3a|ADM|3a:co#80:li#24:\
cl=^Z:
```

The terminal type is ADM3a, ADM or 3a. The terminal has 80 columns (co#80) and 24 lines (li#24). The screen is cleared if the character ^Z (Control-Z or 032) is sent to the terminal. The backslash (\ ) is used to continue an entry over several lines.

To clear the screen on an arbitrary terminal you must determine the terminal type, retrieve the relevant termcap entry and then use the character sequence value of the cl property. The terminal type is normally available in the shell environment variable TERM. To do the rest of the job, you use the following functions from the termlib library (you need −ltermlib on the cc command).

```
/*
**    'tgetent' fills 'buffer' with the termcap entry for
**    terminal type 'name'.
**    It returns −1 if the termcap file is inaccessible
**            0 if there is no entry for the terminal
```

```
**          1 if the entry is found
*/
int
tgetent(buffer, name)
char    *buffer;
char    *name;

/*
**  'tgetnum' returns the integer 'capability' for the
**  current terminal type
*/
int
tgetnum(capability)
char    *capability;

/*
**  'tgetflag' returns the boolean 'capability' for the
**  current terminal type.
*/
int
tgetflag(capability)
char    *capability;

/*
**  'tgetstr' returns the string 'capability' for the
**  current terminal type.
**  The argument 'area' is a pointer to a pointer
**  to the result string.
*/
char *
tgetstr(capability, area)
char    *capability;
char    **area;
```

The termcap entry for a terminal type is returned by tgetent. Its first argument is a pointer to a buffer area for the termcap entry. This should be at least 1024 characters as some terminal descriptions are very large. The second argument is a pointer to a string containing the terminal type. The function returns −1 if the termcap database file is inaccessible, 0 if there is no entry for the nominated terminal and 1 if the entry is successfully retrieved.

You can retrieve the terminal capabilities with the functions tgetnum (for numeric values), tgetflag (for true/false properties) and tgetstr (for string values). Both tgetnum and tgetflag require a string argument giving the name of the capability and they return an integer containing the value (0 or 1 in the case of tgetflag). You give tgetstr a string argument with the capability name but it also needs the address of a pointer to an area for the result string. It returns a pointer to the result string and the area pointer is set to the next free location.

You can move the cursor on a terminal using tgoto which returns the character sequence to move the cursor to a particular line/column.

```
/*
**    'tgoto' returns the character sequence to move cursor
**    according to the cursor motions capability 'cm',
**    to the column 'destcol' in 'destline'.
**    It returns an appropriate character sequence.
*/
char *
tgoto(cm, destcol, destline)
char    *cm;
int     destcol;
int     destline;
```

Certain operations on some terminals require delays, and tputs sends a string to the terminal (using a user specified function, outfunc) inserting delays where necessary.

```
/* global declarations */
char  PC;          /* pad character */
char  *BC;         /* backspace sequence */
char  *UP;         /* up line sequence */

/*
**    'tputs' sends the 'string' using the function 'outfunc'
**    It inserts padding characters as necessary for the current
**    terminal type and the number of 'lines' affected.
*/
void
tputs(string, lines, outfunc)
char    *string;
int     lines;
int     (*outfunc)();
```

Sometimes **pad** characters are required by a terminal and tputs inserts these as well. The pad character is taken from the global variable PC.

We illustrate the use of termcap with the following code that clears the screen, moves the cursor to the middle of it and writes the message "Welcome to UNIX":

```
#include      <stdio.h>

char      *getenv();
int  tgetent();
int  tgetnum();
char      *tgetstr();
char      *tgoto();

char      buff[1024];      /* to hold termcap entry */
char      area[1024];      /* to hold string capabilities */

main(argc, argv)
int       argc;
char      *argv[];
{
    char      *name; /* terminal type name */
    char      *ap = area; /* capability storage area */
    char      *cl;     /* clear screen string */
    char      *cm;     /* cursor motion string */
    int       li;      /* number of lines on the screen */
    int       co; /* number of columns on the screen */
    char      *msg = "Welcome to UNIX";

    if ((name = getenv("TERM")) == NULL)
    {
        fprintf(stderr,
            "%s: cannot find terminal type (TERM)\n",
            argv[0]);
        exit(1);
    }

    switch(tgetent(buff, name))
    {
    case -1:
        fprintf(stderr, "%s: termcap file inaccessible\n",
            argv[0]);
        exit(1);
    case 0:
        fprintf(stderr, "%s: cannot find entry for %s\n",
            argv[0], name);
        exit(1);
    }

    cl = tgetstr("cl", &ap);
    cm = tgetstr("cm", &ap);
    co = tgetnum("co");
    li = tgetnum("li");
```

```
        printf(" %s%s%s \n", cl,
               tgoto(cm, (co/2) − (strlen(msg)/2), li/2), msg);
}
```

Some versions of UNIX, such as System V, provide an alternative to termcap, called terminfo.

7.16 Miscellaneous

There are many other function libraries available for UNIX. Some, like the standard library, termcap and plot, are supplied with most UNIX systems. Others, such as the screen handling library, curses, are in the public domain and available from user groups. Still others, such as database access functions, are sold commercially.

7.17 Perspectives

The main lesson of this chapter is that you should be alert to the existence of a considerable range of standard functions. The C library distributed with UNIX contains a wide variety of useful functions written by experts and tested over many years.

We also emphasize that you should check the error codes returned by library functions. A very common source of error in C programs is the programmer's failure to do so: the program continues as if all were well. Should it fail, that may happen long after the error occurred. This type of bug can be very difficult to find. Worse still, the program may never fail but continue to completion, producing incorrect results. Another common error involves a mismatch between the type of an argument in the function declaration and the type of the same argument used in a call. For example, if an argument is declared as an integer and the function is called with a floating point number, strange results ensue. Regular use of lint can find such errors.

SUMMARY

The full set of functions we have discussed is summarized below.

Input and output: standard I/O functions:

- character I/O: getchar, putchar, fgetc, fputc, getc, putc, ungetc, gets, puts, fgets, fputs

- formatted input: scanf, fscanf, sscanf
- formatted output: printf, fprintf, sprintf, atoi, atof, atol
- files other than standard input and output: fopen, fclose
- binary I/O: fread, fwrite
- file positioning: fseek, ftell
- file status: feof, ferror, clearerr
- pipes: popen, pclose
- buffer control: setbuf, fflush

Input and output: system call I/O:

- error handling and system calls: perror and the variable errno
- basic I/O: open, read, write, close, creat, unlink
- temporary file names: mktemp
- positioning: lseek
- interface with the standard I/O package: fileno, fdopen
- pipes: pipe
- file status and control: stat, fstat, link, chmod, umask, access, chdir, dup
- device control: ioctl

Storage allocation:

- malloc, calloc, realloc, free (salloc, srealloc)

String handling:

- string length: strlen
- copying strings: strcpy, strncpy
- concatenating strings: strcat, strncat
- comparison and scanning: strcmp, strncmp, strchr, strrchr
- common uses and errors

Character types: isalpha, isupper, islower, isdigit, isalnum, isspace, ispunc, isprint, iscntrl, isascii

Sorting and searching: qsort, bsearch, regcomp, regex

Assertions: assert

Non-local goto—long jump: setjmp, longjmp

System interface: declaration of main, arguments, environment variables, getenv, environ variable

- initiating processes: execve, execv, execle, execl, execvp, execlp
- parallel execution: fork, wait, system
- controlling a process: exit, pause, nice, brk, sbrk
- process information: getpid, getuid, geteuid, getgid, getegid, times
- process monitoring: profil, ptrace
- interprocess control: signal, kill, alarm
- user information: getpwuid, getpwnam and structure passwd
- time of day: time, ctime, localtime and structure tm, asctime, timezone

Other libraries:

- mathematical: sin, cos, asin, acos, atan, atan2, sinh, cosh, tanh, exp, log, log10, pow, sqrt, abs, fabs, floor, ceil, hypot, cabs, rand, srand
- plotting: openpl, erase, label, line, circle, arc, move, cont, point, linemod, space, closepl, plot filters
- terminal capabilities: termcap file, tgetent, tgetnum, tgetflag, tgetstr, tgoto, tputs

Chapter 8
Program Development

As in most applications of computers, we start with a *problem* that we want to solve and we design a *solution*. The design process involves deciding the role that a program might play, selecting the form of that program and, finally, its implementation. In designing and writing a program, we illustrate:

- the *tools* design approach that is well supported and exemplified by UNIX

- the use of existing UNIX utilities as well as standard functions to reduce the effort involved in implementing a system

- programming techniques and style
- examples of complete working functions which perform some *idiomatic* operations that arise in similar forms in many applications
- the organization and management of program sources including the use of separate compilation, lint and make.

8.1   Introduction: the problem

The problem we want to address is the management of a mailing list for use by an organization with up to 1000 members or clients. This mailing list, be it manual or automated, needs to record the following information about each person:

- their name
- postal address
- status information about their membership
- any other comments.

Some of the operations we need to do are:

- address envelopes for a mailing to each person on the list
- address envelopes for a certain group of people, such as full members only or those who live in certain postal areas
- print these labels in various orders, including alphabetical and postal code order
- print form letters with personalized fields within them.

Now a manual system that allows all this is very labour intensive even for quite small mailing lists of fifty or so. Nevertheless, let us consider how a manual system might operate so that we can gain an appreciation of the task at hand and approaches to automating the process.

A common manual system for maintaining mailing lists involves keeping an index card for each member with name, address and other details. New members are added by writing a new card and placing it into the sequence of cards in alphabetical order. When a member leaves the organization, it is a simple operation to find their card and remove it. Modifications are also easy: the appropriate card is located and the information modified. When information is to be mailed to all members it is a simple (but tedious) process of going through the cards and writing each address on to an envelope. Finally, we can sort the envelopes as required.

A computer system can follow this manual system closely. The names and addresses can be kept in a computer file. The additions, deletions and modifications can be carried out using an editing program. Placing the addresses on envelopes can be done by another program that reads the membership file and prints the addresses either directly on to envelopes or on to adhesive backed labels. A program that prints addresses can also select them on various user-defined criteria. Entries in the mailing list file may contain information other than name and address: the grade of membership, personal interests, financial status and other information can also be stored.

Form letter generation can be done by a program that scans the mailing list name and address file, printing a copy of a form letter for each selected entry. The printed letter can be modified to include the name and address and other information from the mailing list entry.

8.2 Designing the mailing list system

Having analysed the problem, we decide that a program has a good deal to offer over a manual system. The first decisions we need to make in designing the program are:

- the form in which we store the mailing list
- the major operations we need to perform on that mailing list and the structure of the system in terms of the programs that we need to write, the function of each program and the way that they fit together
- the program's internal representation of the data for each person on the mailing list.

Once we have made these high level design decisions, we can begin the lower level design of the individual programs. In general, design of a system is not a straightforward task: we typically need to explore several possibilities for various aspects of the design and we may well need to revise the design as we attempt to implement it. In this chapter we do not go into the full range of design choices that we could have explored. Instead, we describe and justify our design. But be warned! You cannot normally expect the design and implementation of a system to flow straight through as smoothly as our description in this chapter. Rather, you can expect to have to explore blind alleys, back up and re-view decisions.

One aspect of our design approach involves building **tools** as we go: these may be viewed as useful **primitives** for the problem at hand. Creating these makes a good starting point in the development of a program and they make it easier to explore different design possibilities. Our overall approach to design is **top-down**, starting with overriding and general issues before details. But we combine it with the construction of useful tools for the program and this constitutes a partial **bottom-up** approach. This combination seems to work well.

8.2.1   The file structure

Our first step is to select the representation of the membership mailing list file. This is a critical choice since the structure of the file affects operations on it and the complexity of the resulting suite of programs that manage it. Given that our 'database' is quite small (less than 1000 entries), we decide to store the data in an ASCII text file. This decision immediately removes the major programming task of writing a program to edit the data file. The addition, deletion and modification of entries can be carried out with any text editor available (for example ed or vi). The mailing list can also be printed and manipulated with normal UNIX utilities.

A text editor is quite adequate for maintaining the mailing list file so long as we do not need to make too many changes. This is almost certainly the case with a small mailing list such as we are considering. When the volume of changes increases it may be worthwhile writing a special purpose data entry and editing program. Another important reason for writing a special purpose program might be that a conventional text editor is unsuitable if several operators need to make changes simultaneously. Perhaps the greatest weakness in keeping the mailing list as an ordinary ASCII file that is maintained using an editor is that it is easy to put incorrect text into the mailing list and corrupt it. Given our approach, we can plan for a program to maintain the mailing list for a later version of the system.

8.2.2   Major program operations

The major operations we need are:

- selecting the required members' entries for the current printing
- sorting entries into the required order
- printing labels and
- printing form letters.

First we consider the printing programs and we decide to have a separate program for each printing task. While it would be possible to amalgamate the two functions into a single program and select the required operation using a command line argument or flag, it is simpler to separate them. The two programs will, of course, have some functions in common and we make these available to both programs. We call the label printing program labels and the form letter generation program letters.

Now we consider the task of selecting required parts of the mailing list. One approach is to add a selection feature to both the labels and letters programs, but in the UNIX environment it is more natural to have a separate program that does the selection, passing the required entries to either labels or letters. This is an obvious application for a filter, which we call select.

select must read the name and address file, skipping over all but selected items; these are sent to the standard output file. A UNIX pipe can direct the output of select into the input of labels with the following shell command:

select *selection flags* | labels

The output of labels can itself be piped to the UNIX lpr program for printing on a printer (presumably containing the labels). This approach localizes the selection code into one program (select) rather than two (labels and letters). It has the added bonus that it can be used as a component for any other pipelines that process the address file.

We take much the same approach to the sorting operation. We have a program called sortml and we use it in a pipeline like this shell command:

select *selection flags* | sortml *sort flags* | labels

which selects entries, sorts them and then produces labels.

8.2.3   File format

Having decided that the data file should be a simple ASCII file, we must impose some form on the data so that the programs (and users) can find the various components of each entry. There must be some mechanism for designating the various parts of the entry. For example, we need to be able to distinguish the name part and the address part.

We choose to place each field on a separate line and each complete entry is followed by a blank line. If a field is too long to fit on a single line, we need a convention to indicate that it is continued on the next line. Because we would like to allow that some fields be omitted from an entry, we need to specify the start of each field and its type. We have chosen the following structure:

- The field type is indicated by a word at the beginning of the line followed by a colon and the field value comes after this field label.

- Field continuation to subsequent lines is indicated by leading white space on the continuation lines.

- Entries are separated by at least one blank line.

An example entry is

```
Name: Kim Dent
Address: 42 Brown St,
         Sydney 2001
         Australia
Comments: unfinancial member
```

This form is fairly easy to manipulate with a text editor and the program we are about to write. We have the following field names:

Name:	*full name including title if necessary*
Address:	*address excluding postal code, but formatted as we would want it to appear on an envelope or letter.*
Postcode:	*postal code*
Descriptors:	*one or more single word descriptions separated by white space*
Comments:	*comments about the entry*

Each of the programs in our package must be able to read and manipulate files with data in this form. We should ensure that the programs are structured so that new field types are easily added. This means that we must allow that some fields be omitted from any particular mailing list entry. We also bear in mind that these fields may be given more structure in a later version of the system. For example, we may want the Name field structured so that a program can readily extract the title or family name.

8.2.4 Data structures

Each component of a mailing list item is a string. So a natural representation for a mail item is

```
struct ml__item
{
    char    *name;          /* full name */
    char    *address;       /* address */
    char    *postcode;      /* postcode */
    char    *descriptors;   /* descriptors */
    char    *comments;      /* other information */
};
```

Since we need this structure in many parts of each of the programs, we define a typedef:

```
typedef struct ml__item Ml__item;
```

This statement associates the identifier Ml__item with the type struct ml__item. A subsequent declaration

```
Ml__item *m;
```

declares m to be a pointer to a structure for a mailing list item, ml__item.

The ml__item structure contains pointers to the strings, rather than the actual values of the various fields. We could have declared the structure entries to be character arrays and put the field values into the actual structure. This has the disadvantage that the size of the arrays is fixed at compile time. Our choice of size may be too small, in which case some field values may not fit. On the other hand if we choose a large size then space is wasted for most fields. Some fields, such as the postal code, may have a known fixed size and we could have an array within the structure to hold them. However, this would introduce a special case and so we have decided to store pointers to each field in the structure. In addition, even postal codes differ between countries and we prefer to avoid unnecessary restrictions. Representing each field as a string gives great flexibility.

Our problem of field storage still remains. If we declare fixed size arrays for the fields we have the same problem as before. A better way is to use the standard library functions for storage allocation: malloc (its safer form, salloc), calloc, realloc (its safer form srealloc) and free. Storage can be allocated as needed with exactly the right amount for each field.

We follow the usual practice of placing common declarations, like that for the mailing list entry structure, in a separate **header** file which we include at the beginning of each program file that requires the common declarations. By convention, the header file name has the suffix .h and we call our declaration file ml.h. This file will grow as the program development proceeds.

8.1 Our system design places the mailing list in an ASCII file with modifications being made with a text editor. Consider how the rest of the system design is affected by the use of a simple database package to store the information.

8.3 Implementation of the label printer

We now begin our detailed implementation of the programs. We start with labels, but as we design it we keep the other programs in mind so that components can be shared by each program in the system.

The overall form of labels is

> for each item in the mailing list
>   read the item from the mailing list file
>   print the name, address and postal code for the label

We note that the reading of an item from the mailing list file should be common to the other programs in the system (letters and select). This is fairly typical of substantial programs, where there are many *primitive* operations that we can define and implement for use at several points in the system.

At this early stage, we also need to consider how we deal with errors. Given that the mailing list is an ordinary ASCII file, it could easily contain text that is not in the form required by our system. Should we encounter odd text within the file, we want to be able to tell the user about it. We decide to maintain a line count in the mailing list file as we read and we can report the line number at which an error occurs.

8.3.1 Reading an item

We want to read mailing list entries from the standard input file. This involves reading the ASCII representation and converting it into the internal form of an Ml_item. We call this function readml:

```
/*
** 'readml' reads a mailing list item into 'tmp' from file 'mf'
** On correctly read item, it returns 'OK'.
** It returns EOF on end of file.
** Other errors cause an exit.
*/
int
readml(mf, tmp)
FILE      *mf;      /* file to read item from */
MI_item   *tmp;    /* pointer to structure to read into */
{
    /* skip white space (including newlines) */
    if (skipover(mf, " \n \t " ) == EOF)
        return EOF;

    for (;;)        /* read each field of this item */
        switch (readfield(mf, tmp))
        {
        case ERROR: exit(1);
        case END:   return OK;
        default:    break;  /* redundant but clearer */
        }

}
```

The first parameter to readml is a standard I/O package file pointer. This means that the calling program can read items from any open file (including stdin) using this parameter. The second parameter is a pointer to a mailing list item structure which has been allocated by the calling program. We could have allocated the storage in readml but it is more flexible to let readml just read a mail item into a preallocated storage area.

The action of readml is to first skip any blank lines and then read each field into the appropriate structure item. We use skipover to skip over any number of characters in the given set: it uses ungetc to ensure that the next character read is not in the given set. (We leave writing skipover until later.)

The call on the function readfield is the heart of readml. The code for readfield appears below. readfield must first read the field name so that it can work out the type of the field. To do this, it must find the field identifier which is a sequence of characters terminated by a colon. Then it reads the data for the field into a dynamically allocated area.

Note that on an error in reading the mailing list, we exit. In this application, we choose not to risk printing incorrect labels. In other situations, it might be more appropriate to print error messages on stderr and continue.

readfield could determine the type of the field, by reading the first word of the line and looking it up in a table using strcmp. We simplify things by observing that the first letter of each of our field names is different and so we can use a simple switch on the first character of the field to determine the field type. This might be an advantage if users of the program prefer to abbreviate field names or if they are likely to mistype a field name. An even better strategy might be to allow the user to enter as many characters of the field identifier as they wish and the program would match all that are provided, reporting an error if the input does not match any of the field identifiers. Note that this stage of our design affects the user's view of the system: this is typical of programming in that problems are not usually tightly defined at the start. Now, readfield has to read a field in the following form:

> *field-identifier: field contents*
> *blank space at the beginning of continuation lines*

where the field continuation lines are optional.

```
/*
**   'readfield' reads the next field from file 'mf'
**   into mailing list item struct 'tmp'
**   returns OK on a correct field
**          END on last correct field (on reaching EOF)
**          ERROR on error in field
*/
int
readfield(mf, tmp)
FILE      *mf;      /* file to read field from */
MI_item   *tmp;    /* structure to place field into */
{
        int     c;
        int     ftype;              /* field type character */
        char    errmess[BUFSIZE];/* error message buffer */
        char    *linep  = NULL; /* pointer to each line of field */
        char    *fieldp = NULL; /* pointer to complete field */

        /* read the character that defines the field type */
        if (((ftype = readch(mf)) == EOF) || (ftype == ' \n'))
                return END;

        /* set field type */
        switch (ftype)
        {
```

```
case 'N':    tmp->name        = fieldp;    break;
case 'A':    tmp->address     = fieldp;    break;
case 'P':    tmp->postcode    = fieldp;    break;
case 'D':    tmp->descriptors = fieldp;    break;
case 'C':    tmp->comments    = fieldp;    break;

default:     sprintf(errmess, "illegal field type <%c>",
                   ftype);
             error(errmess);
             return ERROR;
}

/* skip the rest of the field label */
if ((skipto(mf, NAME_END) == EOF)
|| (skipover(mf, WHITESPACE) == EOF))
{
    error("EOF while reading field");
    return ERROR;
}

/* read each line of the field */
for (;;)
{   /* read a line and check for EOF */
    if ((linep = getline(mf)) == NULL)
    {
        error("EOF while reading field");
        return ERROR;
    }

    if (fieldp != NULL)
    {   /* add this line to the field */
        fieldp = srealloc(fieldp, strlen(linep)
                             + strlen(fieldp) + 1);
        strcat(fieldp, linep);
        free(linep);
    }
    else
        fieldp = linep;

    /* check if the next line is part of this field */
    if (strchr(WHITESPACE, c = readch(mf)) == NULL)
    {
        unreadch(c, mf);
        break; /* end of field reached */
    }
    (void)skipover(mf, WHITESPACE);
```

```
        }
        /* by this point the whole field has been read */

        /* remove last newline from field */
        *(fieldp + strlen(fieldp) - 1) = ' \0';

        return OK;
    }
```

So our **readfield** function only has to read and save the first character of the field name. It then skips to the character that indicates the end of the field name. We have defined (in ml.h) that character to be a colon. We do this with a function called **skipto** which is nearly the opposite of **skipover**, in that it skips characters *until* it finds a character in a given set and it actually reads that character (whereas **skipover** does not). After finding the colon, **readfield** skips over white space (tabs or spaces) and then reads the rest of the line using **getline**. It then checks for leading white space on the next line which indicates that it must keep reading the current field on that line. After reading the entire field value, it assigns a pointer to the appropriate value in the MI_item structure. Note that we have defined WHITESPACE and NAME_END in ml.h. We also delegate the task of printing error messages to the **error** function.

In reading a field, we use **getline** to read the remainder of the current line, allocating just enough storage to hold the text read (and the terminating \0). As it reads additional lines, it uses **srealloc** to allocate space for the field so far, the line just read and the terminating \0. (Remember that **strlen** returns the number of characters in the string, *excluding* the \0.)

getline is very similar to the function given on page 132 of Chapter 5. It reads from mf until it reaches the end of the current line. The first BUFSIZE characters are stored in an area allocated by **salloc**. Since we cannot know the size of the field needed until we actually read it, we use **srealloc** to enlarge the area as necessary. Before getline returns a pointer to the area, it calls **srealloc** to reduce it to the exact size needed for the string and its trailing \0.

```
/*
**    'getline' reads a line from file 'mf'
**    It allocates space for line.
**    It returns pointer to line.
**    On EOF, it returns NULL.
*/
char *
```

```
getline(mf)
FILE     *mf;     /* file to read from */
{
    char    *line    = salloc(BUFSIZE);
    int     len      = BUFSIZE;
    char    *cp      = line;
    int     count    = 0;
    int     c;

    do
    {
        if ((c = readch(mf)) == EOF)
        {
            free(line);
            return NULL;
        }
        if (count >= (len - 1))
        {
            line = srealloc(line, len += BUFSIZE);
            cp = line + count;
        }
        *cp++ = c;
        count++;
    } while ( c != ' \n');

    *cp = ' \0'; /* add string terminator */
    return srealloc(line, ++count);
}
```

EXERCISES

8.2 Write the skipover function described on page 261 and used in readml. It should use unreadch to ensure that the next character that the program reads is *not* in the given set.

8.3 Write the skipto function used in readfield.

8.4 Write the error function.

8.3.2 Labels

We are now almost ready to complete the last details of the program that prints mailing labels. The actual code for the main loop looks like this:

```
for (;;)
{
    item = talloc(MI_item);

    if (readml(mf, item) == EOF)
        exit(0);

    printlabel(stdout, item);

    freeml(item);
}
```

A mailing list item structure is allocated (using talloc), and readml reads the next item into it. The item is then printed on the standard output file (by printlabel) and the item structure deallocated. This loop repeats until we reach the end of the file.

We still have to write the functions printlabel and freeml. The latter is easy since it has only to deallocate any field strings allocated when the item was read. Since some fields may be missing from any particular mailing list item, we need to check before deallocating a field string:

```
void
freeml(item)
MI_item    *item;
{
    if (item->name        != NULL) free(item->name);
    if (item->address     != NULL) free(item->address);
    if (item->postcode    != NULL) free(item->postcode);
    if (item->descriptors != NULL) free(item->descriptors);
    if (item->comments    != NULL) free(item->comments);

    free((char *)item);
}
```

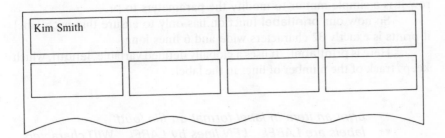

Figure 8.1 A typical layout of address labels.

The printlabel function is a little more complicated and we need to know the size of the labels we are using. Address labels are often arranged in rows of four or more as in Figure 8.1. This means that we have to print our labels four at a time since the first line of the first four labels appears on the first line printed. To do this we have to read four entries at a time and print them all together. This is not particularly difficult but it would make printlabel unnecessarily complicated and we would be embedding the details of the stationery in our code.

A much simpler approach is to leave the problem of side by side labels to a separate program. Our labels program can assume that the labels appear one per row and print accordingly. The output from labels can then be piped into a program that prints successive columns side by side as necessary. This might sound like postponing an inevitable programming task but UNIX has a program pr that can do the job. pr is designed to format data for printing and has options that allow you to specify the paper width, paper length, number of columns to use, column separator character and page header. Its full facilities are described in pr(1).

Given that our labels are exactly 33 characters wide and 6 lines high and there are 4 labels per row and 11 rows per page, this shell command prints labels for the mailing list file mailfile:

labels mailfile | pr -4 -t -w128 -l66 | lpr

The options on pr indicate that the data are to be formatted in four columns, with no page header, and that the paper is 128 columns wide and 66 lines long.

This approach has the added advantage that we can easily alter the stationery. For example, if our new stationery has the labels two per row it is a simple matter to modify the parameters to pr.

So now our printlabel function has only to ensure that each label it prints is exactly 32 characters wide and 6 lines long.

Here is printlabel. It uses a globally defined variable, length, which keeps track of the number of lines in the label:

```
/*
**    print an item in label format on file 'outf'
**    labels are LABEL__LEN lines by LABEL__WID characters
**    with 1 line space and 1 character space between each
*/
void
printlabel(outf, item)
FILE        *outf;
MI__item    *item;
{
        if(item->name == NULL || item->address == NULL)
        {
                fprintf(stderr,
                    " Name or Address missing from item:  \n" );
                printml(stderr, item);
                return;
        }

        length = 1; /* printing on first line of label */
        lab__field(outf, item->name, ' \n');
        lab__field(outf, item->address, ' ');
        lab__field(outf, item->postcode, ' \n');
        while (length++ < LABEL__LEN)
                putc(' \n', outf);
}
```

It leaves the task of printing the correct width form of each field to the function lab__field.

EXERCISE

8.5 Write the function lab__field that sends a given field to a file. The field must not exceed LABEL_WID, the width of the label and the label must not be more than LABEL_LEN lines long.

8.4   Program source management

At this stage, our system consists of only the label printing program which has the following functions: main, readml, readfield, getline, skipover, skipto, readch, unreadch, printlabel, lab_field, lab_char, error, freeml, salloc and srealloc. These give about 400 lines of code. In this section, we discuss the management of the source code of these functions as we develop the program. We show how to use lint, how to organize the functions into several files and to use make.

8.4.1   File organization

It is possible to put all the functions into a single file and use a command like

        cc labels.c −o labels

to compile it. However it is far better to break the program text into a number of files each with a small number of related functions, like this:

File name	Contents
labels.c	main
readml.c	readml, readfield, getline
	skipover, skipto, readch, unreadch
printml.c	printlabel, lab__field, lab__char
util.c	error, freeml, salloc, srealloc
ml.h	various global declarations
	and defined symbols

From the section of Chapter 4 on compiling multifile programs, you should be able to work out that we can compile the program when organized as shown in the list with the following command:

        cc labels.c readml.c printml.c util.c −o labels

This recompiles all the functions in all the files. During program development, we typically alter only some of the functions at each stage in the development cycle and we can compile each file separately and produce the object code for it. When all files are compiled to object code like this:

```
cc −c labels.c
cc −c readml.c
cc −c printml.c
cc −c util.c
```

they can be linked with this command:

```
cc labels.o readml.o printml.o util.o −o labels
```

Whenever a function is changed, only the file with the change needs to be recompiled to object code and then the object code files relinked. For example, after a change to readfield, only the file readml.c needs recompiling, like this:

```
cc −c readml.c
```

The object files can then be relinked:

```
cc labels.o readml.o printml.o util.o −o labels
```

For small programs of one or two files this approach is often adequate. However, with any more files the amount of typing soon becomes tedious. The command line for relinking the labels program has about 50 characters. After each recompilation of a file you have to retype it. You can avoid some typing by using shell expansions and by creating a shell command file or script with the relinking command.

A much more serious problem with this approach is that it is easy to inadvertently use 'old' object code versions of programs. This can happen if, for example, you change a variable declaration in a file that is included by several program files. After making a change to ml.h *every* program file that includes it must be recompiled before relinking. Unfortunately, it is very easy to forget this and to create an executable program with some functions that were compiled with the old declarations. Havoc can result!

8.4.2   Make

The make utility is one of the most important UNIX program development tools. Its main purpose is to *make* an executable program from text and object files. It does this according to a set of rules, some default and others defined by the user.

Let us see the make commands that help us maintain labels.o which is the object form for the C program in labels.c:

```
labels.o:      labels.c ml.h
               cc −c labels.c
```

These commands indicate how the *target* file labels.o can be created: it *depends* upon the files labels.c and ml.h and it can be *made* with the shell command cc −c labels.c. These rules would normally be kept in a file called makefile. When we type the shell command

make

the make program uses the makefile in the current directory.

make operates by examining the files labels.o, labels.c and ml.h. If labels.o does not exist then the action cc −c labels.c is carried out and so labels.o is created. If labels.o already exists then the time that it was last modified is compared with the last modification times of labels.c and ml.h. If either of labels.c or ml.h has been modified more recently than labels.o, it needs to be recreated and so the action cc −c labels.c is performed. With rules like this, make ensures that new versions of the program are properly compiled: if declarations in the include file ml.h have been modified, make determines that labels.o needs to be recreated.

In general, a make rule has:

- a **target**, the name of the file you want to make
- one or more **dependencies**, the files upon which the target depends
- an **action**, a shell command that creates the target.

A target of one rule may also be a dependency in another rule. Here is a makefile with a complete set of rules for our labels program:

```
#
# First version of a makefile for the labels program
#
labels:        labels.o readml.o printml.o util.o
               cc labels.o readml.o printml.o util.o -o labels

labels.o:      labels.c ml.h
               cc -c labels.c

readml.o:      readml.c ml.h
               cc -c readml.c
```

```
printml.o:    printml.c ml.h
              cc -c printml.c

util.o:       util.c ml.h
              cc -c util.c
```

The first three lines in the file are a comment: comments in makefiles start with the # character. The last four rules in our file are similar to the previous example. These make up to date versions of the object code files that are linked together to form our label printing program. The first rule has our labels program as target and the object code files as dependencies. The action of this rule is a command to link the object files and produce the executable binary file labels.

In large programs, the chain of dependencies in the makefile can become quite long. make builds a tree of dependencies from the rules with the target at the root of the tree. make then starts from the leaves of the tree and creates the intermediate targets by invoking the necessary actions. It works its way back to the root of the tree and so, eventually, makes the final target. The final target is, by default, the target of the first rule found in the makefile. You can specify a different target by quoting it as an argument to the make program. For example:

```
make readml.o
```

recreates the file readml.o.

make has a set of *built-in* rules. A particularly useful one creates an object code file from a source file: when make finds a target name ending in .o and there is no rule specifying how to create it, make searches for a file with the same name but ending in .c and then it applies a default action, invoking the C compiler to create the .o file from the .c file. If there is no .c file in the directory, make tries a sequence of built in suffixes. If make cannot find a dependency for the .o target it gives an error message.

Using the built-in rules we can change our makefile to be slightly more compact:

```
labels:       labels.o readml.o printml.o util.o
              cc labels.o readml.o printml.o util.o -o labels

labels.o:     ml.h

readml.o:     ml.h
```

```
printml.o:    ml.h

util.o:       ml.h
```

We can further simplify this makefile because we can combine targets for which we specify the same dependencies and actions:

```
labels:       labels.o readml.o printml.o util.o
              cc labels.o readml.o printml.o util.o -o labels

labels.o readml.o printml.o util.o:    ml.h
```

As we develop each part of the program, we also need to use lint. This is especially important with functions spread over several files because the compiler does not check for consistency between actual and formal arguments to functions in different files from their caller. We can write a rule that makes it easy to run lint as required and we make it a rule with no dependencies, as shown below:

```
labels:       labels.o readml.o printml.o util.o
              cc labels.o readml.o printml.o util.o -o labels

labels.o readml.o printml.o util.o:    ml.h

lint:
              lint labels.c readml.c printml.c util.c

clean:
              rm *.o
```

Rules like the lint rule can be used to specify actions other than those that create object or binary files. We invoke this rule with the shell command make lint. We have another rule without dependancies. It cleans up the directory by removing all the object code files. Assuming there is no file called clean, the command make clean causes the action rm *.o.

make also has simple string macros that allow you to keep repeated strings or lists in one place and have them inserted at various points in the makefile. Macros are similar in form to C identifiers but the convention is to use upper case letters. Assignments to macros have the form

variable__name = any sequence of characters

and the value of a variable is substituted elsewhere in the makefile using

        $(variable_name)

In our example makefile we can use a variable to avoid the list of object code files in three places:

```
#
# makefile for the labels program
#
OBJECTS = labels.o readml.o printml.o util.o

labels:                 $(OBJECTS)
                        cc $(OBJECTS) -o labels

$(OBJECTS):             ml.h

lint:
                        lint labels.c readml.c printml.c util.c

clean:
                        rm $(OBJECTS)
```

If we add another file to the program, we need only alter the first line of the makefile.

In addition to built-in rules, make has some predefined macros. For C programmers, the most useful of these is CC. The default value of the built-in rule that converts a C source file into an object code file uses the CC variable instead of cc. You can use a different C compiler by specifying a new value for CC at the beginning of your makefile. This is useful in testing new versions of the C compiler or when using compilers for different target machines.

Another important variable is CFLAGS which enables you to specify arguments to the C compiler. It is commonly used to tell the C compiler to run the object code optimizer by including the following line:

        CFLAGS = −O

You can change both the built-in rules and suffixes by including special rules in the makefile. For details you should consult the description of make in Volume 2 of the *UNIX Programmer's Manual*.

8.5   Implementation of selection program

Now we deal with the program that selects the required mailing list items for a particular mailing. It is a filter that provides input for the labels program we have already written as well as letters and sortml (which we write in the next sections). To produce labels for a selected set of entries we use a command like this:

select *flags* <*file* | labels | pr −t −4 −w128 −l66 | lpr

where the *flags* indicate which entries should be selected from *file*. The labels program reads the selected entries from its standard input file and processes them as usual.

The main loop of our selection program looks like this:

```
for (;;)
{
    item = talloc(MI_item);

    if (readml(mf, item) == EOF)
        exit(0);

    if (selected(item))
        printml(stdout, item);

    freeml(item);
}
```

We already have readml to read mailing list entries. We still need to write the functions:

- selected which applies the selection criteria, returning a value indicating whether or not an entry is to be selected
- printml which takes a mailing list structure and writes it to the standard output file in exactly the same format as the input file.

But first we need to decide on the type of selection criteria and how these should be described to the select program.

8.5.1   Design of the selection mechanism

We want to make selections on the basis of field values. Some examples of selections we want to be able to make include the selection of entries for people:

- in a given postal code area
- in a given suburb and
- who are office bearers of the society.

We also want to be able to select entries that match a combination of requirements like:

- those for people in a given suburb *and* who are office bearers
- entries in several postal districts.

In designing this part of the program, we bear in mind that the standard library has functions regcmp and regex that match an arbitrary pattern against a string. The form of these patterns is used in many UNIX tools including editors like ed, vi and sed. The first function of the pair is regcmp, and it takes a pattern and *compiles* it into an internal form for the matching operation. It returns a pointer to the compiled form. The second, regex, takes a pointer to the compiled pattern and a pointer to the string and returns a NULL value if they do not match and a non-NULL value if they do.

So now we can allow the fields and patterns to be specified as command line arguments to the select program like this:

select −DF −P″ ^2″

which selects mailing list entries for people who have an 'F' in their descriptor field or a postal code starting with '2'. (The circumflex indicates the beginning of the field.) Each field/pattern pair is a separate argument and has the general form

−*field-character pattern*

where *field-character* is the first letter of the field name and *pattern* is the regular expression that is to be matched against the field value from each mailing list entry. Since patterns can contain characters that are interpreted by the shell, it may be necessary to quote arguments to the select program. When a number of arguments is used, entries matching *any* of the patterns are written to the output.

This design allows selection of one pattern *or* another but we have not explicitly provided for matching one pattern *and* another. We handle this, albeit not very efficiently, with multiple invocations of the select program in the same pipeline. For example, if we want entries for people with postal code 2006 and who are members of the executive (exec in the descriptor field) we can use this command:

select −P2006 <mylist | select −Dexec | labels | ...

which acts on a file called mylist.

8.5.2 Implementation of the selection mechanism

We store the field and pattern information in an array of structures, each containing a pointer to the compiled pattern that regcmp returns and the character which indicates the field:

```
typedef struct ml__pat
{
    char    ml__type;    /* field type */
    char    *ml__regex;  /* compiled regular expression */
} MI__pat;

static MI__pat    patterns[MAXPATS];
```

Now we can write the code to scan the program arguments and initialize this array:

```
for (i = 1; i < argc; i++) /* for each command argument */
    if (argv[i][0] == '−')
        makepat(argv[i][1], &argv[i][2]);
    else
        filename = argv[i];
```

You might like to amend this to do tighter checking on the arguments. As it stands, it treats any argument with a minus sign as a selection flag and any other as a filename. The makepat function calls regcmp to compile the regular expression and put it and the field designator character into an MI__pat structure:

```
makepat(field, pat)
char    field;
char    *pat;
{
    if (strchr(FIELD__NAMES, field) == NULL)
    {
        fprintf(stderr, " %s: illegal field type − %c \n",
                        myname, field);
        exit(1);
    }
```

```
            patterns[numpats].ml_type = field;
            if ((patterns[numpats].ml_regex = regcmp(pat, 0))
               == NULL)
            {
                fprintf(stderr, " %s: illegal pattern - <%s>\n",
                        myname, pat);
                exit(1);
            }
            numpats++;
        }
```

Note that FIELD_NAMES is defined as follows.

```
#define FIELD_NAMES    "NAPDC"
```

We now write selected which takes a mailing list entry and goes through the array of pattern structures, using regex to match the pattern against the appropriate field. If a match is found it returns the value 1, otherwise 0:

```
        selected(item)
        MI_item    *item;
        {
            int  i;
            char  *s;

            if (numpats == 0)
                return !NULL;  /* select all if no patterns specified */

            for (i = 0; i < numpats; i++)
            {
                switch(patterns[i].ml_type)
                {
                case 'N':   s = item->name; break;
                case 'A':   s = item->address; break;
                case 'P':   s = item->postcode; break;
                case 'D':   s = item->descriptors; break;
                case 'C':   s = item->comments; break;

                default:    error(" illegal pattern type" );
                            exit(1);
                }
                if(regex(patterns[i].ml_regex, s, 0) != NULL)
                    return !NULL;
            }
```

```
        return NULL;
    }
```

All that remains is to put these functions together in one or more files and adjust our makefile. We can put the makepat and selected functions together in a file along with the declarations for patterns and numpats. The variables are declared as statics since they are not needed elsewhere.

8.5.3   The printing function

The printml function takes a structure containing a mailing list entry and writes it to a specified file in the same format used in the input file:

```
        static int    length;
        static int    width;

        void
        printml(outf, item)
        FILE          *outf;
        MI_item       *item;
        {
            printfield(outf, " Name" , item->name);
            printfield(outf, " Address" , item->address);
            printfield(outf, " Postcode" , item->postcode);
            printfield(outf, " Descriptors" , item->descriptors);
            printfield(outf, " Comments" , item->comments);
            fprintf(outf, " \n" );
        }
        void
        printfield(outf, field, value)
        FILE     *outf;   /* file for output */
        char     *field;  /* field name */
        char     *value;  /* field value */
        {
            char    *s;

            if (value == NULL)
                return;

            fprintf(outf, " %s%s " , field, NAME_END);      /* print
                                                        field name */
```

```
    for (s = value; *s != ' \0'; s++)
    {
        if (*s == ' \n')  /* newline within a field */
        {
            putc(*s, outf);
            putc(' \t', outf);
        }
        else      /* ordinary character */
            putc(*s, outf);
    }
    putc(' \n', outf);      /* final newline for field */
}
```

The printfield function writes the field name followed by the field value, inserting a tab at the beginning of the second and subsequent lines of the field.

8.6 Implementation of the form letter program

The next program in our mailing list suite is one that prints form letters for mailing list entries. As each copy of a form letter is printed, parts of a person's mailing list entry are inserted at appropriate places in the letter. For example, the person's name and address may be placed in the letter.

The form letter itself is a simple ASCII file. You can create it with a text editor such as ed or vi. Our form letter generator needs to read it and then print it once for each mailing list entry read from standard input. We use the tilde (~) character to indicate a place to insert a mailing list field. Tilde is not commonly used in correspondence but we make it a #define constant so that we can alter it easily if necessary. The tilde is followed by the first character of the field name that is to be inserted, as in the letter shown here in which the name and address are inserted from mailing list entries.

~N
~A

Dear ~N,

     All members of the XYZ Society are requested to attend a special meeting on January 21st to discuss computer processing of our membership records.

Yours sincerely,

Kim Smith (Hon. Secretary)

As the form letter generation program reads each mailing list entry from standard input, it scans through the form letter and prints each character unless it encounters a tilde, in which case the next character indicates the mailing list field to print.

We assume that any form letter will be small enough to fit into memory. So, we need only read it once and then scan it for each mailing list entry.

The main loop of the program is

```
readletter(lf);
for (;;)
{
    item = talloc(MI_item);

    if (readml(stdin, item) == EOF)
        return 0;

    printletter(stdout, item);

    freeml(item);
}
```

The new functions we have to write are **readletter** and **printletter**. The former reads each character from a specified file calling another function, **letchar**, to store them into memory. The **letchar** function needs to allocate memory for the form letter, expanding the area as necessary. Other functions in this program can access the form letter using the global pointer **letter**. Here is the code for **readletter**:

```
char         *letter; /* pointer to form letter in memory */
static int   size    = 0;
static int   index   = 0;


void
readletter(lf)
FILE    *lf;      /* file to read form letter from */
{
    int  c;

    /* allocate an initial area */
    letter = salloc(size = SIZEINC);

    while ((c = getc(lf)) != EOF)
        letchar(c);
```

```
            letchar(' \0');
      }

      /* process next character of form letter */
      void
      letchar(c)
      char    c;   /* next character from form letter */
      {
            /* increase size of form letter area if necessary */
            if (index >= size)
            {
                  size += SIZEINC;
                  letter = srealloc(letter, size);
            }
            letter[index++] = c;
      }
```

The function printletter has to scan the stored form letter one character
at a time, printing either the character or the specified field on the
specified output file. Here is the code for printletter:

```
      void
      printletter(outf, item)
      FILE            *outf;
      MI  item        *item;
      {
            char    *s;

            for (s = letter; *s != ' \0'; s++)
            {
                  if (*s != FORMCHAR)
                  {
                        putc(*s, outf);
                        continue;
                  }

                  switch(*++s)
                  {
                  case 'N':   fputs(item->name? item
                                          ->name : " ", outf); break;
                  case 'A':   fputs(item->address? item
                                          ->address : " ", outf); break;
                  case 'P':   fputs(item->postcode? item
                                          ->postcode : " ", outf); break;
```

```
            case 'D' : fputs(item->descriptors? item
                                  ->descriptors : " ", outf); break;
            case 'C' : fputs(item->comments? item
                                  ->comments : " ", outf); break;

            default:   fprintf(stderr,
                              " %s: bad field specifier in letter \n",
                              myname);
                       exit(1);
            }
        }
        putc(' \f', outf);        /* form feed between letters */
    }
```

8.7 The sorting program

As you would expect, we use the standard function **qsort** to do most of
the work in this program. The main function code looks like this:

```
    main(argc, argv)
    int  argc;
    char     *argv[ ];
    {
        FILE      *mf;
        MI_item items [MAXITEMS];
        int  num items;
        int  i;

        myname = argv[0];

        for (i = 1; i < argc; i++) /* for each command
                                      argument */
            if (argv[i][0] == '−')
                field =    argv[i][1];
            else
                filename = argv[i];

        if (filename != NULL)
        {
            if ((mf = fopen(filename, "r")) == NULL)
            {
                fprintf(stderr," %s: cannot open %s \n",
                        myname, filename);
                return   1;
```

```
        }
    }
    else
    {
        filename = " stdin" ;
        mf = stdin; /* use standard input if no file specified */
    }

    for (i = 0; i < MAXITEMS; i++)
        if (readml(mf, &items[i]) == EOF)
            break;
    numitems = i;

    if (numitems == MAXITEMS)
    {
        fprintf(stderr,
        " %s: too many items in mailing list \n", myname);
        return 1;
    }

    qsort(items, numitems, sizeof (MI_item), compare);

    for (i = 0; i < numitems; i++)
        printml(stdout, &items[i]);
}
```

The only other function we need to write is the compare function:

```
int
compare(item1, item2)
MI_item    *item1;
MI_item    *item2;
{
    switch (field)
    {
    case 'N':    return strcmp
                 (item1 ->name, item2->name);
    case 'A':    return strcmp
                 (item1 ->address, item2->address);
    case 'P':    return strcmp
                 (item1 ->postcode, item2->postcode);
    case 'D':    return strcmp
                 (item1 ->descriptors, item2->descriptors);
    case 'C':    return strcmp
                 (item1 ->comments, item2->comments);
```

```
        default:
            fprintf(stderr, " %s: illegal field <%c>\n",
                    myname, field);
            exit(1);
    }
}
```

EXERCISE

8.6 Write the make file that manages the whole system.

8.8 Conventions for writing UNIX tools

By this stage, you will have seen and used enough UNIX commands to deduce many of the usual conventions. You have probably been irritated and frustrated by programs that do not conform to the usual conventions: these are a constant source of errors and difficulty as users forget the idiosyncratic behaviour of non-conforming commands.

At this point, we summarize some of the commonest conventions for writing UNIX tools. First, we note that the form of a UNIX command must be

> *command-name* [*arguments*]

In terms of this form,

- short command names are the norm
- flag arguments start with minus
- flag arguments come first.

There are many other conventions that are limited to particular systems. Typically, there should be tools to do parsing of command lines that conform to the convention for your system. Unfortunately, there is sufficient diversity between systems that we can give no tighter guidelines on command formats than those above.

Aside from the form of commands, it is usual practice for commands to do the following:

- check arguments
- upon reading a command that cannot be parsed, print on stderr a usage message that reflects the acceptable command formats

- return an exit code of zero on successful termination, using exit(0), and, on failure, return a non-zero code, where the actual value returned may reflect different failure modes.

Finally, you should write a manual entry in the usual form.

8.9 Perspectives

Having completed our version of the mailing list program, we need to stand back and comment on other approaches to the problem. For example, we could have saved programming effort by using awk and troff. These, and many other valuable UNIX tools like yacc, lex and SCCS, are discussed in Volume 2 of the *UNIX Programmer's Manual* as well as in many books about UNIX. Also, at the cost of longer pipelines, we could have used the form letter program to do all but the formatting aspect of the label generation program. Indeed, it is common practice to build a quick prototype system that is composed of available tools pipelined together: only after this has been built and evaluated would we implement parts or the whole of the pipeline more efficiently in C.

Perhaps the greatest shortcoming of our mailing list system is that it does not help the user maintain a correct database of mailing list items. For example, misspelt names may hamper the operation of the select program and we should, as necessary, alert the person entering data if they enter a name or address field that is too large since they may well be unaware of the limitations of the stationery. We could rectify this shortcoming with a data entry program that interacts with the user, checking the validity of new mailing list items and the consistency of the database. This would be a straightforward addition to the existing system.

The system we have created is quite powerful and useful. Its development enabled us to illustrate use of C and UNIX programming support facilities as well as approaches to program design and implementation.

SUMMARY

In developing our mailing list system, we showed how to organize functions in a number of files, with closely related functions collected together in a single file. This

- aids program clarity
- allows separate compilation during program development.

We discussed the need for **make** in maintaining programs, how to write rules in terms of

- targets
- dependencies between files
- commands for creating targets
- comments (# at the beginning of the line)
- macros

and we met default rule

- to create *filename.o* from *filename.c*

and macros

- CC for C compiler
- CFLAGS for flags to the C compiler

Appendix 1
Syntax Summary

program

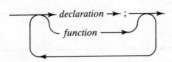

function

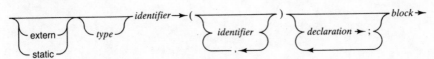

statement

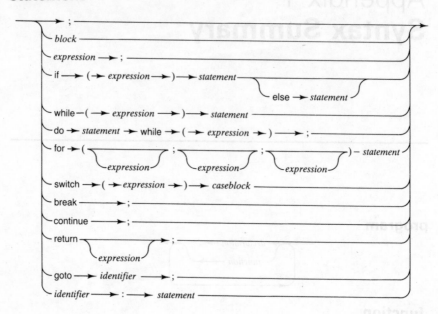

block

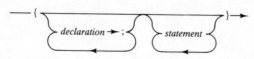

caseblock

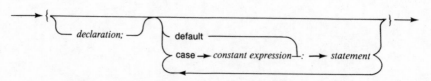

expression

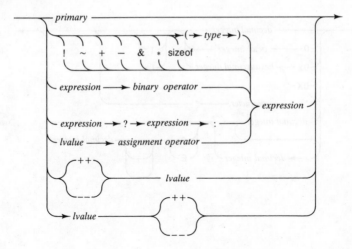

primary

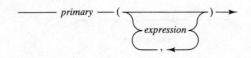

functioncall

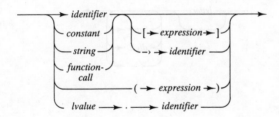

lvalue

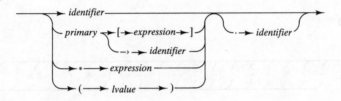

constant

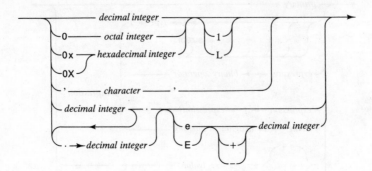

identifier

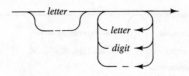

string

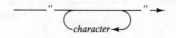

binop

assignment operator

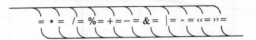

type

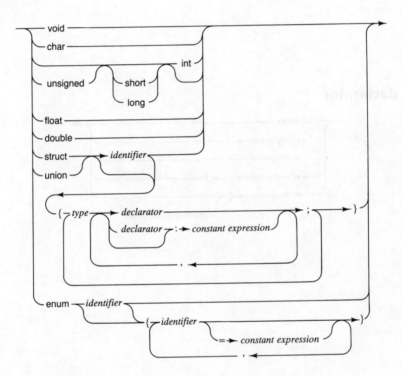

declaration

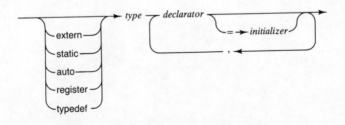

initializer

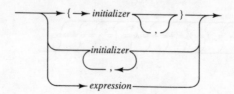

declarator

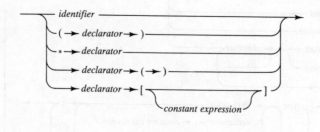

Appendix 2
C Operators

In the table overleaf, horizontal lines mark precedence levels. So, for example, all the assignment operators have the same precedence, regardless of the order in which they are listed, but the if–else operator (?:) has higher precedence. The double precedence lines group the operators with the same left-to-right or right-to-left evaluation order.

Description	Operator
Array access	[]
Structure access	->
Structure access	.
Logical negate†	!
Bitwise negate†	~
Unary arithmetic†	++ -- -
Address of†	&
Contents of†	*
Type cast†	(*type*)
Size of†	sizeof
Multiplicatives	* / %
Additives	+ -
Shifts	<< >>
Comparisons	< <= > >=
Equality test	== !=
Bitwise AND	&
Bitwise EXOR	^
Bitwise OR	|
Logical AND	&&
Logical OR	||
If-else†	?:
Assignment†	=
Arithmetic†	*= /= %= + = - =
Shift†	<<= >>=
Bitwise†	&= |= ^=
Comma	,

Appendix 3
Properties Associated with Storage Classes

Storage models and permitted initialization forms.

Description	Heap	Storage class	
		external static	auto register
Persistent storage model	No	Yes	No
Default initialization to zero (or relevant cast)	No	Yes	No
Explicit initialization allowed	–	Yes	Yes
Constant initializations	–	Yes	Yes
Any expresssion initialization	–	No	Yes
struct and array initializations allowed	–	Yes	No

Interactions between scope and storage class.

Description	Variable identifiers that are declared	
	outside functions	*inside functions*
Visible by all the code after it in the file of declaration	Yes	No
static declaration alters scope	Yes	No
static declaration alters persistence	No	Yes
Can be imported to another file using extern declaration	Yes	No
Permitted storage classes	static	static auto register

Appendix 4
C Standardization

C is of such importance that there is a need for established standards for the language, its preprocessor and the libraries. We have already noted the IEEE P1003 standard (POSIX) for the 'standard' libraries (see page 170). For some years there has been work on an ANSI standard for the language C and this is an important development.

However, the impact of any standard will take some time. This is because a standard can only take effect after there are significant numbers of systems with compilers that conform to the standard. In addition, non-conforming programs may need modifications. So, a successful standard for C cannot diverge too far from the implied language definition as it is embodied in the considerable existing collection of useful C programs.

Our description of C is based on our experience of a large number of C programs that run on many systems. If you follow the main text of this book, you should produce programs that can run on most UNIX C systems and they should be portable between such systems. In other words, you can safely use the material in this book and expect your programs to conform to most likely standards for C.

In this appendix, we outline the types of changes you can expect to come from the standardization efforts and we give details of some of the more significant ones. Should you have a compiler with any of the characteristics described below, we urge that you take care in using them. You may sacrifice portability to the systems that use the large number of existing compilers. You are safer to write code as we have indicated in the body of this book.

Function prototypes

One main change to be expected is that function prototypes may be allowed in external declarations of functions. For example, in

extern int fred(char q, char *s, const char *p, ...);

fred is a function returning int. It has a char as its first argument, a pointer to a char as the second and third arguments. The keyword const indicates the area pointed to by p is not changed by fred. After p, there is a variable number of arguments.

Another new form is

extern int jim(void)

which declares jim to be a function returning an int with no arguments. Note that

extern char *fix();

indicates that the type of arguments is not specified. This is compatible with common current practice.

Types

You can expect that minimum sizes will be defined for various types. For example, a char can be guaranteed to have at least eight bits.

The keyword void may acquire two meanings. A function declared as void does not return a value. In addition, a function declared as a pointer to void should indicate that it returns a pointer to an unspecified object: this pointer could then be assigned to a variable of any pointer type.

The new keyword const will indicate that a variable is read only and never modified.

The keyword volatile will indicate that all reads and writes of the variable must be carried out as indicated in the code and not optimized out. This is useful where a variable may refer to an I/O port or shared memory.

You may see a signed keyword which is relevant for chars and bitfields and a new floating point type long double. The number suffix F (or f) indicates that a constant is a float. The number suffix L (or l) would indicate that the constant is a long double.

Identifiers

Identifiers that begin with '_' may be reserved.

Internal identifiers may have at least the first 31 characters significant with upper/lower case significant. Note that many existing compilers are less generous and it is currently safe to assume only eight significant characters for internal identifiers and for external identifiers, six characters, with case being insignificant.

Character set

Since some countries do not have the same graphic characters as American ASCII, you can expect some standardization of references to these. For example, the UK uses a pound sterling symbol in place of # in the USA and a standard form that means hash everywhere is useful. A likely approach is a three character combination ??= to refer to hash. More generally, this is ??X, where X indicates a particular character.

There may be a new escaped character \a that means 'alert' and is implementation defined but would typically indicate a bell.

Preprocessor

One new command that is likely is

#pragma *identifier*

which indicates an implementation defined action.

Another change would see defined identifiers not being replaced inside strings. (This is incompatible with many old compilers.)

Yet another new feature is that the token #x should be replaced by the definition of x in double quotes. So,

#define qwert   trewq

...#qwert... would be changed to ..."trewq"...

Adjacent strings would be concatenated, so that "a" "b" would become "ab".

Standard include files and libraries

A number of standard include files will be defined, as will the standard libraries.

Summary of areas of change

The main areas in which you can expect to see changes are:

- function prototypes
- types: void, const, volatile, signed, volatile and some definition of the minimum size of types
- identifiers: use of underscore, the number of significant characters
- minor adjustments to the character set
- preprocessor changes: pragma, string related differences
- standard include files and libraries.

Further Problems

Small functions

These are mainly functions that we have found to be useful tools. Most C programmers build up their own small libraries of utilities.

(1)   Write a function called **strrcmp** which behaves like **strcmp**, except that it starts its search from the end of the string. (So it has the same relationship to **strcmp** as **strrchr** has to **strchr**.)

(2)   Write a function which is like **strcmp** but is independent of case. (This would have been handy in our library catalogue examples of Chapter 5.)

(3)   As we discussed in the text, **malloc** is unsafe in the situation where it is unable to allocate the space required. It is also inefficient in the situation where you do not need to reuse allocated space (and so you never call **free**.)
Write a faster, safe form of **malloc** based on the assumption that you never need free storage. Note that you need to manage your own storage area and you must make sure that you catch all calls to both **malloc** and **free** so that these library functions are not called.

(4)   Write a function that reads a file and returns it as a string. Note that any \n that occurs at the end of the file needs to be stripped and that the string must terminate with a \0.

(5)   Write a function that converts a time expressed in seconds into the following, more convenient fixed format:

nnnXnnY

where X and y are the most accurate of the following:

X	Y	for a time expressed as
y	d	years and days
d	h	days and hours
h	m	hours and minutes
m	s	minutes and seconds

(6)   The standard **mktemp** creates a name that is likely to be unique. Study its behaviour carefully and write one that has a better chance of creating an unique name and is more efficient. There is some scope here for creativity but you might consider using more than just the process id, which is unique for all running processes. For example, you might use the current time.

(7)   Write a function that accepts a string and converts all the unprintable characters to the form it takes in a C constant. So, for example, a new line character should be expanded to \n.

Small programs

(1)   Write a program segment that reads and sums a defined number, **N**, of integers.

(2)   Write a program to print the largest of a sequence of integers read from input. Note that UNIX tools make it easy to do this task, using a simple pipeline of UNIX commands like **sort** and **sed**.

(3)   Write a program called **dis**, which is efficient and convenient for displaying information that changes slowly over time. Suppose, for example, that you have a program which produces a display of slowly changing status information about the activity of the system. It might produce a new display every second and much of the information in successive displays would be unchanged. With the aid of the TERMCAP database, use cursor addressing to write to the screen only the characters that have changed since the last display. You should assume that a formfeed character marks the end of each display. (You could test **dis** by piping successive displays of the **date** command, with a formfeed appended to each.)

(4)   Write a program called mc which columnates its input lines across the page (unlike pr which columnates down the page).

(5)   Rewrite any one of the simpler UNIX commands. Compare the efficiency of your version and that of the command supplied.

Some larger problems

(1)   Build a program which prints the same information as the command ls -t but descends the file hierarchy, giving the information for all files that descend from the directory and printed in order of the last change date.

(2)   Construct a shell that runs a program, saving its input and output, correctly synchronized, on a log file. You can add the facility of time stamping the log file.

(3)   Suppose that our mailing program in Chapter 8 had to deal with a large number of entries. Modify the program to use a database you have.

Alternatively, implement a simple database and the front-end programs that add, delete and modify address entries.

Answers to Exercises

Chapter 1

1.2

```
j = 1;
while (j < 26)
{
    if (freq[j] > freq[commonest])
        commonest = j;
    j++;
}
```

1.3

```
for (j = 0; j < 26; j++)
    freq[j] = 0;
```

1.4 The next character is read from standard input and if it has the same value as zot, the function doA is invoked. Otherwise doB. Note that the character read is not stored; it is only used to control the if statement.

1.5 This sets the 26 element array freq to zero. But it is not as clear as the code we gave for the second exercise. Not only does it need to set j to −1, but it combines the loop increment and the loop termination test. We have included it to highlight the fact that the test for loop termination is done at the beginning of each loop iteration.

1.6 This code has exactly the same effect as that in the last exercise. With the increment operator ++ before the variable name, j is incremented and this value is compared against **26**. As we have already noted ++ is used in a range of ways.

1.7 One of the possible answers is to replace loop contents by

```
if (isalpha(ch))
    if (isupper(ch))
        freq[ch − 'A']++;
    else
        freq[ch − 'a']++;
```

1.8 See Chapter 7 and look at some of the other ways to copy a file, on pages 174, 175, 183, 192 and 199.

1.9 A return within the function main terminates the whole program (unless main is recursive).

1.10 You can replace the #include line with

```
#define EOF        −1
```

and the program will behave as before. Because this creates a constant EOF with the value that corresponds to an end of file (−1 as it happens), we could simply use −1 in the test for end of file. But that would be less meaningful than the defined symbol, EOF. There is scarcely anyone who really wants to know that end of file is represented by −1.

Nor are you in a position to change the value of EOF. So it makes no sense to make your own private definitions of it. It is best to use stdio.h to get all the definitions that experienced C programmers have come to know and love.

1.11 One solution below uses the logical negate operator, !.

```
comment()
{
    int lastch, ch;

    lastch = nextchar();
    ch = nextchar();
    while (!((lastch == '*') && (ch == '/')))
    {
        if ((lastch == '/') && (ch == '*'))
            printf(" nexted comment at line %d\n", lineno);
        lastch = ch;
        ch = nextchar();
    }
}
```

Note that we need extra variables and the loop construct is messier. The do while loop (see Chapter 2) gives a somewhat better solution. The form in the main text has the advantage of clarity and easier modification if we need to test for other characters.

1.12 You can print debugging output in several ways.

- Echo the characters as they are read by replacing the getchar in the nextchar function by

     putchar(getchar())

- Simply add a printf statement in nextchar to print the characters as they are read.
- Better still, use a printf statement in nextchar and use the preprocessor facility of conditional compilation (described in Chapter 6) to control its execution.

Chapter 2

2.1 In both cases, action is invoked where x is non-zero. Which is better depends upon the context: the former is better where x plays the role of a boolean flag and the second form is better where x is used as a number.

2.2 Presumably, flagset has a non-zero value when a certain condition holds so we want to call action. Depending upon the particular coding situation, it may be clearer than the equivalent

     if (flagset == TRUE)

where TRUE has been suitably defined as in the comment checker of Chapter 1.

2.3 The if controlling line becomes

     if (gotslash && (ch == '*'))

and the assignment

     gotslash = FALSE;

becomes

     gotslash = 0;

and the other assignment to gotslash can be written as

```
    gotslash = 1;
```

or you can use any other non-zero expression. The original form is much more obvious but this form is so commonly used by C programmers that you had best get used to reading it.

2.4 The problem is missing braces:

```
    if (safe)
    {
        if (val < TOL)
            printf(" Meets tolerance" );
    }
    else
        printf(" dangerous" );
```

2.5 All are acceptable except "num * 2" (because num is a variable) and "84.6" (because case expressions cannot be floating point numbers).

2.6 Any character other than the digits will also cause 'th' to be printed. To make the code effect identical use

```
    if ((digit >= ' 0' ) && (digit <= ' 9' ))
        switch statement as before
```

or we can alter the default thus:

```
    default:     if (' 0'  <= digit) && (digit <= ' 9' ))
                 printf(" %c-th" , digit);
```

2.7 Assuming this is part of a function and we want to return upon an error, one answer is

```
    if (scanf(" %d" , &value) == 1)
        while (value != STOPPER)
        {
            if (scanf(" %d" , &value) != 1)
                return;
            printf(" %d" , value);
        }
```

2.8 You control the loop counter so you know it. This is actually a silly question in C. The value of loop counters on loop exits is only an issue in a language like Pascal that has magical, self incrementing loop counters.

2.9 A simple translation is like this:

```
    initialization;
    while (termination-test)
    {
        statement
    next: loop-increment;
    }
```

We have included the label next for the situation where there happens to be a continue within the for loop. This can be translated into a goto next.

Chapter 3

3.1 The declarations have the effect described below.
(a)   The variable n is declared to be of type int and it is given an initial value of the octal number 170. (Which is 120 in decimal.)
(b)   Rather like the last case, m is an int which is initialized to an octal value but the digit '8' is not one of the octal digits. Older compilers will treat the 8 as octal 10 without any warnings. Here is another use for lint.
(c)   i is a short with initial value hexadecimal 'ab' (which is 171 in decimal).
(d)   j is a long also initialized with a hexadecimal value.

3.2 The type of the constants is:
(a)   0xFFFFFF is a hexadecimal long, since a 6-digit hex number requires 24 bits. (Of course, there is no guarantee that long is actually larger than int on all machines but it usually is so on machines with small word size, as in the case of the PDP11.)
(b)   184000 is a long because it is too big for an ordinary int.
(c)   8l is a long int.
(d)   13L is a long int because this is specified (and in spite of the fact that 13 would fit into an int).
(e)   012L is a long octal constant (10 in decimal).
(f)   8 is an ordinary int constant.

3.3 The expressions have the values:
(a)   1 (but i is incremented after this).
(b)   6.
(c)   1.
(d)   This is a true logical expression with value 1.
(e)   031 (25 in decimal) and u is assigned that value.
(f)   9 since it performs an AND on the last 4 bits.
(g)   79 (inclusive-OR with the last 4 bits).
(h)   70 decimal (exclusive-OR on the last 4 bits).
(i)   72 decimal (this masks the last two bits in a way that is independent of the size of u and will work correctly on any machine).

(j)   This always gives the value of u which, in this case, is 73 decimal.

(k)   This gives 4 for the value of both i and the whole expression.

(l)   This gives 4 and is equivalent to u = u / (s + 1).

(m)   9 (it shifts u three bits to the right).

(n)   0. The higher precedence = = is done first giving 0 which is AND-ed with 1.

(o)   1. The sub-expression (1 & ~017) masks off the last four bits of 1, giving 0 and then the expression 0 = = 0 is true and has the value 1.

3.4 The two lines differ only in that the first has a comma operator where the second has a semicolon. In the first, a is assigned the value 1 and then x is also set to 1. Because = has higher precedence than the comma operator, b is next assigned the value 2. The second line does exactly the same thing. Note, however that the line

```
x = (a =1 , b = 2);
```

would set a to 1, b to 2 and then that value, 2, would be assigned to x.

3.5 The loop is controlled by an expression that uses the comma operator. So, before each loop repetition, e1 and e2 are evaluated and if e2 is non-zero (true), the loop is executed, with doit being called.

3.6 The first printf statement prints the value of x, 1. The last argument, y, is ignored. The second printf statement prints the value of y, 2, since the result of the expression (x, y) is 2.

3.7

```
num = 0;
while (isdigit(ch = getchar()))
    num = num * 10 + ch − '0';
```

However, you should realize that the standard libraries include the function atoi which takes a string as an argument and returns the corresponding integer. (We discuss strings in Chapter 5 and the standard functions in Chapter 7.)

3.8 You need to add a test to ensure that the character is only modified when it is lower case.

```
if (islower(ch))
    ch += 'A' − 'a';
```

or

```
ch += islower(ch) ? 'A' - 'a' : 0
```

Observe that our initial code could have produced quite surprising results had ch been upper case initially.

3.9 One possibility is

```
enum month__type
{
Jan, Feb, Mar, Apr, May, Jun, Jul, Aug, Sep, Oct, Nov, Dec
};
```

3.10 A simple version is

```
switch (getchar())
{
case 'd':    indication = dreadful;    break;
case 'p':    indication = poor;        break;
case 'O':    indication = OK;          break;
case 'g':    indication = good;        break;
case 't':    indication = terrific;    break;
default:     input__error();
}

while (isalpha(getchar()))
    ;
```

3.11   42 b b

Note that if the parentheses were omitted, the pointer itself would have been incremented, rather than the value that it points to. Observe that *cp is the same as *(&ch) which is the same as just ch. Note also that after this printf, num has been incremented:

        43 50

The effect of ++ in the earlier statement is seen here:

        47 47

Both np and ap point to num.

        k k k

These three all refer to the same location ch.

3.12

(a) Floating point constants are handled as double, so 1.0 is a double, it is converted to float before the assignment and the result is float.

(b) kk is converted to double before the multiplication; the right hand side of the assignment is converted to a float before the assignment and the expression is float.

(c) y is converted to a double and the result is double.

(d) 2.3 is double, but is converted to int (2) when assigned to kk. The result of the expression (kk = 2.3) is converted to double and the whole expression is double.

(e) This expression differs from the preceding ones that involved arithmetic and assignment conversions. Here we have an implicit conversion of an integer to a pointer. kk is converted to a pointer to char, the resulting expression is a pointer to char. However, lint and most compilers will give a warning and you really should make an explicit cast like this:

```
pc = (char*)kk
```

(f) x is an unsigned int so 1 is made an unsigned int and the result of the expression on the right hand side is unsigned int. This is converted to float and the result of the whole expression is float.

(g) ch, 'a' and 'A' are converted to int for the evaluation of the expression on the right hand side. Then, this is converted to a char and the result is a char.

(h) This evaluates the int expression kk first. If it is non-zero, the value of k is converted to an int, assigned to kk and the result is int. If the evaluation of kk is zero, the value of y is converted to an int, assigned to kk and the result is again int.

Chapter 4

4.1

(a) sin(.7) is fine because .7 is a floating point constant and hence is of type double.

(b) sin((double).7) has a precise match between actual and formal arguments, but since .7 is a double anyway, this form would be unnecessary and very unusual.

(c) sin(0x1f1) might be all right if you had really set up this constant correctly, but it is unlikely and certainly looks suspicious. lint would complain about this, and if you really wanted it, you should write it as

```
sin((double) 0x1f1);
```

(d) sin(1) is wrong because the argument is an int.

(e) sin(x) is all right if x is declared as either float or double, incorrect otherwise.

(f) $\sin(4 * \sin(3.872) - y)$ is acceptable because the expression is a float (the constants and variables that are not doubles undergo appropriate conversions).

4.2 "doit(&y)" is the only correct call, as it is the only pointer to a char, as required by doit. &x is a pointer to a pointer to an int. &z is a pointer to a pointer to a char, not a pointer to a char.

4.3

```
void
plot(xscale, yscale, fn)
double  xscale;
double  yscale;
double  (* fn)();
```

Note, however, that there is a standard plot library, so you should check its facilities before you write a function like this.

4.4 After the function call, x has the value 1 (because the function's increment of a is purely local and *b in silly is the same as x in the calling code).

4.5 A function type defaults to int if there is no type specified in the function header. Also the arguments default to int if their type is not specified in the header. An undeclared function from a different file is assumed to be int, as is a function that is used earlier in the file than its definition. Similarly, a variable that appears in an extern declaration but has no type specified defaults to int.

4.6 This is an error that is detected by the C compiler. If the declaration of strcpy were omitted, it would take the default type int and the compiler will not allow you to assign it to p.

4.7
(a)   Either move its declaration up before main, or add an extern declaration there.
(b)   Put an extern declaration either in B2 or at the beginning of fileB.
(c)   There would be a loader error because there would be two global variables called b1.
(d)   Because the declaration of b2 in fileB is static, there is no conflict in this situation. It simply creates a new variable that happens to have the same name.
(e)   This has no effect. In fact, it commonly occurs where a program uses #includes to incorporate all the major extern declarations into several files of a program including the one where each is actually defined.
(f)   You cannot import a static function and the loader will report that it was unable to link B2.

4.8

(a)   The **static** storage class is associated with a storage mechanism that makes data live throughout the execution of a program. A **static register** declaration would imply that you wanted to allocate a variable to the register for the duration of the program. This would tie up a register, and as registers are usually a rather scarce machine resource this is not permitted.

(b)   The **&**, address-of, operator can only apply to memory (not to registers).

(c)   Make the header

```
char
fnA(x)
register char    x;
```

4.9   Since external and **static** variables have a default initialization (to 0 or the relevant cast); lint must assume they are set at the time the program starts execution.

Chapter 5

5.1

(a)   Since dot has higher precedence than *, we need the brackets so that this expression takes the value of the member **a** of the structure that **p** points to.

(b)   By contrast, *p.b is equivalent to *(p.b) which is meaningless and may cause an error message.

(c)   This accesses the zeroth element of the member **c** in the structure pointed to be **p**. This form saves you thinking about the relative precedence of * and dot.

(d)   This assigns the structure that **p** points to, to **x**. This means that the whole structure is assigned, including the member that happens to be an array (though you cannot assign a whole array directly).

5.2

(a)   **s = line** is acceptable and sets **s** to the beginning of the array, **line**. Equally, you may see this as setting **s** to the same value as the constant pointer, **line**, that points to the beginning of the 100 element array.

(b)   **s ++** moves **s** to point to the next element in the array.

(c)   **line ++** is *illegal* as it tries to alter the value of a *constant* pointer, **line**.

(d)   s += 7 is acceptable. It makes s point to the array element 7 along.
So, if it was pointing at s[0], it now points to s[7]. This is one way to deal with
subarrays.
(e)   This is just another form for line.
(f)   This is equivalent to line[0].
(g)   This is another form for the address of line[0].
(h)   This is a way of passing a subarray as a function argument.

5.3 The form on page 109 is &a+1 but this is just one byte on from &a. We
need to use ((int *)&a)+1 since a is a char. When it is passed as an argument
it is promoted to an int.

5.4 B[2] [0] has the value 11. *B[2] has the value 11. B[2] gives a compiler
warning and is a pointer to the element with value 11.

5.5

```
*(x + b * i + j)
*(y + d * e * i + e * j + k)
```

5.6
int *A is a pointer to an integer.
int **A is a pointer to a pointer to an integer.
int *B[N] is an array of N pointers to integers.
int C[N] is an array of integers.
int *D() is a function returning a pointer to an integer.
int (*E)() is a pointer to a function returning an integer.
int *(*F)() is a pointer to a function returning a pointer to an integer.
int *(*G[N])() is an array of N pointers to functions returning pointers to
integers.

5.7 Free cannot affect y because arguments are called by value and cannot be
altered by the function. Logically, you should not use y once the memory it
points to has been freed. Problems can arise if you do use freed memory,
particularly if it is reallocated in a later call to malloc.

5.8 Although this code is very similar to the pointer form, C idiom favours the pointer form and, in general, the pointer view gives more natural and elegant code:

```
char *
Array_Detrail(s)
char  s[];
{
    int  last;    /* index of last non-blank in array */
    int  j;

    last = -1;
    for (j=0; s[j] != ' \0'; j++)
        if (!isspace(s[j]))
            last = j;
    s[++last] = ' \0';
    return s;
}
```

5.9 The first declares an array of characters, the second a string. (The compiler puts a \0 after the D.) So the first cannot be used for an **auto** array. We can alter **caps** like this

```
caps = "EFGH";
```

later in the program. This form is not allowed for **specials**. The effect of the assignment to **caps** is to change the value of a single pointer so that it points to a different constant string "EFGH".

5.10 It converts a number in the range zero to fifteen to the appropriate hexadecimal character. Here we have chosen to define a constant string and then, viewing this as a character array, we index into it to find the **n**th element.

5.11 The first line would simply print the message directly as

```
WARNING
Bad data on input
```

and the second would print from the fifth character in the string, which is **N**. The last line is an out of bounds array access and its effect is unpredictable.

5.12 No, you cannot assign a whole array or string. So you *cannot* write

```
s1 = "Hello there"; /* WRONG */
```

and because **s1** and **s2** are *constant* pointers, you *cannot* write

```
s1 = s2;     /* WRONG */
```

Note, however, that the following form is fine:

```
char    *m1;
char    *m2 = " Hello there" ;
...
m1 = m2;
```

and you can use strcpy like this:

```
char    *strcpy();
char    s1[20];
char    s2[20] = " Hello there" ;
...
        (void) strcpy(s1, s2);
```

5.13 The values of a, b and c are printed according to the format that was read by Get_line. This enables you to do runtime formatting; in this case we read the formatting string.

5.14 This is very similar to srealloc:

```
char *
salloc(size)
unsigned    size;
{
    char    *result;

    if ((result = malloc(size)) == (char *)0)
    {
        fprintf(stderr," cannot malloc %d bytes \n" , size);
        exit(1);
    }
    return result;
}
```

5.15 a is a single byte of storage containing the character a, "a" is a pointer to two bytes of storage containing the characters a and \0.

5.16

```
#include  <stdio.h>

#define MAXLINES 20

extern char *Get  line();
char    *lines[MAXLINES];
void    read  lines();
    ...
read  lines(lines, MAXLINES);
    ...
```

```
void
read_lines(l, num)
char      **l;
int       num;   /* maximum number of lines to read */
{
      while ((*l++ = Get_line()) != NULL)
           if (--num == 0)
                return;
}
```

5.17 The declaration treats argv as a pointer to a pointer to a string. Since [ ] is an operator, we could still use the same code. However, code that maintains a view that is consistent with the declaration would look like this:

```
int  i;
char  **next;

next = argv;
for (i = 0; i < argc; i++)
      printf(" argument %d: %s\n", i, *next++);
```

The code that prints the name of the program would become

```
if ((prog_name = strrchr(*argv, '/')) == (char *)0)
      prog_name = *argv;
else
      prog_name++;
```

5.18 Given the declaration of Books in Section 5.7, the following code fragment shows how to invoke qsort:

```
extern void  qsort();

      ...
      qsort((char *)Books, BOOK_COUNT,
                 sizeof (Book_info), compare);
      ...


compare(b1, b2)
Book_info *b1;
Book_info *b2;
{
      /* for simplicity we ignore upper/lower case
      comparisons */
      return strcmp(b1->author, b2->author);
}
```

5.19 This might be a record within a symbol table and here is one form.

```
enum symbol__type {Int, Double, Char};

struct symbol__info
{
    char                *identifier;
    enum symbol__type Type;
    union
    {
        int     i;
        double  d;
        char    c;
    } value;
};
```

5.20 The major difference here is that we scan the file, rather than a structure. We use the standard functions, fopen and fscanf, for which we define the file name as WTFILE, and we need wtf, a pointer to the file. We show the parts of the program that change.

```
        ...
#define NSIZE    50      /* maximum size of place name */
#define WTFILE    "/usr/pub/world__times"
        ...
main(argc, argv)
int        argc;
char    *argv[];
{
    FILE        *wtf;
    int        zone;    /* remote zone */
    int        yesterday = 0;
    char        place[NSIZE];
    ...
    /* open file for reading */
    if ((wtf = fopen(WTFILE, "r")) == NULL)
    {
        fprintf(stderr, "%s: cannot open %s\n",
        argv[0], WTFILE);
        exit(1);
    }

    for (;;)
        /* run through the file, reading places */
        if (fscanf(wtf, "%s %d", place, &zone) != 2)
        {
            /* reached the end */
            fprintf(stderr, "%s:    don't know about %s\n",
                        argv[0], argv[1]);
```

```
                    fprintf(stderr, " look in %s \n" , WTFILE);
                    exit(1);
              }
              else if (strcmp(argv[1], place) == 0)
                    /* found the place */
                    break;
        ...
```

5.21 One approach is to augment the time__diff structure to have the starting and finishing dates for daylight saving. Then we need to get the current date at our local machine, adjust it as necessary for daylight saving, calculate the corresponding time at the target place, check whether it corresponds to a daylight saving period and, if it does, make the required adjustment.

Chapter 6

6.1

(a)   `#define bit0(x)  ((x) & 01)`

(b)   `#define bit(x,n)  (((x) >> n) & 01)`

6.2

```
        main()
        {
            int      i;

            printf(" NUMBER = %d \n" , 50);

            for (i = 1; i < 50; i++)
                  printf(" %d \t%d \n" , i, i*i);
        }
```

Note that the preprocessor only replaces occurrences of the defined identifier. So the word NUMBER in the printf string is not touched.

6.3 It avoids precedence problems.

6.4 You cannot use brackets to overide the default attachments of the dangling #else, so you need to alter the control like this:

```
        #if !A
              ...code C ...
        #else /* A true */
              ...code A ...
        #    if B
```

```
        ...code AB...
    #   endif
    #endif
```

6.5

```
#if DEV=1
    ...
#else
#if DEV=2
    ...
```

and so on.

6.6 There is a dangling else problem. The body of the assert macro could be changed to include a dummy else clause in the if statement.

Chapter 8

8.1 The primary difference is that the selection of mailing list items and their components is much simpler with a database. This means that the input functions in labels and letters change. Other parts of the system remain the same.

Several database packages for UNIX are available and would be useful in a real mailing list management system.

8.2

```
/*
** 'skipover' skips characters in string 'chs' on file 'mf'
** returns the first character not in 'chs'
**        EOF on end of file
*/
int
skipover(mf, chs)
FILE    *mf;     /* file to read from */
char    *chs;    /* characters to skip */
{
     int  c;

     while ((c = readch(mf)) != EOF)
          if (strchr(chs, (char)c) == NULL)
          {
               unreadch(c, mf);
               return c;
          }
     return EOF;
}
```

8.3

```
/*
**   'skipto' skips characters on file 'mf' until a character from
**   the set in string 'chs' is reached
**   It returns OK if a character from the set is reached.
**       EOF if EOF reached
*/
int
skipto(mf, chs)
FILE    *mf;     /* file to read from */
char    *chs;    /* set of chars to look for */
{
      int  c;

      while ((c = readch(mf)) != EOF)
          if (strchr(chs, (char)c) != NULL)
              return OK;
      return EOF;
}
```

8.4

```
/*
**   error prints an error message string along with
**   the program name, file name and line number.
*/
error(s)
char    *s;
{
      fprintf(stderr, " %s: %s at line %d in file %s \n",
              myname, s, lineno, filename);
}
```

8.5 We declare a global variable width that keeps the number of characters in the line currently being printed. We only ever print LABEL__LEN lines. We leave most of the work to the lab__char function that prints each character, checking that the width or length restrictions are not exceeded:

```
void
lab__field(outf, value, ch)
FILE      *outf;    /* file for output */
char      *value;  /* field value */
char      ch;      /* character to follow value */
{
    char    *s;

    if (length > LABEL_LEN)
        return;

    width = 0;
    for (s = value; *s != '\0'; s++)
        lab__char(outf, *s);
    lab__char(outf, ch);
}

lab__char(outf, c)
FILE      *outf;
char      c;
{
    if (c == '\n')   /* newline within a field */
    {
        if (length++ == LABEL__LEN)
        {
            error("too many lines for label");
            return;
        }
        else
        {
            putc(c, outf);
            width = 0;
        }
    }
    else    /* ordinary character */
    {
        if (width++ == LABEL__WID)
        {
            error("field too wide for label");
            return;
        }
        putc(c, outf);
    }
}
```

8.6

```
#
#        mailing list suite
#
SRCS =  labels.c selectml.c formlet.c letter.c sortml.c \
        printml.c readml.c select.c util.c
OBJS =  printml.o readml.o util.o

all:     labels selectml formlet sortml

labels:  labels.o $(OBJS)
         cc labels.o $(OBJS) -o labels

selectml: selectml.o select.o $(OBJS)
          cc selectml.o select.o $(OBJS) -o selectml

formlet: formlet.o letter.o $(OBJS)
         cc formlet.o letter.o $(OBJS) -o formlet

sortml:  sortml.o $(OBJS)
         cc sortml.o $(OBJS) -o sortml

$(OBJS): ml.h

lint:
         lint $(SRCS)

clean:
         rm $(OBJS)
```

Bibliography

General

Bell Laboratories (1982) *UNIX Programmer's Manual* (revised and expanded version), Volumes 1 and 2. Holt, Rinehart and Winston

These are essentially the printed form of the online manual and documents. However, they are extremely useful even where you have access to the online forms. Aside from the convenience of a printed document that is bound, they include a helpful index.

    The second volume is particularly useful for its documents on many of the tools available with UNIX. For several, it provides excellent tutorial introductions.

Kernighan, B. W. and Plauger, P. J. (1976) *Software Tools.* Addison-Wesley

This is the book which described what has come to be known as the *tools approach* to programming.

Ritchie, D. and Thompson, K. (1974) 'The UNIX Time-Sharing System' *Communications of the ACM,* **17**, No. 7, July 1974, pp 365–375.

This is the classic paper by the creators of the UNIX operating system.

Kernighan, B. W. and Ritchie, D. M. (1978) *The C Programming Language.* Prentice-Hall

This was the first book about C by its creators. It has dated somewhat in terms of coverage of the language and rather more so in terms of style. It also places little emphasis on the use of the large library of standard functions that is available in the UNIX environment.

329

Algorithms

Gonnet, G. H. (1984) *Handbook of Algorithms and Data Structures*. Addison-Wesley

This is a collection of classic algorithms for searching, sorting, selection and various arithmetic operations. It gives the algorithms in C (and Pascal). It also has extensive references for the algorithms it describes and makes an excellent starting point to further study of these important and widespread algorithms.

Korn, D. G. and Vo, K. P. (1985) 'In search of a better malloc' *Proceedings of the 1985 Summer Usenix Conference*, Portland, Oregon

These authors studied various algorithms for malloc. If you need a better management for your heap storage, this paper is a good place to start.

Books on UNIX

Kernighan, B. W. and Pike, R. (1984) *The UNIX Programming Environment*. Prentice-Hall

This is an excellent book for a serious programmer. The authors are at the hub of UNIX development and give the reader the benefit of their extensive experience as very productive programmers in the UNIX environment. However, it is quite advanced and if you have little computing background and find UNIX foreign, you may need to start with one of the more basic books. This book also leads the reader through the development of some substantial C programs, illustrating major tools like yacc.

Bourne, S. R. (1982) *The UNIX System*. Addison-Wesley

This is a good book at an intermediate level. Its author was the creator of the so-called Bourne shell, the command interpreter for UNIX.

Brown, P. J. (1984) *Starting with UNIX*. Addison-Wesley

This is an excellent book at the introductory level. It devotes some time to central concepts underlying the design and operation of UNIX as well as providing a functional description. It would not be sufficient for a serious programmer but it serves as a very good starting point for anyone who has little previous experience of similar operating systems.

C and other programming languages

Feuer, A. and Gehani, N. (eds) (1984) *Comparing and Assessing Programming Languages: Ada, C and Pascal*. Prentice-Hall

This is a collection of articles. Many are very entertaining and bitingly critical.

Stroustrup, B. (1986) *The C++ Programming Language*. Addison-Wesley

Describes and discusses C++, a preprocessor for C, that provides constructs like Simula's classes.

Index